A Promising Career

Christy Brown was born in 1932. He was one of 23 children born to a Dublin bricklayer. A victim of cerebral palsy, he could not control his speech or his movement, apart from his left foot. This enabled him to paint and to type his autobiographical novel, MY LEFT FOOT. His other novels are A SHADOW ON SUMMER, DOWN ALL THE DAYS and WILD GROW THE LILIES, and he also published his poetry in COLLECTED POEMS. Christy Brown died in 1981.

CHRISTY BROWN

A Promising Career

Minerva

A Minerva Paperback

A PROMISING CAREER

First published in Great Britain 1982
by Martin Secker & Warburg Limited
This Minerva edition published 1990
by Mandarin Paperbacks
Michelin House, 81 Fulham Road, London SW3 6RB

Minerva is an imprint of the Octopus Publishing Group

A CIP catalogue record for this title
is available from the British Library
ISBN 0 7493 9182 0

Printed and bound in Great Britain
by Cox and Wyman Ltd, Reading, Berks

To my friend and Editor
David Farrer
I hope his patience will be rewarded

PART I
The Present

I

LYING back on the park seat, her eyes closed, feet sprawled out in front of her, she heard the noise of children playing, clustered round the pond close by, sailing their model boats or flying kites fluttering in the hazy air; from time to time there came the noise of wheels on gravel as young wives passed, their infants invisible in the depths of prams; the roar of traffic from Bayswater Road came distantly, pleasantly muffled. The sun, weak in its autumnal last fling, played on her upturned face, a friendly presence glancing down through the heavy yellowing foliage of the trees. She had no idea of the time, having forgotten her watch, but guessed it was late afternoon. Reluctantly she got up, yawning and feeling thirsty, and made her way out through the gates, abandoning the leafy sanctuary of the park, and walked back towards the mews.

She walked along in a kind of alert trance, her steps instinctive, hearing the traffic unceasing all about her, aware of things in a clear yet detached way: a child's cycle leaning against the basement railings of one of the tall dowager houses as she left the main street and gained the quieter avenues, its frame a vivid red in the lengthening sunset; a young couple strolling by hand in hand, in denims, a transistor crackling between them; diamond glint of light as an upstairs window was opened; the muted drone of a vacuum cleaner from some front room. A bright striped ball came suddenly bouncing towards her along the uneven pavements, pursued by two small boys jostling each other to get to it first, their faces flushed and hot with intent, swerving at the last moment to flash past her like projectiles, ignoring her as if she had been a tree or some other mute object in their path. A motorbike revved up somewhere, momentarily drowning the nervous chatter of birds in the thinning branches of the trees. In between the cracked crevices of the paving stones, yellow clumps of grass pushed tenaciously upwards with parched wiry strength. The afternoon hush lay more profound as she turned into the enclosed area of the mews, the houses leaning top heavy against one another as

7

if for support. A few cars were parked in the narrow lane, a well-fed tawny cat curled up on a window sill; no person was in sight. The sky stretched like rumpled vellum high over the sloping tiled rooftops; everything was so still it might have been a hamlet tucked away in a deep fold of hills. She felt for her latchkey, climbed the few steep stairs and entered the flat.

After the light outside, the gloom within was intense and she stood without moving for some moments until the objects in the room assumed their familiar outline and gradually revealed themselves to her. She went into the small lounge, took a bottle from the wall cabinet, poured out some vodka into a glass and drank it straight down, hardly tasting it. She sank into an armchair, holding the drained glass to her mouth as if it were a microphone, mumbling, purring into it, eyes closed in mimicry of concentration, crooning the words, adding a coquettish lisp to her voice:

'How can we get back to where we've been? . . .' She threw back her head and stared at the ceiling. 'The lyrics,' she murmured, 'ah, the lyrics.' She refilled the glass, drinking more carefully now. 'Christ, my love, you write such shit.'

She sat in the chair for some time, sipping her drink, feeling the tiredness slowly ebb out of her bones, grateful to be alone, to enjoy the silence and the comfort of the flat all to herself; the mere presence of somebody else would have grated on her nerves, most of all Art's presence, had he been there on her return; she was almost thankful for the row they had had that morning that had sent him charging out fuming and cursing her and all she stood for with that rather touching fanaticism, that total absence of point he always displayed in his mercurial rages. She vaguely recalled they had been arguing over one of his new songs and he had accused her of making a balls of it up in Leeds last week. She found it difficult now even to remember the words of it, though the tune was droning round and round in her head like a poor trapped mouse in a cage squealing to be let loose. Finally she got up and started to take off her clothes, letting them fall to the floor to form a trail behind her as she moved from lounge to bathroom, taking the glass and bottle with her, humming tunelessly.

She pulled the linen basket over to the side of the bathtub, using it as a table for her drink, and turned on the hot and cold taps until the temperature of the water was to her satisfaction, then she climbed in. She leaned back, sighing; the heat rose shimmering before her, the

8

shape of her limbs distorted and dissolving underwater, the neat dark reddish triangle of hair nestling like a ferny brown cloud between her thighs, tiny tendrils swaying. The steam billowed up, shrouding everything in mist; she felt deliciously drowsy, cocooned, warm and safe, the hard edges of things softly blurred, a slow lassitude creeping through her, voyaging her into half dream.

Something gradually intruded upon the fringes of her senses, a reluctant awareness of being watched, the unwelcome knowledge of someone close by, observing her. Through the haze of steam she looked up and saw Marcie standing in the doorway, a faint smile on her face, looking down at her without any trace of reticence.

'Hi, Jan.'

Janice pulled herself upright in the bath. 'What the hell are you doing here?'

The black girl only smiled more openly, with a hint of her customary insolence, and opened her palm, dangling the key she held there. 'I let myself in.'

Janice scowled and reached for the bottle, drinking from the neck.

'So I see. I suppose my dear husband gave you that?' she added, glaring at the key dangling on its little chain.

'As a matter of fact, yes, he did,' agreed Marcie, nonchalant, leaning her hip against the doorjamb. 'Said he thought you might need some company while he was absent.' Marcie eyed the bottle. 'Seems like you got company already, my friend.'

Janice waved the bottle. 'Company's the last fucking thing I need just now, thanks all the same. I've had three bleeding weeks of non-stop gigs up North, and I won't be needing anyone's company for the next couple of days, except the distilled sort.'

Marcie shrugged. 'That's fine by me, Jan, no skin off my beautiful dusky hide. But you will remember to come to lunch tomorrow, won't you? Simon's expecting you both.'

'Tomorrow?' Janice echoed, frowning. 'Christ – I'd forgotten all about that.'

Marcie gave her a comradely smile and nod. 'Thought as much, but Simon's in one of his brisk business moods, so make an effort to show up.' She swung the keychain between her thumb and forefinger, making a playful little sound. 'Let's hope you and Art are communicating by then. It would be a shame to have one of your usual slanging matches over my canneloni – I'm making the pasta myself.'

9

'Oh, don't worry on that score,' said Janice, relenting, almost liking the note of lazy mockery in the woman's voice. 'You should be used to our little homely hostilities by now.' She placed the bottle back on the linen basket and stood up, holding on to the metal handrail along the wall. 'Throw me that towel, love, will you? Thanks.'

As Janice dried herself in the large fleecy towel Marcie lounged in the doorway, arms crossed, jingling the keychain and observing her with the same cool laconic interest as before, but emboldened by drink Janice did not flinch or become restive under the scrutiny, in no way flaunting her nudity but on the other hand making no coy efforts to conceal it. When Marcie asked if she wanted her back dried Janice consented calmly, and felt herself go drowsy and relaxed again under the pressure of the other's fingers, hard yet indolent, adept in their ministrations as a desultory train of conversation was kept up between them. Marcie's movements were those of a trained nurse, a professional minder of invalids and convalescents, brisk and remote at once, yet now and then her fingers would pause and linger, as if she was thinking of something else, lazily stroking Janice's back like someone fondling a puppy, until Janice growled at her for Christ's sake to hurry up before she froze to death on the wet tiles.

'Drink?' she asked when they were back in the lounge, her hair turbaned in a towel and her body wrapped in a long furry dressing-gown.

'Bit early for me,' answered Marcie, without the slightest suggestion of reproach. 'I'm usually an after-eight lush.'

Janice flopped into the same chair. 'As the song says, "*Fighting vainly the old ennui. That's me.*" '

'Well, if you're sure you can bear to do without my scintillating company,' said Marcie, moving to the door, 'I'll tootle along.'

'Thanks for the rub down.'

Marcie smiled, strong white teeth gleaming. 'Any time. Oh' – she held up the latchkey – 'what do I do with this?'

'Give it back to my one-and-only,' replied Janice. 'He'll want it to get in, if and when he decides to come home.'

'Will do. Ciao.'

Left alone, hearing the sound of Marcie's car receding down the lane, Janice sat in the deepening gloom; after a while she crossed over to the television set in the corner and switched it on, in time to catch the end of the evening news; turning down the volume, she went back to her chair and sat huddled in it, her knees curled underneath her, gazing unseeing at the flickering images on the screen, thinking back to that last performance in Leeds two nights ago, thinking about it as always with the same degree of sadness and pleasure as if it were something that could never be repeated, exactly the way she felt after every performance in the luxurious aftermath of exhaustion; sometimes the sadness outweighed the pleasure, but the reflections were as inevitable as breathing, and it was an immense secret consolation to know that she had still not learned to be cynical about it. She never expected the miracle to occur, but it invariably did, again and again, and each time it took her by surprise, brought her to the verge of nervous tears, filling her with a fierce pride all the more treasured lest one day it should descend into bland acceptance. At such moments she would glance at Art in dread almost that the awareness of this always unique transformation might escape him, and as always his face would be closed to her, bent over his guitar, impervious, caught up in his own inner excitement which he threw off heedlessly, a shield to deter observation, a mask to hide a deeper more turbulent involvement which he could not or would not share with anyone, sitting there inaccessible behind his music even as he threw himself headlong into it, snug and unreachable in the thunder or vibrant calm of the moment. She would look at him, and look away, knowing it was still the same, turning back with familiar hurt to her song, resigned to the old exclusion, to the knowledge that they rarely allowed themselves to communicate to the other what the music meant to them, remaining apart and alienated in the one thing that should have brought them closest together.

It had become night outside, and in the darkness the television set looked like a gross illuminated toadstool squatting in the corner, filling the lounge with moving shadows, casting a static film before her eyes. In the fleecy depths of her robe she shivered, the silence around her empty and no longer companionable; she could no longer pretend she was happy alone with the flat all to herself: it was like trying to delude herself that a cemetery was a pleasant place to be at night. She could not summon the effort to get up and go to bed, and lay dozing in the armchair, the light from the television flickering upon her lids, waking with a start from time to time, thinking she heard a key turning in the lock.

*   *   *

From the bed where he lay in the rumpled wreck of the sheets, his breath still ragged and his chest heaving, matted with sweat, Simon Sandford gazed across with familiar gluttony to where the girl stood at the window, leaning forward on the sill looking out over the morning panorama of the city, her back to him. The convulsion of release that had finally overcome him a few moments ago had still not subsided, had still not ceased its erratic drumming inside him, yet his hunger quickened instantly once more as he stared at the taut symmetry of her bent back, the angular slimness of her hips, her small drum-tight buttocks held rigidly in now as she leaned the upper half of her body forward over the sill, her theatrically long legs slightly apart, her shoulders held at a sharp inelegant angle as she rested her weight on her spread palms. Against the milky light of the window her head looked strikingly martial, the tight dark crinkly hair clamped to her skull like a helmet, making her neck seem longer than it actually was; her body seemed to surge inwardly with nervous tension like an athlete poised on the starting block, ready to sprint forward and launch herself at a given signal into any situation demanding pugnacity, strength and verve, eager to prove her staying power and release the suppressed energy that hummed inside her, masked at all other times by a nurtured indolence which she applied as carefully as most other women apply their cosmetics.

A ray of weak early sunlight glanced suddenly along her left shoulder and hip, bringing a sleek ebony sheen to her skin; hearing a muffled moaning sound from the bed, she turned round, slowly crossed over the carpet and stood at the foot of it, looking faintly scowling down at the large florid man heaped on the tousled bed, peering shortsightedly up at her in pleading pleasure, stumpy fingers grasping the edges of the coverlet, the sweat that had scarcely cooled on him beginning to glisten again.

She shook her head, folding her arms together. 'No, my dear,' she said, as if mildly reprimanding a greedy child. 'Enough is enough. We must start getting ready soon to greet our guests.'

'What time is it?' Sandford muttered.

'Almost ten, by the sound of the bells yonder.'

'Well, then –' Simon wet his lips, eyes devouring her nakedness, the bulge of her breasts over her folded arms, her belly sloping into the hard lean dusk of her thighs and the dark dewy mound of hair that nestled there. He squeezed his eyes up tight, his breathing laboured.

'Christ, you're fantastic,' he croaked, dragging himself with his heels down towards her over the bedclothes. 'Once more, Marcie, just once more – please . . .'

She surveyed him calmly. 'Enough is enough.' She uncrossed her arms and as if absentmindedly her hands wandered to her nipples, brushing them with her palms dreamily. 'Enough *is* enough – hmm?' This time it was more question than reprimand, her hands sliding downwards to move slowly over her thighs, her fingers taut, intimate.

'Don't, Marcie – don't kill me like this . . . again oh again – please – just once . . .' his voice trailed on. For a time she did not move, did not appear to have heard him as she felt and softly fondled herself, body swaying, head held sideways, absorbed in her ministrations, excluding him as if he were not present, as if he did not exist, savouring her private priorities of pleasure, excruciating to him who looked on, trapped in his grovelling need. Her eyes, that had been closed as in fanciful slumber, opened and came to rest on him in a long slow look of disdain tinged with insolent enquiry; she stooped and picked up from where they lay discarded on the floor a pair of tight black leather jeans, studded down both sides with seams of chunky brass beads, a thick brass-buckled belt running through the loops; she slid the jeans over her hips, fitting them to her like a second skin, and clasped the buckle into place with swift brutal precision, all the while not taking her eyes from where he writhed in mute imploring impatience on the immense bed, his phallus struggling erect in tribute, lifting like a small weak phoenix out of its tangled nest, his fisted hands beating out a tattoo on his thighs. Catching at last some of his excitement, her eyes glinting in flinty ironic response, she closed in upon him like a hunter upon a hypnotised prey, and climbed upon the bed, mounting him, straddling his prostrate form like a bridge, her long leather-clad legs bestriding him in a wide arc. Gyrating slowly from side to side, she lowered herself from above him, her hard berry-dark nipples brushing the glistening top of his penis, glancing off its enflamed unsheathed dome as he emitted small lost grunting noises beneath her. Languid at first, dream-like, as if performing a well-known perfunctory chore, she began slapping his face with the back of her hand and her palm, hardly more than light playful strokes to begin with, then gathering momentum – and venom – as well, picking up a certain practised rhythm, until she was striking him really hard, quite viciously on both cheeks, methodical, unerring, causing his head to spin back and forward like a punchbag being hit at well-aimed speed, his eyes puckered up in terrified pleasure, tiny flecks of reddish foam forming on his lips, his mouth opening and shutting in sharp fishlike fashion as he gulped in air, jerking out broken garbled entreaties, his hands making feeble ineffectual gestures, reaching one moment for the swaying brown globes of her breasts dangling above him, then falling weakly away from them as from objects too sacred to touch. Her breathing ragged, her jaw set and eyes arrowed darkly, she pressed down upon him with controlled undulating frenzy, the brass studs sequinned down the sides of her jeans and the heavy embossed buckle of her belt biting cruelly into his squirming limbs, sinking into the soft flabby folds of his flesh as she spreadeagled him, lunging her spiked fury and spite into him, her snarling breath burning past his twisted face as a long protracted shudder ran through his riven length, her teeth clamped, her panting voice cursing him.

Minutes later Simon stood under the shower in the bathroom adjacent to the main bedroom, relishing the cold tingling needle-point jets of water that hissed down on him from overhead, startling his lately quiescent flesh into quick jovial life. He hummed and whistled in tune to the music that was coming over the stereo system.

Simon rubbed and sponged himself, wincing when he touched the raw tender welts left on him from their lovemaking; he grinned in rueful boyish fashion; he prized these bruises and lacerations, thinking of them as victory spoils, noble scars earned on the battlefield of their mutually inordinate and punishing passion, the dominance he was happy and eager for her to assume in bed, the gracious submission she readily accorded him outside of it. It was an arrangement that suited them both ideally, and at times it made him long for similar felicitous juxtapositions in life as a whole, where people were forever stepping into rôles they were woefully unsuited to assume, usually ending up miserably miscast for the rest of their grey scrabbling lives. He sighed, gingerly probing his swollen mouth with his tongue; life would be so much simpler if only people would learn to know and play their rôles better.

Today he felt more keenly aware of his own good fortune; he shimmered with verve and initiative, in control of everything within his circumference, master of his own not insignificant little ship, ready to tackle new enterprises, new schemes, promotions, investments, manoeuvres and manipulations. He whistled louder as the music on

14

the stereo crashed and whirled towards a shrill crescendo. The world, that raucous burrowing back-stabbing little world he had chosen to invade and stride in, was there after all for the taking, a sizeable portion of it anyway, and with such an invaluable asset as Marcie in his business and emotional arsenal he could not fail. To do so one would have to be dedicated to failure, and he was not. He liked to win, which made him no better, no more meritorious than most people, since winning was a human craving most people had, but what raised him above the colourless norm was his unswerving resolution to succeed. Not merely not to lose, which was an ambition any automaton might reasonably be expected to harbour, but to win at any cost and by any means as long as they were not injurious to himself, to rout and demoralise the opposition totally before they were aware that hostilities had even begun. That need, that fierce resolve was always with him, in all moods and seasons, whether he acted like an anchorite of lean ascetic whims and desires, or out-played the grossest most dissipated gigolo about town since Farouk expired in his own fat, the drive to win never left him, but Marcia sharpened it, honed it, fed and fuelled it in a way that was completely beyond the grasp of that other weak affectionate vague and uncertain woman Elinor his wife, existing in nerveless opulence in that other quite separate life of home and family, with their three equally unassertive children and their sullen German au pair girl whose name he could never remember and who always ate alone in her room. He thought of them all as a coterie of rather bovine creatures grazing on rich pastureland, enjoying the plump fruits of his acumen and ambition to the point of dimwitted repletion, chewing the well-nourished cud and only distantly intruding upon his larger life in the city.

With her hard lithe limbs and bruising mouth as much as with her brains, Marcie understood his ambition, groomed, pampered and perfected it, stripped it of excess tissue and made it as lean, cunning and resilient as her own body, as devious in its snares and lures, as forceful in its attraction, as elusive to pin down and slot into easy categories. As he touched the soft places of his flesh where she had left her imprint, he thought of her with great tenderness and respect: being married to her would destroy everything, of course, bring it all down to vapid blinkered perspectives, and he shuddered at the idea; no, as things stood she was invaluable to him in every way, and he was determined to let things stand as they were. Again it was a matter of rôle-playing, and Marcie did it superbly. It was grotesque to think of their relationship in any other light, and it was a source of unending solace to him to know that she felt the same way. The trim insipid little domesticities, the tasteless conjugalities of life in his house in Mill Hill receded out of sight, out of hearing, almost out of memory upon the rush of wellbeing and confidence that swept through him, and he hummed and whistled louder and faster to the music pounding away in the background.

When he had dried himself and tied a towel round his waist, he padded back into the bedroom, where Marcie had already chosen and laid out his clothes on the eiderdown; in this as in most other day-to-day things he trusted her judgement implicitly. He was putting on the light grey suit and silk shirt when she came in, draped in a loose kimono robe, naked again underneath, body glistening from her bath, smoking a cheroot out of a slim holder.

'Janice phoned while you were in the shower,' she said, resting one of her buttocks on the deep windowsill. 'Apparently our erstwhile genius Art strayed after he left here last night and didn't get in till the small hours. She phoned to say they may be a little late arriving for lunch.'

Simon frowned. 'No doubt stopping on the way for a restorative.' He began stuffing the tail ends of his shirt down into his trousers. 'Let's hope they don't start one of their scenes – if they ever do get here in the first place.'

Marcie blew a curling whiff of smoke. 'Oh, I think they'll come – give her credit, when there's business afoot she comes running like a dutiful child.' She slanted her head, giving him a shrewd look. 'Of course she's not to know whether it is to be to her advantage or not, is she?'

He sat down on the bed, pulling on his socks. 'That's right. But she's bright, and she's bound to catch the drift of things sooner or later.' He spoke with a certain crisp satisfaction.

'And then what?'

He looked up, eyebrow raised. 'And then I hope she'll be sensible and not stand in his way.'

Marcie gave him a laconic smile. 'You mean you hope she'll creep off into a corner and not cause anyone any trouble, like a good and loving little housewife?'

He straightened up. 'That would be too much to hope for, my

16

dear, but yes, something like that would be very agreeable.'

She screwed the cheroot more firmly into the holder. 'You really are determined to split them up, then?'

He spread out his hands as if appealing for logic. 'From a purely commercial and one might almost say aesthetic point of view, yes. I think he'd be far better off concentrating on writing songs, and she's holding him back with this rather dead-end duo act of theirs.'

She inhaled. 'You don't happen to fancy her, do you, Simon?'

He thought awhile, mocking. 'I don't think so, my dear.' He got up from the bed. 'Why – do *you*?'

Marcie scratched the inside of her bare thigh, her face impassive. 'I hadn't thought about it. Maybe on a rainy day – who knows? Might put some excitement into her drab little existence.'

He regarded her admiringly. 'I do believe you'd seduce her, just for the hell of it.'

She shrugged. 'That's another grubby little fantasy you can add to your list, free of charge.'

'I'm just overawed by your versatility, my dear, that's all.' He paused in the act of straightening his shirt cuffs. '*Have* you? Seduced another woman, I mean?'

'I'm sure your imagination will supply an answer, Simon.' She smoked quietly for some moments while he put the finishing touches to his dressing. 'So poor old Janice is to be sacrificed, is she, for the greater good of the firm?'

He gave her a sharp reproving look. 'For the greater good of us all, my dear. Don't ever forget that.'

'I'm sure you'd never let me, even if it should slip my mind now and then.'

He became brisk and decisive again. 'Don't get me wrong, dear. I've nothing against Janice personally. I cannot afford the luxury of personal likes and dislikes, not where business is concerned. She's a nice girl, I suppose, but she shouldn't be allowed to delude herself into believing she's got a great voice or anything of that sort of nonsense. The kind of voice she has is going for ten a penny, for God's sake.' He moved slowly about the room as he spoke, with a kind of soft purring feline content, picking up things and examining them dreamily and putting them down again. 'Ten a penny, that sort of voice. You must know that by now, dear.'

'I hadn't quite realised she was that lousy.'

17

'Oh, it's all right for the sort of thing she's been doing,' he said airily. 'One-night stands in Leeds, Birmingham, Manchester. Places where they play bingo in between acts. Where people eat chicken-in-the-*rough* and gulp down pints of ale. That sort of thing.' He sighed. 'I'm afraid her horizons are strictly limited.'

'Poor girl.' Marcie closed her eyes, blowing smoke. 'Maybe I will seduce her after all, if only to show her that somebody cares.'

He smiled lazily. 'That's your forte, my dear – making people feel wanted.' He went on padding softly about the room, making his absentminded inventory of things. 'Our friend Art, however, is something else again, I believe. He's got some real talent, writing songs, but as long as he's tied to her doing those stupid gigs up and down the country he'll never amount to anything.'

Marcie stretched, her thigh showing. 'And you want him all to yourself, eh, Simon, neatly wrapped up in a contract that'll give you exclusive rights over him?'

He nodded. 'I want him to form his own music company, in partnership with me, *that's* what I want him to do. Nothing to it. A hundred pounds down for a licence and you're in business.'

'Sounds incredibly simple.'

'Simple as blinking, darling,' he agreed affably. 'That's the thing to do today. Form your own limited company. High stakes to be made, selling good material to the really top names in the business. As long as you know where to look, and I think you'll agree I've got the right kind of contacts.'

She smiled. 'Your wallet's full of them.'

He managed to look ingenuous and misunderstood. 'I'm just a confirmed hardworking capitalist, like everyone else. Does that make me a latter-day Svengali?'

'Not any more than usual, Simon. I'm just the tiniest bit puzzled, that's all.' She got up from the windowsill and ejected the remainder of her smoked cheroot into an ashtray. 'I mean, that last single of theirs didn't quite sink without trace, did it? It may not have set the world on fire, but it held quite a respectable position in the charts for over six weeks, and it's still played now and then. So how come her voice is so terrible all of a sudden?'

He gave her another look of mild reproof and disappointment, as if she should have known better than to ask such a question. 'My dear, you know as well as I how that record came to be the sort of near hit it was. I promoted it remorselessly and at considerable expense. There was hardly a disc jockey in the country who was free from my blandishments and wiles. God knows what it cost me in parties and secret midnight crates of champagne and cognac left mysteriously at doors of well-known radio personalities. I whored that record around shamelessly for weeks before it even came out. Not even mediocrity comes cheap any more.'

'And what happens to her now, if you succeed in weaning Art away from her? Or is that irrelevant?'

He lifted his shoulders. 'I really don't know. How should I? I can't be expected to provide life insurance to everyone I meet in the course of business, can I?'

'It will be hard for her to start learning to be a mere housewife at this late date, even if she is in the outer darkness of the show business world.'

Simon pursed his lips. 'Your concern does you credit, dear, but what am I to do? I'm in this wretched business for what I can make out of it and not for humanitarian reasons. I daresay the working-man's club and parish hall will be with us for a long time to come, so at least she'll be able to sing for her supper, however humble it may be. She's good enough for that, I think.'

She went over and looked out of the window, ignoring the casual cruelty of his words. 'Poor Janice,' she said again, half to herself. 'Poor bitch. At least I hope she enjoys my canneloni.'

He came up behind her and placed both his hands on her hips, stroking her. 'You're positively overflowing with loving kindness this morning, darling.' He pressed himself against her, his hands sliding down inside the robe, over her thighs.

She twisted angrily away from him, tightening the belt of her robe. 'You met them first in Bradford, didn't you?'

He blinked and compressed his lips. 'Actually it was Barnsley, in some hideous nightclub or whatever. The first and only time I've ever been to Barnsley.'

'I thought Bradford *was* Barnsley,' she said, giving a mirthless smile. 'They sort of merge together in my mind, in one grey murky blob.'

'A pardonable confusion, believe me.'

'What were you doing there, Simon? It hardly seems your kind of place.' She sat on the bed, leaning back. 'I can't quite imagine you straining at the leash to get to Barnsley.'

'I don't really know how I got there,' he said, taking the place at the window where she had sat. 'Probably on some obscure eccentric piece of missionary work – I can't remember now. Anyway, there I was, and there they were – most extraordinary.'

He had found himself sitting at a table directly beneath the stage. All cough and smoke and noise everywhere, nobody taking much notice of what was taking place onstage, which admittedly was not exactly spellbinding, some silly comedy act or other in which two clown-dressed men kept shoving one another about and guffawing grotesquely at their own inane jokes; they had to, since nobody else did. When he next looked up at the stage there was this young couple up there; he had not even noticed that the two comics had finished their atrocious act and had scuttled off. The young man and woman were naively handsome, he with his trim apostolic beard and determinedly unkempt appearance, a thick-chained medallion dangling from his neck as he sat bent over his guitar on a wooden stool behind the girl, who was tall and earnest, with long copperish hair falling over her shoulders, gripping the microphone as if for reassurance, like a spar or lifebuoy. She was white-faced in the glare of the overhead lights and looked scared to death, yet defiant, gallantly making a go of it, while her partner stooped obliviously over his instrument, tightening and loosening its strings, not once looking up from the task. There was something at once so gullible and brash about them that to his surprise Simon felt an unfamiliar stirring of sympathy and curiosity and waited keenly to see what they would deliver. The young man at last twanged sharply on his guitar, striking a challenging note; the girl swallowed, stepped forward blindly like someone about to face a firing squad, and began to sing. The guitar playing was nimble, adept, precise as it followed the singer, whose voice was quite devoid of colour but pleasant enough in its undemanding way, controlled to a clear innocuous pitch of competence. They were no more than a touchingly goodlooking pair of young people performing to the top of their decidedly limited ability, giving a neatly tailored exercise that gave no offence and brought no excitement, and beyond a feeble flutter of applause at the close of each number the audience paid them scant attention and went on noisily drinking and rattling their glasses and behaving in a boorish, raucous amiable fashion, as befitted that type of clientele. Not knowing precisely what he had expected, Simon felt vaguely disappointed and his interest in them began rapidly to evaporate. Still, there was no urgency for him to leave and go elsewhere for any particular reason, so he stayed at his table and ordered another drink.

Then the couple began singing a different type of song altogether, original and trenchant, like vinegar compared to diluted honey, and he sensed a change come about both in the performers themselves and in the audience, a change so tenuous and subtle at first as to be almost imperceptible, no more than a slight stirring of awareness, a sudden pause in the prevailing din; it grew and strengthened, became a pulsing thing that took on a unique identity, so that the revellers quit slurping their whiskies and gins and looked up at the couple on the other side of the footlights with dim surprise, unbelieving, as if something very pleasant and refreshing had just happened to each of them individually, turning their evening inside out, turning it into quite an event, a happy encounter. The dogged pounding of the guitar in the background changed to a live vulnerable thing, thrusting, inquisitive, eager to explore, pluck out new meanings, transcend its own tight monotony and break loose in prankish vibrant freedom; the girl's voice too had somehow changed, as if by the force and depth of the lyrics, letting the words go from her without constraint, without striving after effect, letting them instead assume their own character and direction, letting them travel at their own pace, cleaving the turgid atmosphere like swift bright arrows, demanding to be listened to and received. Intrigued and not a little shaken, blinking his eyes as if coming out of a torpid half slumber, Simon had made his way afterwards backstage to their cramped dressing-room, where he learned that the songs that had so enlivened the second half of their performance had all been written by the young man himself.

A renewed concourse of church bells intruded into his reverie, and he looked up to see Marcie standing, yawning and stretching herself, the belt of the robe again loosened so that it slipped from her shoulders and swung wide, showing her breasts, the dusk of her body framed vivid in the fleecy white cloth. There was nothing flaunting or capricious in the gesture, yet as always her casual nakedness caught him off guard, catapulted him out of complacency, threw into disarray his neat brisk conception of himself, so that he wanted to grovel and crawl to her and lick her feet, to prostrate himself before her and have her trample on him and use him as she wished. She read with ease the expression on his face and smiled, making no attempt to draw the robe together.

'My my,' she murmured, her eyes sardonic, 'we *are* greedy today, aren't we?'

'Marcie – ' he grunted and made a wild fumbling lunge at her, but she laughed, evaded him and went lightly from the room.

'Bitch,' he swore softly, taking out a large floppy handkerchief and mopping his brow. 'Black bitch.' He breathed the words like a tender benediction in her soap-scented wake.

He ambled across to the window and tugged at the swish-cord of the drapes, drawing them fully back from the spacious floor-to-ceiling panoramic sheet of glass. He stood with hands clasped behind him, looking down at the city sprawling away into the distance, like a plunderer who had swept down from the hills and conquered it while the inhabitants lay drugged and slothful in their beds. The morning had not yet come fully awake, slow stirring in its sabbatical indolence, a thin haze shimmering in the air, veiling the lineaments of buildings. The late-rising sun struck tiny arrows of light off the golden cupolas of distant churches, of domes, spires, parapets, turrets steepling the sky.

Simon looked down on it all with pride of ownership, teetering gently back and forth on his feet, watching the dreamy solemn city stir itself lazily and struggle into its more measured weekend stride, a bronzed furore in the air as bells pealed and boomed and sonorously echoed, jingling in musical mayhem above the rooftops and serrated stone steppes of the metropolis. There was a slow glazed magic in it, looking out over London on a Sunday morning from the plush depths of his eyrie, the sun nudging itself forward through a feathery bank of cloud, warm images like wine creeping through his mind like the felicitous fingers of Marcie upon his skin.

He turned back into the room, where the stereo music, having ebbed, was now surging triumphantly once more towards a new crescendo of pounding primitive exaltation; he stood a moment in the middle of the room and closed his eyes, the rhythms crashing about him, drowning the gentler music of the bells beyond the window.

They sat round a low glass-topped table near the open terrace window, sipping gin and tonic, a welcome light breeze on their faces. Simon, annoyed with the latecoming of his two guests and petulantly determined to let them know it, sat a little apart, pretending to be listening with half-closed eyes to the muted sounds of the stereo, but stealing surreptitious glances at them when he thought they were not looking, rather like a sly master trying to catch his pupils out in a childish misdemeanour. This subterfuge was quite lost on Art, however, who bore a ravaged appearance, the unwise festivities of the night before spiderwebbing his face, eyes sunk far back in his head, hunched on the edge of his seat, gripping the square chunky glass in both hands. The stop at a pub in Earl's Court on the way over in the minicab had apparently not produced the desired effects, nor was the second gin and tonic now in his hand weaving any magical formula so far. He wished to Christ they would shut off that bloody music, stop the small talk and just put the gin bottle on the table without further ado, but the social niceties had to be observed, though he was more than content to let Janice make most of the verbal running, which she was doing anyway and with a vivacity that was unusual in her, he noted in the midst of his hangover misery. She sat just as rigid as himself, her face strained, nervous, devoid of makeup, a bit be-draggled-looking in her corduroy jacket and jeans, talking over-loudly at times, vying with the music as if to compensate for his bilious silence. The stop at the pub had in fact been a bit of a disaster, for they had done nothing but quarrel for the ten minutes or so that they were there, and the drink itself had been a dead loss as far as a cure was concerned, so all in all he concluded the day had little or nothing to offer him and he resigned himself to wait for Marcie to offer him a refill as he quietly died in the meantime. He had a vague idea that Simon had some kind of business proposition to put, but he could remember only bits of their conversation yesterday and had not the strength or inclination to think about it now. All he wanted at the moment was another bloody gin and let the rest take care of itself. He moped in limbo.

At least the lounge was cool, the beige and oatmeal-toned walls giving it a spacious airy elegance. Strips of vivid Peruvian rugs broke the glazed dark-brown surface of the woodblock floor; some prints lined the walls, sparse abstracts and samples of poster art in the Beardsley fashion, with here and there one or two originals Simon had got or bullied or otherwise wheedled out of small covens of artistic dilettantes whose style, or lack of it, plainly reflected his own. Plants in terracotta pots threw pleasant green shades across the tiles of the terrace outside. Simon soaked in all this comfort like a sponge, igniting a brief envy in Art before it waned and was submerged in a renewed flood of post-bacchanalian ennui and self-pity.

Marcie, cool and efficient as ever in an oriental-type gown with high prim collar, long sleeves ending in tight-wristed cuffs and with a hip-reaching slit up one side, found herself once more pitying the other girl, her pinched scared defiance as if she felt there was some sort of unvoiced conspiracy brewing between Simon and her husband but was determined to push it from her mind and be cordial to everyone. The late arrival of the two had not affected Marcie in the slightest; she knew it had not really upset her lover either, and that he was only making a silly fuss of it because he felt it incumbent on him as a sort of elder statesman to show his displeasure at the ill grace of the younger generation. She was amused by this, but she also rather despised him for pretending to harbour a grievance he did not really feel in order just to make them uncomfortable and assert his authority. Whatever sympathies she had were entirely on the side of the supposed miscreants, and she thought Simon patently ludicrous in his false injured dignity and bloated pomposity, lingering over his diluted gin, a fat spoilt boy.

Becoming aware at last of her amused eyes on him as she passed between him and the table, he shifted uneasily in his chair, then gave a sheepish grin and drew closer to the others.

'Oh hell,' he said, expansive, laying a paternal hand upon Art's shoulder, 'let's all have a refill, my dears!'

'I was about to do just that,' said Marcie, returning with a large glass jug holding gin and iced tonic.

As she quietly poured, Simon pulled his chair closer and loosened his jacket, looking at Art in sly merry old-boy camaraderie. 'Who was a naughty boy last night then, eh?' He swivelled his head and winked hugely round at the women. 'Drenched in wine and smothered in roses, eh?' He blinked, as if surprised at his own wit, and slapped his knee. 'That's it, eh – drenched in wine and smothered in roses!' He leaned back in the chair and laughed in great gusts at his ingenuity of phrase until his eyes streamed and he fished out the copious handkerchief again to wipe away the moisture. 'And we in our innocence thinking you'd gone straight back to your trusting little wife here!'

In the laying down and lifting of a glass, it seemed, Simon was transformed from a glowering sullen host brooding in a dark niche into a beaming avuncular teddy bear, florid and jolly, dispensing largesse with a bland wave of his soft plump hand, his eyes moist with conviviality sunk in the creased suet layers of his face. Marcie sat down and surveyed him over the rim of her glass, distrusting his sudden spurt of mellifluous hilarity.

Art grinned weakly, the gin slowly working the hoped-for miracle; he was far from cured yet but his misery was becoming more bearable. 'That's about the size of it, Simon,' he confessed, contritely eyeing Janice. 'Went for a bite and a drink somewhere – God knows where – and ended up having more drink than bite.'

'Ah! It was always thus, my boy,' said Simon, beaming broadly, radiating forgiveness, a paunchy priest in the confessional on a good day feeling kindly disposed towards sinners. 'It was always thus,' he smacked his rosy lips. 'And you, my dear,' he said, turning to Janice, 'have you found it in your heart to forgive him yet, or are you still making him grovel at your feet?'

Janice felt a slight churning in her stomach at this overripe sickening geniality, but gave a tight blithe smile. 'I'm afraid Art is not the grovelling type.' She saw with pleasure the quick angry frown forming on Simon's face, and noted how Marcie smiled in comradely response as she tapped her fingernails quietly against her glass. 'I had a nice little evening all to myself,' continued Janice, quite prepared to compromise as long as it did not cost too much. 'Watched television without hearing a word, played some sounds, drank rather a lot of vodka – you know, the usual harmless home-sweet-home stuff.'

Simon joined his fingers together. 'How very domestic. You look none the worse for it.' He managed to inject a measure of smooth malice into the words, though his tone was as fruity and amiable as before. 'How charming to have such an oasis of calm homely leisure in the midst of all the turmoil you two have to endure, tearing up and down the length and breadth of our green and pleasant land playing to orang-utans and other untamed species over the clatter of knives and forks.' He closed his eyes as if in pious contemplation of their plight. 'Such lack of appreciation must be quite daunting at times. I really don't know how you keep going.' He sighed, looking at each of them in turn with soulful admiration. 'There are times, I'm sure, when you wished you were a million miles apart.'

Marcie, intent and alert, saw the muscles in Janice's face tighten at Simon's words, though she remained upright and unshaken in her seat, the same fixed unyielding smile nailed to her face. Again Marcie felt sorry for her and contemptuous of Simon, though still in a remote, rather uninvolved way, keeping herself a mere spectator at an unedifying little show of professional knife-throwing. It would have been so much more charitable, and certainly less unpleasant for all, had Simon simply taken Art out to some pub and put his conniving little scheme squarely to him over a few drinks, without dragging Janice along on the pretext of a pleasant Sunday lunch just to embarrass and humiliate her and possibly goad her into futile retaliation; for Marcie had no doubt Simon would have his way, he would have his mercenary little triumph without much effort.

She let her gaze rest obliquely on Art. She knew very little about him, really, but she did not think he was by choice weak or faithless, just ambitious, which was natural at his age; and this was leading to stresses with Janice which Simon was determined to exploit. Marcie found herself hating the whole unsavoury business, and wishing it was over; the lunch was slowly turning into a marathon test of nerves and Simon was winning hands down. She longed for the apartment to be quiet and restful again, where she had no need to feel sorry for anyone and her means of enjoyment and repose were entirely her own affair.

She put down her drink and got to her feet. 'If you lot can bear the thought,' she said, moving away, 'lunch is just about ready whenever you are.'

Simon gave a little clap of applause and clambered up, patting the protruding hillock of his belly. 'Bravo, my dear – I'm famished! We follow where you lead.'

They seated themselves round the white circular table in the dining recess, a large bowl overflowing with fruit glimmering like coloured glass in the centre. After a quick few glasses of wine, fearful of letting the warm reassuring glow engendered by the gin ebb away, Art began to pick at his food like someone sternly facing up to a test of character; tossed green salad first, then the rich cannelloni itself, beautifully cooked, but which left his stomach no less queasy than before, and as soon as he decently could without giving offence he dived back to the wine, declining coffee. He was determined to be as fortified as possible before Simon began unfolding whatever was revolving busily round inside that glistening cherry-ripe cranium of his; he felt he had to be on his guard whatever it was, and at the same time, rather to his surprise, he felt a strange tenderness towards Janice, as if he had already wronged her without knowing what the hell he was supposed to have done.

Throughout the meal Simon dipped and curved and turned little scintillating verbal somersaults like a performing seal, keeping up a facile flow of chatter, a cherubic caricature of the perfect host, easy and brilliant in his tactics to keep everyone entertained and diverted. Looking on, growing more alert and perceptive with wine, it seemed to Art that Simon was making a special display of being gaily courteous and solicitous to Janice, pressing wine and small delicacies upon her along with an equal amount of compliments, addressing most of his remarks and comments to her and in all bestowing upon her the status of star guest. It was like laying inordinate layers of butter upon a decidedly thin slice of bread. Janice received all this attention with a kind of bemused politeness, sitting as if carved into her chair, eating with studied detachment, her earlier nervous vivacity gone and in its place an attitude of frozen serenity into which she had retreated as though fleeing from an enemy. The only sign she gave of being actually at the table with them was when Marcie spoke across to her, showing then quick unfeigned gratitude no matter how trivial or ordinary the remark might be; it was as though an invisible thread of new and unexpected understanding was being woven between them to the exclusion of the two men, finding themselves sudden allies in a secret battle into which they were being drawn and inveigled against their better judgement.

Art looked down into his wine, frowning, a sense of nagging guilt weighing upon him, dogging his thoughts, making them drag like chains, and not knowing the cause he gradually subsided into querulous and moody silence, defiant and defensive at once, hating all the scented polished luxury and affluence about him, the hard glitter and gleaming surfaces of everything, the stereo music phoney as that piped in pub or supermarket; he looked at the fat florid man opposite him with sudden distaste, wanting to smash his fist into that plump complacent face and see if real blood would flow from it, and the black woman showing her sleek limbs in the slit gown whenever she moved, her cool superior smile and sleepy voice, a bought toy wound up to act on cue, looking as if she belonged behind a glass case, a decorative nerveless artifact, impeccable and remote. He found himself sliding into the elaborate phoniness of it all.

27

When the meal ended, Simon showed no more effect of having consumed so much food and drink than if he had sat down to a mere snack, and sat picking his teeth while the others finished before heaving himself reluctantly up from the table, draining his wineglass as he stood, belching happily and without restraint. He looked round at them with a heavy-lidded smile and again patted his abdomen.

'Amen,' he intoned sonorously. 'Shall we adjourn to the terrace and have our post-prandial libations out there, my dears?' He padded out, leading the way.

The sun, as if in defiance of the waning season, had grown warmer to show it still had strength to make people sweat, to dazzle the mind into a delusion of past languor; the breeze abated as the day lengthened, offering scant relief from the heat as they lounged about, glasses in hand, talking in a desultory fashion, like people in all the hazy lassitude of high summer, leaning on the parapet, picking out telltale city landmarks near and far, embroidering them with little fables and recollections, small patchwork histories ephemeral and half imagined; occasionally a jet plane streaked high and noiselessly across the sky, invisible at the head of the thin silver snail-like trail it left in its wake.

The streets below snored rather than roared, the volume of traffic trim and leisurely as citizens went unhurriedly about Sunday pastimes and meanderings, in no particular hurry to get to one place from another, a placid sedate parade that seen from above hardly appeared to be moving at all. It was a beautiful day, quiet, full of dimmed brilliance and charm tinged with a vague underlying melancholy, a nameless rueful backward-glancing longing for something past and out of reach. More than once Art turned to his wife as if to beckon her aside and somehow warn her in a quick impatient whisper; her face was remote, however, withdrawn, as she stood in a corner of the balcony looking out over the city, in a private reverie, and he turned away from her with the same perplexed hurt and unaccountable feeling of having somehow wronged and betrayed her.

And then he found himself alone with Simon; he had scarcely noticed the absence of the women; they had retired into the coolness of the apartment. Simon was resting his bulk against one of the small outdoor tables, stirring the olive in his drink and looking at him with a pensive enquiring stare. Art was floating happily on a gentle feather-soft balloon of alcohol, and he began to see Simon as a much wiser and kindlier person. With a surge of stoical affection he faced him.

'What is it, Simon?' he asked cheerfully. 'You've something on your mind, right? Out with it, mate!' He topped up his glass from the jug close by, taking care not to appear drunk.

Simon plopped the olive into his mouth, revolving it about with his tongue with the thin stick, sucking on it. 'You're right – I do have something on my mind, concerning you.'

Art grinned, pushing back his shoulders. 'I'm all ears.'

Simon came forward, placed his hand on the other's arm and took him to the edge of the terrace, dropping his voice to a low intimate tone, as if they were about to hatch a plot.

'I did rather hint at it yesterday evening, before you left,' he began, 'but there wasn't much time.' He turned round, rubbing his chin. 'I want you to get this right the first time. The old grey matter's in working order?'

'I'm far from pissed, if that's what you mean,' returned Art with a swagger, holding the glass firmly in his hand.

'Good. You know I believe in your ability, don't you?'

Art nodded, sombre. 'Up to now you've certainly put your money where your mouth is, and we're both grateful to you for that.'

Simon waved expansively. 'Not at all, purely a business venture. I've had some good returns.' He paused and again rolled the olive round on his tongue. 'That's just it. I think the returns could be much greater from now on, for all of us, if – ' he munched the olive, flicking the tiny stick away; 'if you're prepared to listen to what I have to say.'

Art shrugged. 'I'm prepared.'

Simon turned his smiling glistening face to him, sipping his drink. 'How do you see yourself first, Art – as singer, guitarist, accompanist, whatever, or as songwriter?'

The other man frowned. 'Hadn't really thought about it, to be honest – does it matter?'

Simon raised an eyebrow. 'Matter? My dear boy, surely that is the only thing that *does* matter? Hmm?' He waited as if the point could not reasonably be contradicted.

'Er – well, yes, I suppose it is,' replied Art, feeling somehow chastened and ungrateful. 'Yes, I suppose it is, really,' he agreed more readily.

29

'I'm extremely relieved to hear you say so,' said Simon, peeved; he waited, but moved impatiently when the younger man remained silent. 'And how *do* you see yourself, Art? It is rather important that I know.'

'Oh. Well – ' Art looked intently down into the sunlit sauntering streets as if for enlightenment, then up at the sky, seeming to treat it as a matter not to be rushed. He turned at length to his questioner. 'I suppose, behind it all, I think of myself as a songwriter first and foremost.' He glanced dubiously at Simon. 'Is that bigheaded of me?'

'Not in the slightest,' responded the other, highly pleased. 'It's what I was hoping to hear, because it means on that score at least we think along the same lines.' He began to pace slowly up and down, taking the other man with him, clasping his shoulder in a paternal way, lifting his glass now and then in emphasis and continuing to speak in the same confiding cloistered tone. 'You see, it's my opinion that the way we're going we're wasting the best asset we've got – your songwriting. I think you're throwing that talent away by haring up and down the country doing these stupid grubby little gigs – ' he shut his eyes in distaste – 'Lord, what a perfectly nauseating phrase! Those frantic scampering little engagements from one horrid hovel to the next, earning little more than your board and keep and having to hole up in disgusting hotel rooms when you're not travelling half the night in that cramped little van – ' Simon stopped, as if overcome by the litany of horrors he was cataloguing, looking earnestly at his companion. 'I honestly don't know how you have endured it so far!'

'Oh, it's not half so bad as all that, you know,' Art replied, feeling his work style being vilified and rushing to defend it like an old friend. 'We've had some good times on the road, lots of laughs, and met some fantastic people – really kind, you know – '

'Yes, yes,' sighed Simon, resuming his deliberate pacing, taking Art in tow, humouring him as before. 'I don't say it's been all gloom, and it certainly got you the experience you needed, but the point is, I hope you agree, that it's time we put all that trucking and trading behind us and moved on to the next phase in our plan of operation, the next advance in our campaign – '

'You sound like bleeding Eisenhower,' Art broke in, piqued by the brisk thorough manner of his host, which jarred with the slow benevolent progress of the day and his own unhurried thoughts and lazy speculations. 'You make it all sound like a matter of warfare, as if we were moving over a minefield.' He bit his lip, rebellious. 'Looking at it that way takes all the kick out of it, all the joy. Makes it all sound fucking mechanical.'

Simon winced, then nodded in amiable deference. 'Yes, I *do* rather tend to draw on the old military analogy, but don't let that sidetrack you, dear boy,' he continued, clasping the other's shoulder more firmly. 'It doesn't change the thrust of my argument, to coin a phrase, which is simply that I think we'd all be better off in every way by having you concentrate on what you do best of all – write songs.'

Art stopped in his obligatory perambulations and looked at the older man, full of sudden insight. 'Stop the act, you mean, with me and Janice? Quit it?' He stepped back, putting a small distance between them. 'Is that what you mean, Simon – is that what all this is leading up to? You want me to step out of the act with Janice and let her go it alone? Christ,' murmured Art half to himself, more in wonder than anger, 'I've never thought *that* was what was running round in your head all this time!'

Sullen, defensive, stung into retaliation by what he took to be a display of churlish ingratitude, Simon stood his ground stolidly, almost growling in his impatience and need to vindicate himself. 'Don't be so melodramatic, Art, and don't for God's sake be so naive. You're at a dead-end now, a full stop, and you know it, and the only way out of it, the only way you're ever going to get ahead in your career, is what I'm asking you to do now and prepared to back you with all the hard cash and influence you're likely to need. What is so sinister about that, I'd like to know?' he went on. 'I'm only urging you to make full use of the very real talent you've got – maybe the *only* real talent you've got!' He almost sneered, fishing out his copious handkerchief and mopping his steaming face and neck.

'Oh, I don't doubt your motives, Simon,' replied Art, his voice calm. 'I know I can't sing, and as a guitarist I'll never make Django Reinhardt rise from his grave to praise me. I think you're right, as a matter of fact,' he went on in a relaxed ruminative manner, staring at the ground; 'I think whatever talent I have comes out in the songs I write – '

'Well then?' challenged Simon, the epitome of misunderstood logic. 'We don't have a problem, do we?'

Art moved away and placed his glass on the parapet, his back turned. 'There is just one thing I'd like to know, one little thing I'd like to have cleared up before we go any further.'

Simon sighed and ambled heavily up to where he stood. 'You mean Janice, of course?'

Art nodded, not looking away from the city rising below them. 'I mean Janice. What happens to her if I split the act?' His mood had changed once more and his voice sounded querulous rather than angry, as if he were already mentally coping with a whole new set of problems.

Simon noted the change and assumed his former benign Nestorian rôle as easily as slipping on a familiar well-worn coat. 'My friend,' he said, laying a fatherly hand on the other's sleeve, 'I think you do that admirable wife of yours a considerable injustice. Don't you think she wants only the best for you? Don't you think that's her first and highest concern?'

Art gestured nervously with one hand. 'Yes, but what happens to *her*? As it is, her whole life revolves round our stage act; what would she *do*, for God's sake, if that was taken away from her? She couldn't change overnight to just looking after the potted plants and trying out recipes – ' He glowered angrily at the other man. 'You can't expect her to do that!'

Art's voice had risen in his agitation, making Simon glance round anxiously towards the room behind them; he made out the indistinct shapes of the two girls seated on a couch poring over some record albums, and relaxed, knowing they were well out of earshot and that it would be impossible for them to catch anything that was being said over the noise from the stereo player. He took the other man's glass and freshened it without speaking; he came back and put it gently, reassuringly into his hand.

'Let's try and not get too intense about this,' he began. They leaned forward upon the parapet, like two people at the seafront leaning on a promenade railing looking out to sea. 'Let's not jump to any wild conclusions. First of all, this idea of mine is simply a commercial proposition, a matter of business, and not an evil scheme to break up anybody's marriage or private life. Just remember that, will you, please?' Simon sounded grave, like a lawyer advising a client.

Art muttered something, his thoughts jumbled. He knew Simon was right in assessing his ambition and the extent to which he was willing to go to have it released and realised, yet at the same time he resented being found out in what he had almost convinced himself was a weakness, a defect of character, an absence of loyalty. He was not, after all, being coerced into something he did not want, he was not being manoeuvred into a position he had not secretly thought about and coveted for such a long time; it was like having a persistent ache localised and treated after putting up with the pain for too long. His ambition was nothing very remarkable and could not in any sense be thought of as voracious; it was indeed quite orthodox and nothing to be ashamed of, yet he felt he was yielding to a craven desire to promote and propel it at Janice's expense, for already he felt sure she would not be going with him, that it would not be so much a question of her staying behind as being left behind stranded by the impetus of his cornered ambition leaping out of its snare, sprung by Simon's dexterous cupidity.

'It can all be arranged and set up quite cleanly,' Simon was saying, joining his hands serenely together. 'All absolutely above board and honour bright. Only trust me to put things in motion – that's all I ask. Best for everyone, believe me.'

And then suddenly light dawned finally in Art's fuddled mind. He was being asked, for Simon's benefit far more than for his, to betray his wife utterly, to condemn her to the rôle of the little woman who stayed at home. Alone in the rat race of show business into which they had plunged together, she would be lost; and for all their quarrels he loved her. He wouldn't, he couldn't do it. He turned on Simon, his eyes angry. 'I wonder if you know what you are asking me to do. Anyway, the answer is NO!'

At that moment, hearing a movement from behind, they both turned to see the two women come out on the terrace. Simon advanced, apparently in profuse good humour, greeting Janice in particular as if she had only just arrived, placing an arm round her waist and guiding her to a chair, filling her glass, waggish and gallant in turn. Marcie grimaced slightly at this fulsome display and turned aside, trailing her fingers idly through the ferny green filigree of one of the plants, keeping herself away from the circumference of Simon's virulent hilarity as from an infectious disease. Art allowed himself a brief curiosity about her, to speculate on what might lie behind that cool elegance and poise which sheathed her as sleekly as the gown she was wearing; she exuded an air of porcelain remoteness and mystery, a glamour almost forbidding and withering in its secretive glitter, yet he had a feeling that she could prove to be a good friend to him at some indefinite point in the future if ever he plucked up sufficient courage to risk her impassive scorn.

His mind veered fretfully between the swarm of his thoughts, and he walked over and stood above Janice, hoping for some sign from her, of understanding, conciliation, of recognition almost, anything that would break the rigid detachment of her mood as she sat with the same polite smile on her face, accepting Simon's obese pleasantries like an insomniac listening intently to what was being said to her without taking any of it in, hardly a muscle in her face was stirring. He hovered, placed an indecisive hand on her shoulder, but he might as well have touched a statue, and muttering a curse to himself he turned away and moved to where the jug of iced tonic and gin stood on a table.

PART II
Four Years Earlier

2

THE three girls linked arms and crossed the swaying wooden bridge to the island in the middle of the estuary, duffle-coated against the keen wind sweeping over the river. The lights on the embankment behind grew dimmer as they neared the island, looming eerily out of the mist, while jazz sounds lifting in the air strident and plaintive came from a large barn-like timber structure squatting before them like an enormous beehive lit by smoky rings of light. It was towards this they were making their way like everyone else, all roughly the same age, in duffle coats and jeans, fashionably bedraggled and sloppy, lights playing on their faces as they came up to the entrance, giving to each a brief luminous identity, before passing into the avalanche of noise and swirling press of bodies inside.

Even so early in the evening the place was crammed and most of the tables taken, but they spotted a vacant one beside the stage wreathed in smoke and directly beneath the band, which only made it more desirable. They quickly pushed their way through and sat down with a certain air of ownership, loosening the hoods and wooden button-pegs of their coats and looking about them for familiar faces.

'It's packed in here tonight,' one of the three said, 'hardly worth paying to get in.'

'Oh, I don't know,' responded the second. 'It might be fun.'

'God, it's stifling in here,' said Janice, a little loudly. She looked at her two companions, Angela and Susan, almost identical twins, identical also in their plainness, and could not help feeling sorry for them in a superior sort of way, well aware of her own good looks. 'It's really hot.'

Susan nodded. 'Sure is.'

'Well, what about something to drink?' Angela said.

Her sister looked undecided. 'Really, I don't know –'

Janice shook out her thick hair. 'Oh, all right. Whisky all round?'

The sisters looked slightly alarmed. 'My God, Jan, you're not serious!' exclaimed Angela, trailing a gaunt tress of hair through her

35

fingers, her eyes large and earnest, and at the same time waiting to hear what Janice, whom they seemed to regard as leader, would say.

Janice laughed. 'Well, I don't mind a bit – but do you think you two could take it without getting us chucked out?'

The sisters relaxed, seeing they were being kidded. They replied almost in unison, 'Oh, cut it out, Jan.'

'Besides,' countered Susan, still serious, 'what would your parents say?'

'They know I'm corrupted,' answered Janice, affecting a casual air, and added in the same tone of voice, 'You forget that I'm singing tonight.'

Their look of alarm returned. 'You're not really,' said Angela uneasily, 'are you?'

Susan swallowed. 'You're – you're just joking, aren't you, Janice?' She gave a weak simper. 'Always up to tricks, you are, Jan.'

'Of course I'm singing tonight,' said Janice, joining her hands together on the table. 'That's why I wanted to get here early. Frankie's going to announce me during the interval.'

Angela made an effort to look and sound relieved. 'Oh, that Frankie –' she glanced up at a slim young man in a white polo-necked pullover standing at the side of the stage chatting and wisecracking with the customers below on the floor, waiting for the band to finish to resume his duties as M.C. 'That Frankie's always kidding about,' said Angela, trying to convince herself as much as anyone else. 'He'd promise anything just for a giggle.'

'Absolutely,' Susan said, anxious to agree.

Janice smiled. 'Not tonight. It's all arranged.' At that moment Frankie spotted her and waved to her in expansive greeting, blowing her a kiss and pointing to the microphone, as if wanting to know was she ready. She waved back and nodded her head, still smiling. Heads were turning towards their table, people staring at Janice with interest and speculation. Janice basked in unknowing shameless triumph.

As usual, the crowd had gathered to listen to and applaud the band rather than to dance, which was considered secondary to the primary aim of enjoying the music itself. Boys and girls stood about the floor in tight talkative little coteries, holding half-pint glasses of ale in their hands as they listened intently, occasionally breaking into whistles and cheers at certain favourite passages of melody, an intricate solo

36

by a favourite player on clarinet, alto or tenor sax, trombone, bass, piano or drums; shouts of encouragement, demanding encores; a pliant wavering sea of young upturned faces, rapt, glistening with sweat and enthusiasm, moved and swept along by the surging momentum of nervous vivacity and release, joined by the music in a tribal sense of excitation, uninhibited, strangely innocent, virginal, spontaneous as children or young animals sporting and tumbling together in a newly discovered heat of rough bodily contact, herdlike, yet separate, singular, each involved in their own unique fantasy, adapting the music to their private needs and impulses. In the hazy depths of the hall the stage became a dim temple, veiled by swirling scarves of smoke rising like incense from the condensed spaces of the floor.

Inevitably at times the tempo slowed, became a pleasant sonorous undertone murmuring in the background, while the crowds broke apart and dispersed, some to replenish their glasses at the makeshift bar at one side of the hall, others to lounge and lazily smoke at their tables, sharing cigarettes as well as brave tentative intimacies which sustained and buoyed them up more surely than either the nicotine or the stuff they drank out of their glasses with such uncertain panache.

Janice slowly became aware of being under furtive scrutiny from somewhere, and turning her head she saw a tall gangling youth slowly and, it seemed to her, unwillingly making his way to their table. She watched him with some interest; he had a rather downtrodden look about him, a look in which pride and defiance struggled to break through, and he kept shoving his thin long-wristed hands irresolutely in and out of the pockets of his jeans, as if not quite sure what to do with them; his face, angular and perplexed, was blemished with pimples, frail lashes drooping over pale eyes that kept flitting nervously about as if searching for somewhere to rest. As he made his reluctant way up to them, he lifted his hand to his ear, tugging furiously at the lobe, fixing his gaze at a point slightly above Janice's head, like a lone traveller adjusting his compass to make sure of his path, quite ignoring the other two girls, who giggled at his approach.

'Here comes Romance!' sniggered Angela, putting her hands to her mouth to smother her laughter while her sister managed to look demure.

The youth slouched to a halt a few feet away, gulped, and tugged at his earlobe even harder. 'Er – care for a drink?' he muttered, fixing his eyes momentarily upon Janice.

She looked him over unhurriedly before replying. 'Are you talking to me?'

This seemed to send him spinning into greater confusion. 'Eh?' he spluttered, dropping his hand from his ear. 'Oh – er – yes. You.' He looked suddenly abashed and wrung his lank hands tightly together. 'Yes – you – miss – care for a drink?' There was a politeness in his voice and manner now which he seemed afraid others would hear and observe, for he threw an apprehensive glance over his shoulder.

Following the direction of his glance, Janice saw that a group of youths had gathered a little way off, and were grinning and nudging one another, exchanging winks as they observed the progress of their ill-at-ease comrade; they looked casually away when they saw she had discovered them, but kept up their snickering and taunting vigil.

Janice turned back to him, smiling calmly. 'Thank you very much. I'll have a glass of cider, please.'

Her speedy favourable response took him by surprise.

'Eh? You will?'

Janice kept smiling. 'A glass of cider, please.' As she spoke the cluster of boys edged closer for a better vantage point and the twins seemed to be in two minds whether or not to be offended at not being included in the offer and finally decided to be just mildly amused. Janice added, to the boy, 'It's very kind of you to ask.'

He blinked. 'Oh – er – not at all.' He backed away, bumping into some people on the floor, finally tearing his gaze away from Janice and making for the bar on the other side of the hall, pursued by his mates ensuring he would not squirm out of the dare that they had obviously foisted upon him.

Angela cleared her throat. 'Well, fancy that. Love comes out of the blue.'

Susan looked intrigued. 'Are you going to let him see you home, Jan?'

Janice laughed. 'Don't be silly, but I couldn't let him down.'

The sisters stared. 'What do you mean, let him down?'

'I mean in front of his friends. He only did it for a dare.'

Angela showed her annoyance. 'You've a heart of pure melting gold. And he completely ignored us.'

'As if we were not here,' agreed Susan.

'But I got the impression you disapproved of him,' Janice pointed out.

Angela smiled rather smugly. 'He's no first prize, is he? But that's not the point. He should at least have let us refuse him.'

'I'd never take a drink off a strange bloke,' Susan said. 'And he *is* a stranger. Anyway, he won't come back. Bet you anything.'

Janice shrugged, and looked about her with bright interest. On the stage the musicians were having a break, gathered over a barrel of ale, from which they filled their glasses, tuning and fiddling about with their instruments. They were mostly middle-aged balding men with paunches and abstracted expressions, some of them carrying a permanent look of resignation and disillusionment, as if what they were doing was very different from the sort of dreams they had not quite put by, a drab second-rate existence compared to the images that had once fired them, taking melancholy refuge now in the very music that had failed them, or which they themselves had failed; a loquacious sadness seemed to pervade them that sometimes found relief in their playing in dim basement clubs to small audiences, and then trudging home through silent lachrymose streets in the drizzle of the anaemic light of dawn.

Janice often wondered about these men and what lives they might lead away from the smoke and din of the places they played in; she felt sure that somehow behind the exotic aura that wreathed around them on stage they were as ordinary, sad and harried as most other people in the world, which made her a little sad also, a sadness that she could not understand, romantic rather than sharp and actual. She thought of them only as an extension of their music, the music was real only while it lasted, which might invest the men who played the music with certain brief enigmatic identities.

Her musings were cut short by an involuntary gasp next to her.

'My God,' whispered Angela, grasping her sister's arm, 'he's coming back!'

Janice looked to where Angela was pointing and saw her admirer returning, pushing his way through the throng with grim determination, his face strained with effort, two half-pint glasses of cider held aloft, his tongue protruding slightly from the corner of his mouth as he concentrated on his task. Holding the glasses on high, the sleeves of his short denim jacket shot up, exposing his bony wrists and enhancing the resemblance he bore to an overworked valiant scarecrow: the same group of boys trailed after him still, making fatuous comments, and by the time he reached her table his face was steamy with sweat and the glasses were spilled to nearly half their normal measure. He set them down nonetheless with almost a swagger of triumph.

'I – er – I spilt some,' he said, panting slightly, rubbing the palms of his hands along the sides of his jeans. 'Hope you don't mind.'

'Won't you sit down?' invited Janice, looking around to see if there was a vacant chair anywhere within range. The youth still continued to ignore the presence of the other two girls with blithe unawareness, as if he genuinely believed Janice was alone and unconnected with anyone else in the hall.

'I – er – won't sit down, thanks,' he replied, picking his glass up and contemplating its sudsy contents. He looked at her, unsure. 'Well – er –'

'Oh, cheers,' she answered lightly, lifting the glass to her lips and taking a sip. She set it down and inclined her head with a certain feeling of buoyant malice at the sisters. 'Do you know my two friends, by any chance?'

He flicked a glance at them with a stiff movement of his head. 'I – er – no, I don't think so.' He took a quick swallow of his drink.

'Angela and Susan,' she announced. 'Sisters, as you may have noticed.'

He looked at them once more. 'Sorry – would you – um – like something to drink?'

'Well, actually –' began Angela.

'We're far too expensive,' said Susan, 'and anyway our escorts should be here any minute.'

'Don't mind these two,' said Janice, 'they're retarded. Are you sure you won't join us – can't you find a stool or something somewhere?'

He shook his head. 'That's all right – I'm with company –' he winced as he said this, throwing another wary glance over his shoulder. 'I – er – I'll be getting along –'

He seemed acutely aware that, having performed his little act of gallantry, he should now withdraw with as much grace as possible before he overstayed his welcome and spoiled the effect, but he lingered at the table in a state of growing indecision, as if he had something else on his mind. He was looking at her as if seeking her help.

'Was there something else you wanted to ask me?' she enquired gently, noting how tightly his fingers gripped his glass.

He squared his shoulders, emboldened by her kind directness.

40

'Well, yes, as a matter of fact –' he stopped, biting his lip and then went on in a rush. 'I was wondering if – er – if you'd care to dance, later?'

A spluttering sound of hastily suppressed laughter came from the sisters; Janice smiled with even greater composure and nodded. 'I'd be delighted.'

He looked again at her for a moment, frowning with uncertainty as if trying to make out whether she was in earnest or mocking him; he smiled tentatively in return, convinced of her sincerity, and began to withdraw. 'Thanks – that's great – thanks.'

He was edging away, a happy, rather foolish look on his face, when she called after him, half rising from the table, 'Wait – your name – I don't know your name.'

He halted. 'Oh – it's Richard.' He raised his voice above the din to make sure she heard him. 'My name's Richard!' He turned away and went boldly up to the group of taunting boys, almost strutting, holding his head at a new challenging angle.

'Well!' said Angela abashed and admiring at once: 'You certainly led him on. What if he comes back looking for that dance?'

'Yes, absolutely,' piped in Susan. 'What then?'

'Oh, he'll come back all right,' said Janice, placidly.

'Watch it,' warned Susan, 'your tiara's slipping.'

'Oh, shut up,' said Janice goodhumouredly.

The chirpy young M.C. in the polo-necked sweater was tapping the microphone and repeating 'One, two, three, testing' into it again and again, grinning down at the people on the dance floor, cracking jokes with the band, going through the drill with poise and assurance, with all the versatility of a veteran. With a flourish he brought the leader of the band forward, the trombone player, a small dark gnarled man, both hands glittering with rings, flashing his teeth in a grin as the applause went up. The M.C. held up a hand in mock protest, grinned, engaged in more banter, made engagingly disparaging remarks addressed exclusively to the young ladies, and in all performed his duties well. Then he started to sing; his voice lacked balance, poise, sophistication, but he carried the medley of songs through with élan, and at the end the applause was loud and generous, interspersed with good-natured boos and whistles. As the noise subsided he held up his hand for attention as though he had an important announcement to make.

Without warning the spotlight veered to Janice's table, seeming to strike directly at her, making her blink, almost blinding her: the two sisters gave a little shriek and held up their hands as if to ward off a blow.

'And now a little surprise packet!' the M.C. called out, his voice booming over the crackling microphone. 'A big hand, lads and lassies, for one of our very own – are you ready, Janice? You are? Great!' He beckoned, all smiles and white teeth, making a flourish. 'It's all yours, little lady!'

She could never quite remember afterwards how she got up from the table and onto the stage: she seemed to move like a puppet propelled and controlled by invisible strings, but there she was, facing the crowd, or rather the tide-like ebb and flow of a crowd, a multitude to her, hidden in the darkness. She clutched the microphone, more to stop herself from swaying than anything else, and started to sing. At least she opened her mouth to sing, and she must have sung something, and rather well at that, for they cheered and clapped loudly as she finished, and yelled for an encore. She just stood there foolishly, not remembering a word of the song, feeling unreal, a bit cold in spite of the heat from the overhead lights and the sweat on the palms of her hands. Frankie, the M.C., came over and gave her a hug and kiss and persuaded her to sing again, which she did, with the same trance-like feeling as before, and then it was over and she found herself back at the table with Angela and Susan, as if she had never left it, as if it all had been a dream or something she had mimed in her sleep.

'You were terrific,' said Angela.

'Yes, terrific,' echoed Susan.

They seemed strange, altered, a little shy, as if speaking to somebody else, someone they were meeting for the first time. They looked at her in a new way, not quite full on, almost timid, and unaccountably Janice felt annoyed, puzzled and sad, wanting to know why the hell they were looking so sheepish, but she said nothing.

'Didn't know you could sing like that,' said Susan, and it sounded as though she was trying to make conversation. Angela gave a small nervous laugh. 'They'll be asking for your autograph next, queueing up.'

'Just imagine,' Susan went on, as if wound up and unable to stop, 'in a few years time we'll be able to say we knew her when –'

'Oh, for God's sake!' Janice snapped, and immediately felt sorry, they looked so hurt. 'I mean, it was just a bit of a lark, really.'

'You did very well,' persisted Angela, stubborn and loyal, jutting her chin out.

'Thanks,' said Janice, chastened.

The crowds were on the dance floor again as the band swung into its routine after the intermission; girls danced with each other in a casual companionable fashion, shunning the boys, who responded at first by pretending not to notice, drinking ale and smoking, chewing gum: the boards shook and shuddered under the furore of feet, the music picked up momentum, drawing the dancers inexorably together.

Janice, standing aside, was conscious of a certain giddy nausea, like someone suffering from vertigo; she thought how cool the night air would be outside, the lights of the city mirrored in the water, broken into innumerable bizarre cameos of colour; the breeze would be tainted by the river smell and the sulphurous drift from the city, but it would be cool and pleasant on her skin, carrying with it a soft illusion of peace after the noise and smoke, the sweat of bodies, the endless commotion inside the hall. The amplified noise swept upon her in flurries, like a window being opened to let in the crash of waves, then closed again, the noise receding, falling to a deceptive murmur. She had made up her mind to leave when she saw, standing a little distance away, uncertainly, as if trying to gather the courage to approach her, the boy who had said his name was Richard. She smiled and nodded to him and, encouraged, he came up.

'Have you come to claim your dance?'

'Is it, you know, alright?'

'Yes, of course,' she answered, 'but I'm afraid I'm not very good at dancing. Are you?'

He shook his head. 'Not very good, but if you'd like to take a chance –'

'Why not?' She held out her hand. 'See you later,' she told the sisters, who stared rather wistfully after her as Richard, fumbling to take her hand, led her on to the floor.

And then a change came over him; it was as if he had taken on a new identity, a new personality, moving into the rhythm of the dance with ease, with a swift unstraining assurance that took her by surprise: he was no longer awkward, inelegant, but possessed of a natural mobile

43

grace, as if he had glided at last into his own domain, his own element where he knew every move and step, where he was at last master of himself, sure of his way and able to act without painful hesitancy or doubt.

'You're good,' she said, raising her voice to make herself heard above the noise. 'You're very good.'

He grinned. 'Not bad, I suppose, once I get started.' He moved closer, keeping pace with the tempo. 'I heard you sing – you were marvellous.'

'Oh – like your dancing, not bad.'

'Your first time, was it?'

She nodded, somewhat hard put to keep pace with him. 'And my last, no doubt. Must've been mad.'

He shook his head vigorously. 'No, you're marvellous – honest. Will you keep it up? I suppose you will –'

'Oh, no, I don't think so. I'm a nervous wreck as it is.'

They talked like two old friends, in a light-handed way as they moved and circled each other in the dance, the music having at once a stimulating and tranquillising effect, putting them at ease with one another, free of any need to please or impress. He no longer moved like someone in shackles; as he danced he became animated with purpose, older and more decisive, responding to the music with smooth facility, creating his own little space on the floor and filling it with lithe command and assurance. By contrast she felt her own movements to be stiff and blundering, all sharp angles and slithering uncertainty, as if skating on ice for the first time, and was glad when the band took another break.

They stood on the edge of the crowd, unsure, each seeming to wait for the other to decide what they should do next: she did not want to go back to her table just yet.

'Er – would you like some cider or something?' he asked, a trace of the stammer coming back into his voice.

'Yes, please,' she answered with alacrity. 'That would be nice.'

He hurried off towards the bar, and left alone she thought about him, amused and puzzled, more than a little intrigued. He was such a strange boy, clamping up tight as an oyster at the least pressure or most tentative approach, yet displaying a muffled restrained eagerness to venture out of his shell, out of the carapace he carried about with him like a snail, to creep out into the world inch by timorous

44

inch, a bit bewildered by what he encountered, willing to trust and confide, but fearful of rejection, of being hurt and prodded and made to look ridiculous for the benefit of others out of the same dread of repulsion and dismissal. She was sure it was more a question of fear, a need to be accepted even at such a shallow level, rather than weakness of character, that made him fumble his way so painfully into the affections and activities of others. She wondered what part of the city he came from, what sort of background and family he had, what he thought about things, whether he worked or was still at school; her mind was full of little commonplace curiosities about him, which rather surprised her, for it was unlikely that they would ever meet again after tonight; these sort of chance meetings were always happening, she told herself, especially in dance halls and other such places where people congregated, and seldom anything of a lasting friendship came of them, which was as it should be, perhaps, since people usually turned out to be so hurtful to each other, so sadly different from what they had at first seemed. She was full of bright brittle young wisdom which afforded her the illusion of being able to see the variegated patterns of life in sharply defined terms. She was prepared to entertain a certain romantic sadness about the almost certain fact that she would not see him again after tonight. Then she heard someone cough quite close behind her, and thinking it was him, turned round with what she hoped was a suitably melancholy and pensive smile.

'You're back –' she started to say, then stopped, confused and feeling quite silly, realising that she was addressing herself to a total stranger, who was staring at her very hard and appearing to have been doing so for some time.

'Why – have I been away?' replied the young man, grinning at her in a most audacious but inoffensive way. He was dressed in a black leather motorcycle outfit with a white helmet on which the face of a tiger snarled; under his arm he carried an instrument case with a zip up one side. He loosened the straps of his helmet and came closer, the grin still on his face.

'Sorry – didn't mean to stare. Bad manners.' He pulled up a vacant stool and straddled it, putting the instrument case across his knees. 'You're the girl who sang just now, aren't you? You've the makings of a good voice.' His tone was relaxed, conversational and absurdly senior considering he was just about her own age. 'Very good indeed.'

'Thanks – but I don't recollect asking your opinion,' she replied primly, finding his attitude and composure distasteful and turning away from him.

'True,' he admitted, unruffled, taking off his thick motorcycle gloves and placing them on his lap. 'You don't know me from Adam and I don't know you from Eve. I didn't mean to be rude –'

'Which you are,' she interjected, rigidly on her dignity, looking away from him at the crowded dance floor.

He nodded. 'Which I am. Sorry about that. I've noticed you here before, once or twice, but didn't know you sang.' He stopped, her silence proving effective at last, and shook his head. 'Not getting very far, am I?'

'Nowhere,' she retorted, enjoying his momentary discomfort yet annoyed with herself for not ignoring him completely.

'I enjoyed your singing,' he went on stubbornly. 'You sang like a professional. Are you? A professional, I mean.'

Somewhat mollified by the change in his approach, she glanced at him and shrugged. 'Hardly.'

'You mean it was your first try in public?' he asked, leaning forward with interest.

'Just about.' After a moment's further hesitation she said, 'Yes.'

He regarded her with a sort of canny wary respect. 'You carried it off well. Have you taken singing lessons or anything like that?' He paused again and smiled, more diffidently this time. 'Don't mean to be nosey, I'm just interested. You came over ever so good, it's hard to believe you've never sung before – in public, you know.'

She turned to him resolutely, wanting to terminate the conversation with as little fuss or offence as she could manage and let him get on his way. 'I've never had singing lessons and tonight was my first time to get up and make a fool of myself in public. I hope that satisfies your curiosity.'

He continued to look at her, quite oblivious to the sharp formal tone of her voice. 'You think you made a fool of yourself?'

'That's right.'

'The way the crowd clapped and cheered,' he pursued, '*they* didn't think you'd made a fool of yourself.'

She gave him a wintry smile. 'Most of them were my friends.'

'They're usually the worst.'

'You talk like a professional yourself,' she said, interested in spite of

46

herself, interested in what might lie behind his conceit and arrogance, her glance going involuntarily to the instrument case spread across his knees, though she immediately looked elsewhere.

He saw the look and smiled. 'I do a bit here and there, playing this thing,' he said, tapping the case. 'Guitar. But a professional –? Far from it. I pluck out a few things, make up a few things as I go along.'

'You mean you write songs?' she enquired, forgetting to feel annoyed with herself, her interest deepening.

'Oh, I wouldn't say that exactly,' he rejoined, seeming to make an effort to sound modest. 'Bits and pieces of things, you know, strung together in a sort of loose fashion. Maybe someday – who knows? But I'm talking too much as usual.'

His brashness was beginning to grate less and less, it was so without artifice and somehow desperately innocent; it was as if he were standing before a mirror, combing his hair first one way, then another and asking her which style she liked best, more to suit and please her than himself. She could not explain why she should think this about a stranger – he seemed to be waiting for the slightest sign of approval from her to light up and become something unique and quite marvellous. She still considered him rather objectionable, but he was becoming less so as the moments slipped past.

'How about having a beer with me?' he asked, half rising.

'Oh – no, thanks,' she answered quickly, taken a bit off guard. 'My friend's gone to get something.'

He sat down again. 'Fair enough. Will your friend be seeing you home, do you think?'

She imagined she detected the faintest hint of mockery in his voice, but she was determined not to let him see that she noticed. 'I usually find my own way home.'

He shrugged. 'If you're stuck I'm the proud owner of a broken-down Yamaha that still works, and you're welcome to a lift, as long as you don't live out in Tunbridge Wells or anywhere foreign like that.'

'Thanks just the same. Well, here's my friend –'

She waved ostentatiously as Richard emerged through the crowd balancing two half-pint glasses of cider in his hands. He came up and handed her a glass, breathing hard and smiling with relief, not

47

immediately aware of the interloper sitting nonchalant and at ease nearby.

'Sorry it took so long,' he said. 'There was such a queue –' Becoming aware of the other person, he swivelled his head round and looked at him, unsure.

'Well,' said the newcomer, getting to his feet and slinging the guitar case up on his shoulder, like a labourer hoisting a spade. 'Adios.' He turned to her. 'I still think you've a good voice.'

'Thanks,' she said drily.

He lingered a moment. 'That offer of a lift still stands.' He placed his gloves in a side pocket of his leather jacket.

She sipped her drink. 'Thanks again.'

He strolled off, saying, as if an afterthought, 'My name, by the way, is Art – Art Devlin.' Then he made for the makeshift bar, managed for the evening by two women, one middle-aged, sour and snappish, the other young, chatty and flirtatious, her blouse like her eyes overflowing with promise as she worked the taps and basked in sly rude compliments.

Richard stood, shifting from one foot to the other. 'A – um – a friend of yours, that bloke?' he mumbled, his eyes not coming fully to rest upon her.

'Never saw him before.'

He brightened. 'Oh, is that so? I thought maybe you knew him –'

'Only as well as I know you,' she replied, smiling, 'which is hardly at all.'

He looked relieved and abashed at once, as if he felt he had perhaps intruded too much already upon her good nature, but unable to disguise his delight that he did not have to share her attention with anyone else.

Suddenly the whole atmosphere inside the hall became again oppressive, clogging; she felt almost trapped, like being in a cell with the door locked and the walls closing in on her.

'It's weird,' she said, handing him her glass, 'but would you mind taking this? I've got to get some air.'

He looked alarmed. 'Are you ill? Shall I get your friends?'

She shook her head. 'No – thanks. I'm all right. I just want some air.'

'Shall I come with you –?' He hovered, uncertain what to do.

'No, of course not,' she answered sharply, and immediately regretted her acerbity. 'I mean, I'll be all right, really, once I'm outside.'

'Well, if you're sure –'

'Yes, I am.' She saw the hurt puzzled look on his face and, angry with herself, was almost prepared to blame him for her confusion. 'Look, I'm sorry, but I must go outside for a while.' She forced a laugh. 'Hope I don't sound too Garboish.'

'No, I understand – it is hot in here.' He stood, irresolute, self-consciously holding the two glasses in his hands. 'As long as you're okay.'

'Oh, I am, thanks. If you see my friends – the two girls I was with –'

'Yes, I know. I'll tell them.'

She remained a moment longer, almost deciphering the question she felt sure he was trying to frame.

'I'll probably be back soon,' she said. 'I'll likely see you again sometime.'

'Yes. Yes, I hope so.'

She left him quickly and made her way through the crowd towards the exit, feeling foolish and avoiding all the eyes that she felt were upon her, hardly believing it possible that only a short time ago she had stood before them on the stage in the full glare of the lights.

3

THE low whining hum of the lawnmower came from the front garden, a sound associated in her mind with warm suburban Saturday afternoons in summer, mingled with the crunch of tyres on hot tarmac as cruising cars ambled by, radios audible through lowered windows. She stood watching her father through the swaying lace curtains, seeing how tautly he gripped the handle of the mower, as if trying to restrain a headstrong steed, moving stiffly like a robot, legs out-splayed, shoulders rigid, a look of grim stolid concentration on his face as he moved up and down, forward and back across the small sloping lawn, flicking the tip of his tongue from time to time to skim the drooping edges of his moustache, the white cloth cap pulled low over his forehead. His shirtsleeves were rolled up to his elbows, showing the corded sinews on his forearms bulging with effort; now and then the sun caught the dial of his wristwatch and made it flash like a snake's tongue, leaving angry asterisks shimmering in the air.

The top of the morning paper stuck like a baton out of the back pocket of the faded pair of trousers he wore, his light shoes stained by the damp grass; the old-fashioned black braces criss-crossed his back like a harness, patches of sweat showing through his shirt. She felt sudden pity for him as he bent rigorously to his task, the mown blades of grass flying before him; she wanted to cry out and break the heavy dumb solitude that hung upon him as he trundled ox-like about the railed-in little plot of garden, minutely observing his own handiwork, moving in a kind of trance or browbeaten premature dotage, stolid as a tree or concrete block, moving with elaborate mindless method and precision, up and down, forward and back, never raising his eyes from the brutally shorn grass.

It struck her as wrong that he should be cutting grass as though the whole purpose of his existence, the whole drive of his nature were concentrated in that mechanical effort and nothing else had meaning for him outside of it. The sap that was in the grass now being mercilessly trimmed was in her too, rising sure and tenacious as life, and she felt a pang of outrage at the shuttered oblivion with which he went about his self-appointed duty, like an executioner taking no pleasure in his work but grimly resolved that it should be done well and to his own insular satisfaction. It amounted in her mind to a brutal denial of all that made her quicken with life, seeing him walk like an automaton behind the spluttering machine, a denial of something that might still lie within himself, a hope, a flash of defiance not quite vanquished under the grey tyrannical toil of his life, an urgency that would recall him to real life for a moment and enable him to see and feel and taste it sharp and burning as she knew it to be in all her hunger for it. Anything but this terrifying beastlike absorption that impelled him now, moving up and down, forward and back, eyes riveted to the ground, the clouds of sliced grass flying before him, staining his shoes and the ends of his trousers with juice.

Compassion as well as fury worked an obscure panic in her, making her want to run to him and shake him out of his industrious torpor, to look up a moment and perhaps see something that had remained hidden from him before – the green vivid green of the grass, the valiant little rose bush in the lower corner of the garden splashing its display against the wall, the dry calligraphy on the bark of trees along the avenue; anything that would make him pause and submit his senses even briefly to a glad invasion of life as it grew and breathed and throbbed in every crevice and pore about him. But even as the urge to reach out to him struggled for expression within her something told her it was already too late, and she moved away from the window, from her silent unseen scrutiny of him, unaccountably close to tears.

Turning back into the cool cloistered room, a little blinded by the sun, she almost blundered into someone standing close behind her, and fell back a step, startled.

'Didn't see you, Mom,' she said, laughing a little nervously; something in her mother's face made her stop. 'What is it?'

For a time her mother looked at her absently, as if she did not quite recognise or remember who she was, the look remaining in her eyes like a shadow; then she brushed back her greying hair from her forehead a little tiredly and shook her head.

'Oh – nothing, nothing at all,' said her mother, rubbing her hands in her apron in her usual vague preoccupied fashion, moving away. 'You slept late today, Janice.'

'A bit, I suppose,' replied Janice, feeling guilty.

'Almost twelve,' pursued her mother.

'Oh – is it?'

She tried to sound casual, as if only mildly surprised at or interested in what was being said to her, wanting to skirt and ward off the confrontation she felt was bound to arise any moment because of the lateness of her arrival home the night before and the usual disapproval about her frequenting dance halls and the like, especially the one on the island in the estuary which her parents regarded with the utmost suspicion and had repeatedly warned her about, all their fears being based entirely on rumours which only made the peril all the more real to them. So Janice was already shaping her answers and making her defence, angry as usual at having to do so when everything was so innocent and ordinary, but her mother had wandered to the window again, standing as she herself had stood moments before, looking out at the square-shouldered stolid figure in the garden with fretful concern, the same look returning to her eyes.

'He drives himself so hard,' she murmured, half to herself, fingers absently toying with the curtains. 'Out there since nine this morning, and on his day off . . .'

Janice went about making herself some breakfast, eggs and bacon and tea, having a good appetite and no fashionable superstition about putting on weight. As she shifted the eggs and bacon about in the pan, playing the transistor radio at a moderate pitch, she thought about the look she had seen passing over her mother's face; she had seen it before, in off-guard moments, veiled and fleeting, like a curtain being raised and swiftly lowered again, hinting at rather than revealing what might lie behind the look. It was like a landscape whose outlines and contours were as familiar to her as the lines in the palm of her own hand, being overshadowed by a persistent cloud and rendered suddenly strange, secretive and withdrawn, making her doubt what she thought she had seen there before, making her fumble and grope trying to find her way back to the old clear vantage point of certainty where everything was laid out cosily in front of her and nothing was left to speculation.

At such times, when that look of her mother's came and her father's face remained impassive over a book or newspaper or simply staring into space, she came to realise the private and exclusive lives her parents led, separate and independent of her own, a map she could no longer read with facile unthinking ease, a suddenly barred and enclosed area she could not penetrate or wander into without losing direction and losing her way. She had accepted as natural and inevitable that there should be a certain tacit distance between her life and them, but the idea that the reverse might equally be true had not really loomed upon her with any strength or significance until now, seeing her mother stand at the window hidden behind the same look.

The new concept filled her with vague alarm, bringing with it a perverse sense of hurt and resentment, as if she had been hoodwinked into a false feeling of security and must now face the truth that it had all been a cunningly contrived charade in which her parents had moved and spoken and gone through a repertoire of gestures and required responses without once revealing their real selves to her except at random moments, and then only to withdraw into deeper recesses away from her. She knew the chagrin she felt was unreasonable, that it was not brought about by anything her parents had set out to do, but she clasped it like an ally in a new and intricate battle and nursed it as a shield against even deeper hurt and imagined acts of duplicity.

As she sat down at the kitchen table and began her breakfast, her mother wandered in from the front room and sat opposite, taking the cup of tea her daughter handed her and setting it down carefully before her, as if she had something to say.

'I heard you come in last night, Janice,' she commenced, folding her arms on the table. 'It was very late.'

Janice cut away the bacon rind and pushed it to one side of her plate. 'I suppose it was, Mom. I'm sorry.'

'I could see the clock quite clearly,' continued her mother. 'It was gone two.'

'I'd no idea it was as late as that.'

'Your father was asleep, but I was not.' She raised the cup and sipped at the tea. 'I'm waiting, Janice.'

'Waiting, Mother?' said Janice, using the name she always used when she was on guard and expected to be obedient.

'You know perfectly well what for,' said her mother patiently. 'An explanation, if you please.'

It seemed suddenly pointless to lie or try to fabricate a shallow deceit on such a bright morning, so Janice told the truth of where she had been last night, and as she did so a pained look crossed her mother's face and she put down her cup resignedly.

'You know how your father and I feel about that place, Janice. You will get a bad name going there.'

'Oh, Mom, that's old-fashioned and foolish!' she blurted out, both amused and angry and spluttering a little on a forkful of bacon and egg. She saw the unchanging expression on her mother's face and tried to be earnest and dutiful. 'Really, Mom, nothing happens there. We just go for the music –'

'And drink.'

'What?'

'There's drink served, I believe.'

'Oh, there's cider, if you call that a drink –'

'I certainly do, and so does your father, I should imagine.'

'Well, I only have half a glass or two,' said Janice, volunteering the information as if a serious charge had been made against her.

'And there are police raids from time to time,' added her mother, quietly implacable, lifting the cup to her lips again. 'Under-age drinking.'

'I've never seen or heard of any raids,' answered Janice. 'And if the police do make their silly raids,' she continued, tilting her head at a scornful angle, 'it shows they've nothing better to do with their time.'

'That is hardly the point. Your father and I just don't want you going there. Isn't that enough?'

Not being able to eat any more, stung into retaliation by what seemed to her the glaring injustice of it all, Janice put down her knife and fork, trying not to make a rattle, and confronted her mother across the table. 'But why must I stop going? What harm am I doing? It's so unfair!'

'Unfair or not, it is what your father and I wish,' her mother replied, her voice calm and unemotional, as if merely putting forward a logical balanced argument, showing neither anger nor over-protective concern. 'Naturally we like to think you will respect our wishes by not going to that dreadful place again. Do I have your promise that you will not?'

The glow was steadily waning out of the morning but the rebellion and hurt were strong within her. 'Please don't ask me to promise that, Mom.'

Her mother's gaze did not waver, rooted in its own expressionless righteousness. 'Why not, may I ask?'

'Because I won't be able to keep it.'

No trace of a frown disturbed the placid width of her mother's forehead. 'You mean you won't keep it – you don't choose to keep it?'

'I won't be able to keep it, Mother.'

A shadow interspersed itself between the table and the bright little pantry window, and looking up Janice saw her father standing hesitantly looking at both of them in turn, cloth cap in hand, as if reluctant to break in upon a private conversation.

'Douglas,' said her mother, pushing her cup a little distance away from her without turning round to look at her husband. 'I was speaking to Janice.' Her voice had become formal, as if she were in some way rebuking him.

He nodded and put the cap away. 'So I gathered.' He rubbed his hands along the sides of his trousers, eyeing the kettle on the stove. 'I could do with a cup.'

Janice got up and poured him out some tea, and he sat down, taking the newspaper out of his back pocket. 'Well,' he said, with a weak attempt at jollity, 'what was it I interrupted?'

Her mother stared ahead. 'I was asking Janice never to go to that awful dance hall place again, Douglas. She refused.'

The way her mother said it made it sound like a stark indictment, making her feel like a hardened chronic criminal lost to redemption, placing her in the dock with a placard round her neck enumerating her heinous misdemeanours, and her mother's flat unemphatic drone of voice made it all sound even more chilling, the staid parchment-dry voice of a judge pronouncing sentence and craftily leaving it to someone else to carry it out. She resented being cast in the rôle of mere callow rebel, crassly intent on getting her own way, when she saw things in such a different light, feeling that what was really at issue was justice, and honesty, and trust; what was really being put on trial, she felt with increasing ardour, was her parents' own ability or willingness to trust *her*, and not tarnish her motives with their own sour adult suspicion, not crush everything blindly beneath the heavy stamp of parental authority just because they did not wish her to go to a certain place or mingle with a certain 'type' of people. They were 'typing' everything and everybody and it was odious and monstrously unfair since it all came out of their own uninformed prejudices and suppositions. She found herself almost wishing she *were* a hardened chronic criminal, for she could then take it all in her stride and not feel bruised or betrayed, not feel she was being hounded into a corner reserved for inveterate offenders all because of something that was natural and enjoyable and completely unblameworthy.

She looked at her father hopefully, wondering if he felt even a trace or tincture of what she was feeling, but he merely went on munching on a slice of bread and butter and sipping his tea, and she was sadly certain that all he wanted to do just then was to escape into the little side parlour and immerse himself in the financial pages of the paper, as he did every Saturday morning until well past midday, constructing imaginary monetary empires in his head as he followed the rise and fall, the indices and indexes of the stock market like someone piecing together a mosaic or elaborate jigsaw puzzle with infinite methodical care and pleasure, his world of insurance, indemnities and life policies spread out before him like an intricate set of coloured bricks to be joined and dovetailed and welded together to form certain set shapes and patterns in his dry mind's eye, where he was in deft control of everything and where accident, chance, mutability were things that could be contained and calculated in terms of pounds, shillings and pence. Instead of which he now sat at the table, mild and attentive to what was being said to him, but with an underlying weariness, an inertia of will, sorry he had come in from the garden in the first place, brushing tea and breadcrumbs off the bristly edge of his moustache in rather a mournful manner, looking at his daughter dubiously, trying to make up his mind what to say to her in order to measure up to what his wife obviously expected of him. He sighed, cleared hs throat and shifted in his chair.

'Well now, what is one to say – ?' he began, then looked across at the transistor radio babbling away on the kitchen sink. 'Er – would you mind toning it down a little, Janice?' When she had done so and took her seat again, he resumed, looking at them both in the same nervous uncertain manner, blinking and fluttering his lashes over his very pale blue eyes. 'What I must ask you, Janice, is – is this true, eh? Did you in fact refuse to promise your mother not to go to that – um – that dance place again – eh?'

'Surely, Douglas, you don't deny my word?' said her mother, her neck stiffening and spearing a look of disdain at him.

'What? Oh no, no, my dear, not at all,' he answered hastily, almost stammering. 'Certainly not. It is just that I would like to hear it from Janice herself – I would like her to admit it.' He took a quick swallow of tea, hoping he had extricated himself from a tight situation, and

56

fixed his pale worried gaze on Janice patiently. 'Did I understand your mother correctly – did you refuse to promise?'

'Yes, Dad.'

He blinked rapidly, as if surprised by the directness of her reply.

'You refused? You refused to comply with your mother's express wish that you wouldn't go near that place again?'

She nodded mutely, too furious to reply in words.

Douglas finished the last of his bread and butter and brushed his fingers drily together. 'Ahem. And may I ask why you did not promise your mother when she asked you?'

'I couldn't, Dad,' she said through tight lips.

'You couldn't? I don't understand –'

Her mother sighed heavily, still staring at the wall behind her daughter, hands folded on the table. 'I should think it's obvious. She evidently feels I am being unreasonable in asking her to stay away from that dreadful place clearly because it holds some unwholesome attraction for her –'

'That isn't true at all!' cried Janice, stung into speech. 'It isn't in the least dreadful or unwholesome –'

'That surely is for your father and I to decide,' her mother went on implacably. She inclined her head ever so slightly towards her husband, as if acknowledging for the first time his part in the debate. 'I may add that she didn't get home until two o'clock this morning, and if *that* is being unreasonable –'

'Yes,' interrupted Douglas, rustling the newspaper abstractedly. 'I heard Janice come in.'

Vera looked at him with a certain bright venom, as if she had been betrayed. 'You heard her come in? You were not asleep?'

Douglas shook his head complacently. 'I was not asleep.'

Vera compressed her lips, her locked fingers tightening. 'And you knew the time?'

Douglas returned her look, his face blank and at the same time contemptuous. 'Certainly I knew the time. My sense of time is excellent as you well know, my dear, day or night. It seldoms errs.'

'And you said nothing?' she reproached with absurd bitterness. He shrugged. 'My dear Vera, at two in the morning there would hardly be any point, would there?'

She chafed inwardly because he had with his usual inconsiderate casualness spoiled what she thought would have been her triumphant little surprise in informing him of their daughter's insensitive disregard of their feelings by coming in at such an hour, when he had known all along and had not spoken a single word about it all morning, not even to her over breakfast; he had stayed silent and let her make a fool of herself in Janice's sharp discerning eyes, and not even out of spite, which at least would have been positive, but simply because he had not thought of mentioning it to her or of sharing her concern; he had simply not given it a second thought, and it was this that she found galling and unjustifiable, and she despised him with an intensity she had not felt in a very long time in any of her feelings for him. She hoped her eyes would tell him this, but he was looking down at the paper in his lap with comic longing, immensely unaware of her even then, and the pang of rejection that darted through her was utterly real and took her totally by surprise. She turned her gaze resolutely back to the wall beyond her daughter's head.

'Now that you have had time to consider, Douglas,' she said, pursuing her grievance with severe sarcasm, 'what do you think should be done, or do you need more time?'

His hand strayed across his mouth. 'Hmm?' He looked at her vacantly, then nodded with unwanted vigour, as if to show he had been following the line of argument closely from the beginning. 'Oh, I agree with you, my dear. Two o'clock in the morning is much too late for a girl of – of –' he stopped, swallowed and ran his fingers nervously over his moustache. 'Of fifteen,' he announced, waving his hand in order to disguise his momentary confusion over his daughter's age. 'Of course – naturally – *much* too late.' He settled back in the chair, feeling he had performed his paternal duties admirably and hoping the whole wretched overblown business was now at an end.

Vera, however, remained immovable. 'And the question of her frequenting that dance hall or night club or whatever it chooses to call itself – what about that, or don't you have an opinion?'

His shoulders slumped as he looked dolefully at his wife. 'What? Oh, that – well, that's settled, isn't it? I mean, I think we've made it clear –' he turned purposefully to his daughter, once again clearing his throat. 'Janice, you are forbidden to visit that place again. Do I make myself clear?'

'Yes, Father.'

'So we have your solemn word, do we?' Douglas persisted, buoyed up by his own success, 'your solemn word, that you will not go near that place again – eh?'

She looked at him and he quailed at the stricken expression on her face, the evidence of broken trust and failed hope he saw there, as if he had violated her self-respect and pride by taking the strap to her before an audience of sniggering onlookers. That look seemed to jerk him up out of his chair and he got clumsily to his feet, ramming the newspaper down into his pocket.

'I do have your word, Janice?' he swallowed, the words coming raggedly from him, near to entreaty.

'Yes, Father,' she answered dully, not bearing to look at him, at the crumbling authority in his face and voice.

He stood a moment, irresolute, looking perplexed and saddened from wife to daughter, from woman to woman, as if caught between two adult adversaries both of whom he was expected to gratify and appease, failing miserably on both counts. He swallowed hard, dawdled a moment longer, then turned and blundered from the room, all illusion of peace and privacy gone, making his way out into the garden again, and the noise of the lawnmower when it reached their ears once more sounded strangled, as if with impotent rage.

Vera rose and went to the window, taking up her vigil like a nanny supervising the antics of a difficult slow-learning child. 'You've upset him again,' she said, her voice calm. 'You've upset him by your stubbornness, and he spending all morning in the garden, making it nice for us.' She put her hand before her eyes, as if shading them. 'It's really too bad of you, Janice – why do you do it? You don't seem to realise how much we care and worry about you. You're a girl, after all, and . . .' Her voice trailed off.

Janice felt very odd, being spoken to and yet being completely ignored; it was like being left in a room with a stranger and not knowing what to say or how to conduct herself next. Her mother could just as well have been alone, talking to herself, thinking out loud, engaged in a soliloquy, moving about in a private reverie, unattached to anything in the present. Janice looked on, hurt and bewildered, watching this gaunt large-boned loose-limbed woman with greying brown hair and preoccupied eyes, who suddenly seemed to her someone who had aged in the space of a single morning into simply another mid-fortyish matronly nonentity with haggard features and a permanent air of going nowhere, as if rooted in the same spot all her life, doing and saying and thinking the same things in a never-ending forever-spinning roundabout of grey tireless repetition, moving and speaking with profound tenacious placidity, drugged with the unremitting tedium of her existence ticking away inside her with the patient pitiless persistence of a clock, merely waiting for it to stop, tidying up the contents of her life conscientiously, without zest, impelled by nerveless gravity. Yet though she willed it fiercely at times, she could not feel the same pity for her mother as she felt so often for her father, the pity she had known for him earlier that morning, for instance, watching him trundle about the garden like some obedient beast tied to a yoke; there was something about her mother that repelled facile compassion and made it redundant, craven, ignoble, something to be secretly ashamed of, like feeling pity for a blind person, a deaf-mute or cripple, a cheap cornershop commodity that could be bought any hour of the day or night. Her mother was like a solitary island that could not be reached by any sort of conventional bridge; one was beheld and surveyed from a distance beyond which one could only approach at a given signal, and to detect and interpret that signal was such an arduous intricate business that the invitation that led to its being given was often as not withdrawn and cancelled long before one realised it had ever been extended. The strongest emotion her mother evoked was a wary vigilant respect that had at times something of the potency of fear in it.

Janice tidied the breakfast things away and went quietly from the room, but for all the notice that her departure and absence received she might have left it an hour since.

'In disgrace again, eh?' cackled Gran happily, sitting up in bed, hands clasped contentedly together on the smooth green quilt, sleek hair still abundantly dark in places tied back in a bun leaving the wide temples clear. 'Head-on clash with the authorities again, eh?' The bright eyes twinkled and beckoned invitingly. 'Tell me all about it, child, and don't spare a word, mind!'

Coming in from the strong sunshine of the backyard glancing off asphalt and concrete walls, Janice rubbed her eyes in the gloom of the little maisonette at the rear of the house where Gran had taken up almost permanent residence since she fell and fractured her thigh three years ago; the place had been built for her many years before, and it was distinctly her own domain where she abode in the midst of the happy muddle of her eccentricities, but since the accident she seldom ventured out of it, leading a firmly self-contained existence spent mostly in bed, listening to the radio, reading books and drinking sherry with a buoyant lack of discretion from the stock she kept under the bed more for convenience than concealment. From the outside it was just another squat one-storey suburban outhouse at the top of the back garden, complete with its own toilet and tiny kitchen, which at least made it different from many others of its kind. Inside, however, Gran had stamped her own mark everywhere, books strewn about and overflowing from the small bookcase in the corner, framed photographs on every conceivable flat surface, mostly of herself as a young woman, ample and unashamed evidence of her blithe egomania and exuberant conceit; trunkfuls of old letters from admirers and lovers long joined in earthy brotherhood with the worm; old theatre bills and posters of a mildewed era adorning the walls, conjuring up resonant echoes of favourite performers from vaudeville to drama. It was a rogues' gallery of second-hand euphoria and vividly imagined bonhomie with the famous and infamous, the renowned and obscure, the clowns and gigolos, the dwarfs and giants of music-hall and stage with whom Gran conversed and held court and claimed kinship simply because of the fact that she had been born into the same generation as they and felt herself entitled to some of the light and aura that surrounded them.

Many attempts had been made early on to clean up the chaos and impose some sort of domestic tidiness on the place, mostly by her daughter-in-law Vera when she had been interested enough to care, but Gran had resisted these unwanted incursions upon her privacy so fiercely and with such fine rhetoric that they had rapidly waned and soon ceased altogether, so that now she was left pretty much to her own glad devices of benign nostalgia and reminiscences of things and people she had known and met only in the country of her fancy, unmolested any more by civilised attempts to 'tidy up' her life and turn it into a trimly packaged item like the majority of lives about her.

She fed and pampered her clutch of eccentricities as zealously as most other people spoil and fondle their household pets, and chief among these personal manias was her eldest grandchild Janice; she acknowledged the existence of her three other grandchildren only as one would acknowledge the existence of toothache and neuralgia and other infirmities of the human saga, but to Janice she was utterly and painstakingly devoted and with enough blatant egocentricity as to suggest that in Janice she saw a clearer and more laudable reflection of herself, and she did nothing at all to check this impression or dilute it with an infusion of acceptable modesty and altruism; she *did* see herself in the girl and the girl likewise in her, and that was that, nothing more to be said, no song and dance about it please. Vanity was what silly unimaginative people like Vera and Douglas called it; she rather preferred to call it the honest truth.

As Janice was about to sit on her allotted place on the side of the bed, Gran made a familiar motion with her hand, pointing downward, and knowing the signal well her granddaughter smiled and, feeling under the bed, brought forth a half-full earthenware jug of sherry and filled the waiting tumbler on the little wicker bedside table, waiting until Gran had tasted it and approved with closed eyes and puckered lips before replacing the jug beneath the bed and sitting down. 'How are you today, Gran?'

'Oh, don't mind me,' said Gran impatiently, then shot a shrewd look. 'Why do you ask – what's so special about today that I shouldn't feel as well as I do on any other day?'

'Don't be so suspicious, Gran,' laughed Janice. 'Only old people are suspicious, and you can't use that as an excuse.'

Gran made a face, but she was pleased. 'You have a way of getting round me that is positively indecent. You pander to my vanity, and there's no resisting that. So,' she asked brightly, taking another appreciative sip, 'what's the latest on the warfront? What have you done now to disgrace the family name?'

'I sang last night.'

'You what?'

'I sang last night. In that place I told you about, out on the island.'

'You mean,' said Gran, dipping further into her glass to give herself reassurance, 'you mean you got up and sang before a hall full of people? How brave – how gorgeous!' she chortled. 'No wonder you incurred parental wrath. Did your father have a seizure? Did your mama faint away into the nearest chair?' She grasped Janice's wrist in her hard bony fingers. 'Tell me, child!'

'Oh, it wasn't my singing that made them angry,' said Janice. 'They don't know about that. It was because I didn't get home until two. God knows what would have happened if they knew about the singing. As it is, they've forbidden me to go there again.'

Hearing the sad disappointment that lay behind the girl's words, Gran stroked her hand fondly where it lay on the quilt, feeling a swift anger at the plodding stupidity of people going through life busily grinding away at their own brittle little axes, hoisting their own jaundiced little phobias and timid panics upon others too decent and faithful to fight back and tell them what they so needed to be told. She knew she was being passionately prejudiced and unfair to her son and his wife, who were after all parents and therefore quite another species, but knowing this did not lessen the violent dislike she always had for people who took themselves seriously and exercised whatever moral authority they had in such a mean-spirited blinkered fashion, usually out of no great moral concern for the individual within the scope of that authority, but more often than not merely to play variations of tunes on their own trumpet attesting to their virtue and wisdom.

Her own experience as a parent had been so brief, so ephemeral and so long ago that it hardly mattered to her now and did not endear her either to the ranks or the cause of parents in general and her son and daughter-in-law in particular. They believed so vehemently in the frail fallacy of family life that almost anything must be imposed and endured in order to keep it glued together and not let the cracks show. It was all a game, and a very silly one at that. Sometimes all the rules of the game were forgotten, and then it got vicious, warping people and grinding them down into ugly facsimiles of what they had been or might have been, burrowing blindly along rutted narrow paths to grubby ignominious little ends, expiring before they had fully drawn breath, straitjacketed into the belief that they had only done their duty.

'And like a dutiful subject,' said Gran now, rousing herself from musing and speaking with a touch of sarcasm, 'you'll obey the latest edict?' She lay back on the pillows in a combative attitude, pulling in the corners of her sunken mouth.

'I suppose so,' replied Janice, her eyes thoughtful. 'I wouldn't want to make them any more unhappy than they are.'

Gran gave her a shrewd look. 'So you think they're unhappy, do you?'

Janice nodded. 'I think they're very unhappy. Maybe not within each other, like most married people who are unhappy, but more with themselves, as persons.' Her fingers toyed gently with the quilt.

'They're not very happy with each other, but without each other perhaps they'd be worse – *I* don't know.' She fell silent a while, staring intently ahead in a way that was oddly reminiscent of the way her mother had sat staring earlier in the kitchen; then she stirred. 'I'd hate to grow into that kind of person, Gran, grow into that kind of situation.'

Gran made an impatient movement and pulled herself forward and upright. 'You don't have to grow into anything! People have a choice,' she added, taking a disdainful sup of sherry, 'and if they don't take it they've only themselves to blame – which is the last thing they do, of course, preferring to put the blame on whoever happens to be most convenient at the time.'

Janice considered this a moment. 'Isn't that a little harsh, Gran, a little too cynical?' she said gently.

'And what's wrong with being cynical, may I ask?' snorted Gran, two red spots of indignation appearing in her pallid cheeks. 'Do you think old people shouldn't be cynical – do you think they ought only to be tolerant and liberal and compassionate and all the rest of it and not say a harsh word about anything?' Her eyes were quite fiery and her hand shook as she raised the glass to her lips once more, drinking with vigour.

'No, of course not, Gran,' said Janice, marvelling at the old lady's ire and in no haste to soothe or dispel it by any inept faltering of apology or appeasement. 'It's just that we haven't got your strength of purpose –'

'Nonsense – utter nonsense!' cried Gran, as if she had been insulted. 'Flattery won't work this time, my girl. The thing is,' she went on, with an effort making herself calm and restrained, 'what happens is, people are in such a fever of haste to be happy that they end up being confused and miserable. They become boring to themselves and to everyone else around them. They become insufferable when they realise that what they've done is merely to swap one illusion for another – the illusion of belonging to themselves, and the other illusion that they could in some deep mysterious way belong to someone else. That's the crux of the whole matter, my dear!' pronounced Gran, smacking her sherry-moist lips, pleased with herself.

'Do you think so, Gran?' asked Janice, looking doubtful. 'Is it all that simple?'

'Simple?' echoed Gran sharply. 'Who said it was simple? But it needn't be as complicated or tortuous as people make it out to be. They start off on the wrong foot, that's all. They've been bamboozled into believing that being attached to someone will make them happy, so they go off and form these grand romantic made-in-heaven attachments and thereafter proceed to lead semi-detached lives with hardly a word to say to each other or a thought in common. They buy houses, raise families, go into debt and work till they drop, all to make themselves happy, and then one day when it occurs to them at last that not only are they not happy but very *un*happy –' Gran snapped her fingers, making a derisive sound – 'Whoosh! everything's over, finished, at an end – except of course it isn't. They find they can do nothing but go on living drearily together, being more miserable and boring than before and making everyone suffer because of it.'

The old woman stopped, breathing quite rapidly by now, the colour rising in her cheeks, contemplating the glass in her hand almost with a glare. 'That's how people are, child, so watch out that you don't fall into the same old trap!'

'And how do you avoid it, Gran?' smiled Janice.

'Ah, now there I can't help you,' said Gran resignedly. 'That's where the sticky bit comes in. You just have to go and make a fool of yourself in your own way, after your own fashion.' She drained her glass and held it out, making the same downward signal as before. 'No,' she continued when the sherry jug had been brought forth and put back again in its place under the bed; 'there's no way out but to go and make a fool of yourself if you really want to find out –' she looked at her granddaughter ruefully – 'and I suppose you do?'

Janice stooped and kissed the old lady's forehead, which felt dry and taut as toasted bread. 'Just as you did, Gran.'

Gran patted the sleek flowing hair of the young girl tumbling about her. 'I don't know if I ever found out.'

Nobody knew, least of all her son Douglas, just how old Gran really was; the only information she would volunteer on the subject herself was to say cryptically that being sixty held no terrors for her any longer but being eighty was still shrouded in mystery. Even when her favourite granddaughter, out of the gentlest fun, pressed too near the question, Gran would say the subject of age bored her intensely and pass on to something else. She was well aware of the fact that she was very much something of a local enigma and had long since passed into neighbourhood legend and lore, the theme of endless speculation and mythologising by next-door or next-street savants who had never set eyes on her and whose imaginations were subsequently all the more enlivened and set twitching by the invisible presence of their quarry.

At times during the summer weather the nearest snoopers would catch glimpses of her sunning herself, protected by an old-fashioned parasol, under a withered old elm that had seen better and greener days, its bleak canopy of leaves affording scant shade; they would peer from upper back bedroom windows or through spaces in the bushes and hedges that separated the back gardens, hoping for a closer look, and some of the more adventurous would come to the front door on one pretext or another, hoping to achieve a local breakthrough by being the first to observe the local lady of fable at close quarters, perhaps so close as to ascertain the number of buttons on her blouse or the approximate number of wrinkles on her face, an experience tantamount in their minds to the unsealing of the tomb of an Egyptian mummy. So endless spools of myth and fancy were spun round her, again like so many layers of embalming bandages, encasing her in perennial mystery and make-believe enriched and sustained by the juice of imagination.

Gran was aware of all these exotic parables created in her image, and it afforded her a certain grim rueful satisfaction to know that she was causing more excitement and attracting more attention, with her life creeping placidly towards its close, than she had ever known or been responsible for at any point in her life before as a young woman with more than a sizeable portion of the world at her feet. It was another of the innumerable small ironies of life that seemed to grow and increase in a weird ratio to the number of years, months, weeks or days remaining to one on earth. Irony was something that became more potent and real as life went on, replacing idealism as the medium through which one looked at the world; how else would it be possible for an old woman lying half crippled in bed with only her memories as daily companions to become the focus of so many other peoples' fantasies and rabid hyperbole? It annoyed her now to think that, despite the raiment of lurid glamour conferred upon her by local hearsay and gossip, she would probably die a very tame and ordinary death with the usual staid ritual of candles, crisp linen sheets and shaded windows, a few muffled prayers and polite murmurs of condolence and then a couple of flying shovelfuls of earth and gradual unremembrance in the minds of the inconsolable bereaved. Sometimes merely being alive was a high price to pay for the dubious bounty of life and its consequences. Yet it was so hard to let go, she thought, her fingers tightening automatically on the edges of the quilt; so hard.

She looked at her granddaughter moving about in the untidy little room, touching things in a musing pensive way, as if in a museum, looking at faded photographs, a half smile on her face, picking up books, handling them delicately; everything she did, everything about her was gentle, thoughtful, treading her way sensitively through the lives of others, careful not to disturb by an incautious movement any of their treasured private possessions or jar by a discordant note the rhythm of their preoccupations. There was light wherever she moved, a singular felicity of tact and sensibility, yet at times a shadow would stir deep in her eyes like a faint premonition of nameless sadness already advancing upon her out of the future, causing Gran to fret and silently rage against the unknown forces that might already be in league to blight the exquisite promise she discerned surrounding her grandchild like an aura.

At such times she would want to cry out a warning and clasp the girl to her fiercely, harbouring her against danger, against all the mean subtle treacheries that would encroach upon her and turn her away from the true possession of herself in confusion, bewilderment and the hurt that never leaves the heart once it enters, the hurt of having the love that she once gave out without question thrown back in her face like a soiled rag, but Gran knew she could not utter that warning because it was not hers to give, not even love could enable or entitle her to sound it, and besides there were no words ever forged or created to give utterance or shape to it. Inarticulate and mute as love ever made anyone, she could only watch and pray for the safe deliverance of this special child into peace and happiness with the minimum of pain. It was one of the more bitter illusions of life that one could ever bequeath anything of value to anyone else; a door closed, inevitably, and there was seldom anything worth leaving behind in the empty little bubble of space where one had existed. All that she could leave to Janice was all that she could never say if she had lived another hundred years; it would all be lumped into the grave with her bones, every scrap of wisdom and courage and charity she had ever acquired during her life, and maybe it was as well, for surely these things were as useless to anyone else as a beggar's rags when they finally fell from his back.

Janice ceased her wandering about the room and came slowly back to the bed, a framed picture in her hand which she looked at intently, then regarded Gran, lying back on the pillows, her eyes half closed; the girl in the photograph sat on the parapet of a bridge looking wistfully into the camera, a profusion of hair falling about her face lit by the sunset behind her, in a long muslin dress that reached the ground and holding in one hand a wide-brimmed picture hat with trailing ribbons; the faint outline of a castle could be seen in the far background. The expression on the girl's face was at once poignant and mischievous, as if briefly pondering life's mystery and purpose before starting up again and running laughing into another adventure.

'Where was this taken, Gran?' asked Janice, sitting on the side of the bed once more, holding the picture in her lap.

'What?' mumbled Gran, pretending to be miles away; she glanced at the picture. 'Oh – the castle gives it away. Scotland.' She sipped sherry. 'Somewhere in Scotland.'

'Was it on your honeymoon, Gran?'

Her eyes opened fully. 'My honeymoon? Why do you ask that?'

Janice studied the picture some more before answering. 'Well, you look so happy and well, sort of honeymoonish, I guess. That pretty dress and hat and – everything about it.'

'Not my honeymoon.' Gran was silent, holding the glass in both hands like a chalice, resting it on her shrunken chest. 'I hardly remember where or when it was taken.'

'I think you remember very well, Gran,' said Janice, reaching over and placing the photograph on the bedside table. 'You do remember, don't you? You remember everything.'

Gran's face remained stern for a few moments longer, trying to look inscrutable, then she smiled. 'Hardly everything, darling. Like most people I try to remember only the things I want to remember and forget the rest.'

'And that picture, Gran,' persisted Janice, nodding at it. 'Do you want to remember or forget it?'

Gran turned her head and looked at it silently for some time, vanity and remorse struggling for expression in her face. 'Oh, take it away, child,' she said finally, turning back on the pillows. 'It's not one of my best. A frivolous little nincompoop looking into the dead eye of a stupid machine. Who wants to be remembered like that?' She shifted restlessly in the bed and held out her glass again.

'I think it's a lovely picture,' Janice said, retrieving the sherry jug and pouring. 'I think you're beautiful in it.'

'But she's gone,' said the old woman, taking her refilled glass and lying back on the pillows, eyes closed. 'That girl on the bridge is gone.'

4

A THREAT of rain hung on the air, no more than a faint premonition carried on the wind that brushed the bronzed surface of the river and rustled the sparse branches of trees along the towpath. Sluggish coppery clouds moved ponderously across the sky, swollen with impending menace, so low and near they appeared touchable, obscuring the maze of spires, gasometers, pylons, factory stacks, mastheads and ships' rigging and the sprawling labyrinth of tower blocks and offices rising like begrimed subterranean monsters out of the shrouded city on the far side of the ship-heavy barge-laden lugubrious river. Fumes and snaking spumes of thick industrial fog smudged the splintered skyline, giant dirty fingermarks scrawled in indiscriminate greed and contempt, leaving their imprint upon everything visible, a lurid pall of smoke rising from cramped human warrens like a miasma; gulls swarmed the air, wheeling and swooping, wailing in wretched avarice and hunger, defeated and despoiled by the city, poisoned by its breath, sinking their beaks and talons into the murky water in thin ravenous high-pitched rage, scavenging for scraps of sustenance. Tugs like over-fed terriers crawled upon the river, rolling and listing indolently, hooting in remote melancholy greeting and camaraderie, borne on the wind like distant cries of puny distress, strangely comforting, telling of men at their taciturn toil estranged from the ant-like frenzy of life ceaselessly broiling along the violated banks of the great river and in the bruised catacombs of streets beyond; at intervals sounded the deeper boom of large ocean-faring ships returning from alien hemispheres or else setting sail upon the tide of routine adventure on errands of commerce, vessels of imposing or meagre aspect, sleek-sided and lithe with proud purpose, or creaking and crabbed with ill-usage and neglect, resonant with hope or harrowed with despondency like the human cargoes aboard them, whose skill, expertise, ambition or need coaxed or bullied them forth upon the waves in pursuit of minted fulfilment or transient escape from common nightmare. The farther

70

stretches of the river were hidden in mist, imbued with a dull deceptive allure enhanced by distance, like a false dawn or premature sunset, wherein mysterious phantom shapes rose and subsided without seeming to move; tiny arrowheads of haloed light flared briefly in the gloom, momentarily piercing the enflamed atmosphere before dying out abruptly, like matches hastily extinguished. The wind freshened, sharp and chill, slicing across the turgid water, pungent with brine and wastrel city odours, shaking the lachrymose trees in dry spasms of commotion; the bruised glow widened and deepened in the sky, grew denser, more livid, streaked with stripes of leaden hues; it began to rain.

Janice moved slowly along the towpath, huddled in her anorak, absently scuffling through fallen leaves as she walked beneath the trees, catching random snatches of talk as people passed overhead on the embankment, the noise of the city hushed by the fog creeping over the river. The mood of the night entered into her, at once melancholy and expectant, vibrant with threat and promise; summer was ending imperceptibly, and she felt something inside her too was coming to an end, giving way to something else, something she could only guess at remotely as some indeterminate point in the future towards which she was travelling slowly but with unerring direction, drawn by an obscure gravity. The sense of grievance she had felt throughout the summer since the ultimatum her parents had given her about visiting the island still weighed heavily inside her, though as summer waned it too had grown less strident, less heated, and was now folded inside her like the leaves at her feet, more of a sad pensive awareness of injury and injustice than the quick violent resentment it had been at the beginning.

Then, with the fine unclouded rashness of the young mind, she had quite clearly decided that her life was just about as good as over as far as expecting any justice from it was concerned; she went into a kind of voluntary exile at home and her room had become her cell wherein she lived as rigorously as any anchorite of antiquity, leaving it only for meals and to do whatever household chores were allotted to her and returning to it as soon as these tasks had been performed. Her small record player had remained resolutely unplayed and unused, gathering dust under her bed; she had not bought a record in months, and had politely but firmly declined to accept any pocket-money from her father, who distributed small amounts between his children at weekends; buying records was the only thing she had ever spent it on, and since she no longer bought them she had no further need for pocket-money. Playing and listening – merely listening – to music had suddenly seemed such a wooden mechanical pastime, such a mindless inane way to spend one's time, sitting hunched on the bed or cross-legged on the floor in front of a squat little box of machinery, a thing of wires and knobs, nuts and bolts, screws and soldered bits of metal, with the disc spinning round and round emitting its feeble scratchy imitations. Shutting herself up in her room, locking the door, drawing the curtains as if to erect a solid barrier between herself and the world beyond the windowsill, then plugging in the socket, turning the knob, twiddling about with tone and volume control, knowing she had it in her power to heighten, lower or throttle altogether the music as it spun round on its pathetic revolutions – it all struck her as perfectly insipid, arbitrary, devoid of surprise or excitement, leaving her completely uninvolved, outside of anything the music might otherwise have held.

Music, she told herself passionately, vehemently, music should be like love or prayer, spontaneous, unpremeditated, stripped of dry ritual, flowing out of the moment, igniting it, casting a spell frenzied or sublime; it should not be at the beck and call of habit, switched on or off at a whim, a caprice of temper, trimmed to accord to the position of the hands on a clock, the idiosyncrasies of households. It should be a celebration, again like love or prayer, a celebration either joyful or sad, of thanksgiving or regret, hello or farewell, but whatever it was it had to be free, genuine, uncramped in its expression, not an empty observance, not a ghostly dance of shadows and disembodied voices, a chalice without wine. So Janice in those early days of summer and hurt quietly seethed and fulminated, full of bitter enlightenment as to the ways of adults, supremely sure of her right to feel persecuted and wronged, the legitimacy of her emotions fixed in her mind beyond self-doubt. So she kept to her room and hoarded her solitude like a secret cache of diverse riches, feeling serenely vindicated and utterly miserable.

She took care to be pleasant and polite, doing whatever was asked or expected of her without complaint, surpassing the deference and respect she had always shown her parents, treating her two sisters and small brother as kindly as ever, listening to their prattle and woes and in general performing her duties as eldest child without once incurring a single rebuke or frown. She had indeed become something very nearly approaching a paragon, greatly to her own surprise and the sore perplexity of her parents, but in the process she had also changed into a mystery, a considerable enigma, causing her parents to look at each other with troubled faces and wonder what nameless wrong they had done her to make her so submissive and self-effacing, such a model of obedience and at the same time so withdrawn and unreachable as to become almost a stranger in their eyes. At first they had accepted as a sign of her growing maturity the unconditional way she complied with their wishes, and which they had also put down in no small way to their own wisdom in handling her, but there was such a joyless air of discipline in everything she did, such an automatic response to whatever they asked of her, that their confidence gradually waned and they almost looked forward to any sign of open rancour on her part. None came, though, and she continued to obey and defer to them to an almost monotonous degree, tidying up, putting things in their proper place, making beds, washing and drying dishes, ironing, scrupulously doing her own housework and helping the other children with theirs whenever she thought it prudent to do so, turning herself virtually into a latter-day Cinderella and when her chores were completed retiring to her room and locking herself in, ensconced in profound silence, without as much as a single raucous blast from the record player to reassure her parents that her admirable but abnormal placidity was over and she was herself again.

As always the only person who could strike any response from her throughout this period of withdrawal was her grandmother, who knew perfectly well what was going on inside her and did not need to probe with words or resort to affectionate subterfuge in order to draw her out. Just entering the room where Gran lay and sitting by her bedside, not speaking much, was in itself an act of confession and trust that told the old woman all she needed to know; yet even here Janice maintained a certain unfamiliar distance, an unwillingness to impart more than what she could not help revealing, as if the rest were too painful to be spoken or shared.

Coming to a bench, one of several that were laid at intervals along the towpath, she sat down and looked across the river to where the city glimmered and glowed. She sat and watched, feeling sad herself, but in a strangely elated almost buoyant way, wanting to laugh and cry at the same time and with equal unreason, the tears that moistened her eyes springing from nowhere. The long inertia that had hung upon her like a heavy cowl for months past began slowly to lift as she sat down under the trees, the brazen metropolis ogling her across the river, leering, luring, flaunting its brilliant spurious enticements before her like innumerable strings of artificial gems; she imagined its coruscated neon-lit miles of misadventure and gala, its mounds of glittering glamour and squalor, its treachery and fable-gathering where dreams walked and laughed and beckoned and faded into shadow spun out of violent beginnings and veering to yet more violent and savage ends; she looked yearningly across the river to the breakneck Babel-loud city and longed avidly to be part of it, its gilded dangers and temptations, its panic and challenge, its insatiable appetites and gluttonies; she longed to be swallowed up in its commotion, to be swept past the narrow restraints of dull logic into vivid confusion and exuberant precarious freedom, where nothing was certain and everything was feasible, where greed was as different from avarice as hunger was from mere gluttony since it was greed after adventure, wonder, excitement and the possibility of happiness and bravery. She sat on the bench and hugged herself, dreamy and in turmoil, pensive and agitated, incapable of staying still, yet not wanting to stir from where she was, the river before her was teeming with subdued life, the incandescent sprawl of the city in the spangled distance whispering fables in her ear and setting her heart racing; she saw her future written in bright letters in the heaving broken wastes of the sky above the city, crude, ungainly, but clear, hanging like a fiery prophecy.

5

'I NEVER thought I'd see you again.'

His voice was low, hushed, with a faint ring of reverence in it, as if he were in the presence of a mystery, toying nervously with the salt cellar on the table to hide his tenseness, his coiled excitement. In the unreal glow that fell on them from the strip of fluorescent light overhead in the tiny booth, his face was sallow, thin, cheekbones hollowed in shadow; his wrists, as he idled with the salt cellar, were slim and vulnerable, yet possessed of a supple strength, flexible, agile; flecks of rain still glistened on his hair, soft brown, tousled, tumbling on his forehead, and the shoulders of his short leather jacket were also wet; he had unzipped it to half way, showing a dull wool cardigan beneath. She felt his alert eyes moving rapidly over her face, like one scanning a familiar landscape come suddenly upon after a lengthy absence, seeking welcome and reassurance in its every remembered aspect, as she busied herself taking off her scarf and shaking out her massed hair.

'I honestly never thought I would,' he repeated, in the same quiet tone.

The booth was cramped, narrow, stall-like, with just the small rickety table between them, its formica top stained and chipped at the edges, and she knew she had only to reach out and touch his wet sleeve, yet he seemed quite a distance from her, unreachable, enveloped in strangeness, subtly withdrawn, hidden, even as she felt his gaze upon her, watching her every movement intently, something that she almost resented even as it pleased her.

'How are you, Richard?' she asked, leaning her elbows on the table, hands cupping her chin, studying him in turn. 'How – and what – have you been doing? Tell me.'

'Oh, nothing much,' he replied, his voice oddly guarded, obviously reluctant to talk about himself. 'I read something about you, a – a few – a few months ago,' he went on, a trace of the old hesitancy coming into his voice. 'You were singing – was it up North? Yes, up North, I think.'

She nodded. 'Yes, in Bradford, during the summer. But that's unfair, you know,' she gently reproved, leaning forward in an attentive, listening attitude. 'I asked first. Tell me about yourself.'

He concentrated with a further comic vigour on the salt cellar, avoiding her eyes. 'There's nothing to tell – really.'

'After two years? I can't believe that.' She joined her fingers together, throwing back her head and giving him a long, shrewd, slanting glance. 'You look older, more important. You haven't been just vegetating – I can see that. So what have you been doing?'

There were few people in the café, some customers sitting on stools at the counter, reading newspapers, absently munching sandwiches; others, mostly young couples, huddled over cups of coffee in some of the other thinly partitioned booths, smoking or holding hands, talking in desultory whispers, inhabiting private worlds, taking little note of the dingy surroundings, the cheap blinds on the window, the fading black-and-white squared linoleum on the floor muddied by footprints and soiled by spilled coffee, the walls of bleak dull glazed stone patterned into vaguely aquatic murals, the spotted glass panels behind the counter steamy and smudged with grease; swing doors led to the kitchen at the back, whence came pungent coffee odours and the sizzling of pans each time they were pushed inwards or outwards by the one rather slatternly young waitress who was serving the tables, carrying trays back and forth in a zombie-like fashion, her face blanched and expressionless, like a convict dawdling up and down a prison yard. A white-coated bespectacled youth stood idly behind the counter, lounging against the glass panels, arms crossed, staring into space, coming lethargically to life only when he rang the cash register as customers paid and went on their way.

Richard had not answered her, and presently she became aware that he was looking at her hands, looking quite hard, peering at them, as if unmindful of the fact that she was also watching him. She stretched her hands out towards him, opening her fingers, divining his thoughts and smiling.

'No rings, Richard, nor bells on my toes,' she said, striking a light note, wanting to ease the atmosphere between them. 'Unhitched, if a little unhinged.'

She almost felt his furious blush as he twisted his face away. 'Didn't mean to stare,' he mumbled. He looked about, seeking release, refuge from his trapped, absorbed awareness of her, betrayed into confusion.

'That waitress is taking her time,' he said, making an ineffectual attempt to catch the girl's eye as she passed with an empty tray.

'There's no rush. You still haven't told me a thing.'

She saw the tense outline of his shoulders against the wooden partition, and knew she was making him uncomfortable, but in a perverse way, a way she could not explain to herself, she was enjoying it, exerting a power over him, and she really was curious about him, about how he had filled the two years since she had last seen him. He, too, she felt, was being perverse, obstinate in the way he held back, retreating into a safe void, and this at once annoyed and stimulated her; after coming upon him in the rain and chill raw dark of the early evening, she felt a compelling urgency to know how the pattern and shape of his life might have gone, what made him so new and unknown to her now. She felt a quick vibrant thrill at the romantic randomness of their meeting in the street as they had, a feeling that she knew was absurd and naively childlike, but it was there, very real inside her still, and she did not try to banish it with any pretence of grown-up clear-headedness, with any attempt at foolhardy practicality. It was silly to deny that she was not excited, intrigued about seeing him again, literally bumping into him out of the hurrying throng of people bustling along the garish lit pavements; it was something that happened in films or plays or novels, something that happened to other people, never to one's self, except in daydreams. It had happened to her now, and although she knew that it was not in itself remarkable, since she was after all back among places and haunts where she might very likely have met him in any case, sooner or later, she was not going to be cheated of this warm pleasant sensation of glad surprise she was now feeling by speculating upon mere nerveless logic. She knew she was reading far too much into it, but she did not reproach herself for this, and was more determined than ever to know all she could know of him before she caught the bus home. So she waited, facing him across the table, unrelenting, like playing a game of chess, waiting for the other to move.

'I work in a garage,' he said finally, worn down by her scrutiny, resigning himself to the inquisition; he gave a brief, self-mocking smile, seeing her interest. 'Not as a mechanic – no. I just pump petrol into cars. Not what you'd call a demanding job.'

'Still, necessary,' she said, not meaning to sound flippant or cruel, and knowing she most probably did.

'Oh yes,' he answered, his sardonic mood lingering. 'One of these jobs that somebody must do to keep the country running, and the pay's not bad, with overtime.'

'Go on,' she said, when she thought she had waited long enough for his moroseness to pass, wishing he would stop his silly fiddling about with the damned salt cellar.

'What do you mean, go on?'

'What else have you been doing?' she asked, impatient, feeling he was being deliberately dense.

He seemed to press further back against the partition, away from her, his fingers tightening round the squat utensil as if it were a life-support apparatus. She could feel almost tangibly the tense obstinacy and aversion to talking about himself flowing like electric current from him, but she ignored it, her face slightly upturned, resting once more on her hands. As he continued to sit in silence she smiled, wanting to prod him into response, even to make him retaliate, anything to breach the barricade he seemed intent upon erecting between them.

'Why are you so secretive, Richard, so tight-lipped? You haven't become a crook, have you, or an urban guerrilla? That would be exciting.'

Slowly, almost forlornly, he relaxed, easing his shoulders; he put the salt cellar down on the table, folding his arms. 'Nothing like that. The garage takes up most of my time. I work all days Saturdays, sometimes.'

'Don't you go dancing or something?'

He gave her a slow and strangely charming smile. 'I've still got two left feet. I do a bit of writing now and then,' he added casually, as if it were of no possible consequence or interest to anyone else, without the faintest trace of pretended modesty or self-effacement.

'Writing?' she echoed, trying not to sound surprised or too drastically taken aback. 'Now that I think about it,' she laughed, 'you do look rather literary. Much too much like a writer to actually be one –'

'Oh, don't talk like that, Janice,' he said, quite sharply, admonishing her in his own quiet manner. 'I'm not a writer – of course not. I just – well, doodle, I suppose you'd call it, like some people do funny little squiggles on bits of paper without really knowing what they're doing.' He sounded quite sure of his own insignificance, as if he took

78

comfort in it, as if it afforded him some sort of solace, some immunity from obscure perils. 'That sort of thing.'

'Ah, but it's different, Richard – it's got to be!' she cried, not to be sidestepped out of her heightened interest in him. 'You must know what *you're* doing. You have to know, if you're putting sentences and things together, putting thoughts on paper, commas and semi-colons and full stops and all the rest of it. That's not doodling!'

'You'd be surprised,' he intervened dryly, remaining cautious and stoical in the rush of her enthusiasm, warmed as he was by it. 'You'd be surprised how deliberate doodling can be. It can take all your attention, hour after hour – '

'You're being facetious,' she broke in, not liking the initiative passing from her, at the same time strangely elated by the authority in his voice. 'What do you write – what sort of things – have you shown them to anyone – submitted them to anywhere? I want to know, Richard!' she ended in a flurry of impatience and excitement, hounding him.

He was saved from the need to answer her by the arrival of the tattily dressed waitress, carrying the coffee and sandwiches they had ordered on a tray that was sloppy from previous use.

'Two coffees 'n 'am sandwich,' she said in a mechanical, bored voice, not asking if the order was correct but merely stating a fact, setting down the cups and saucers and plateful of sandwiches on the table like a card player dealing out a hand, and slouching away without another word or look when her task was done.

Janice gave a small delighted giggle. 'It's sleazy here, isn't it?' she whispered. 'Lovely and sordid – '

She felt him go tense again. 'Sorry, I didn't know – never been here myself – '

'Oh, Richard, don't be so solemn!' she laughed, taking up the cup and sipping her coffee. 'I love it. So grotty and run-down – terrific! I love this kind of place. But,' she said, lowering the cup, 'you haven't told me. Did you show your writing to anyone, did you send it anywhere?'

He looked down doubtfully at the plate of sandwiches. 'Don't think we should tackle those, do you? They look unhealthy.'

'Oh, all right,' she replied, curtly. 'I'm not hungry anyway. And please stop evading the issue. Have you or haven't you shown your writing to anyone?'

'My writing!' He took up his cup and sipped carefully, taking his time. 'You make it sound literary,' he said, steam from the coffee rising before his face. 'It isn't, not in the least. I just do it to amuse myself, odd bits and pieces now and then, when I'm in the mood and have nothing better to do.'

'Yes, but odd bits and pieces of *what*, for God's sake?' she asked, exasperated, unconsciously picking up a sandwich and starting to munch on it.

'I don't know – sketches, I suppose you'd call them,' he answered slowly. 'Might be about people, or places, empty houses, shops – anything, really. And animals sometimes.' He looked at her sternly, disapproving. 'Do you think you should eat these crummy things? They look poisonous to me.'

She stopped chewing, as if only becoming aware of it, and put the rest of the sandwich back on the plate. 'Never mind that. Has anyone seen what you write – that's what I want to know.'

'Well, I did have one or two things printed,' he said, again quite slowly, as if first thinking it over carefully in his head.

'Printed?' she said quickly, leaning forward, eager, attentive, her eyes shining. 'You mean published?'

'Well – yes. Just one or two things, little stories, descriptive things.' He sipped his coffee again, as if anxious to terminate the subject. 'Are you still living with your family? How long are you home for this time? I know you do quite a lot of travelling.' His eyes seemed dark and remote behind the steam rising from the coffee.

'Why do you keep warding me off, Richard?' she said in a level, hurt tone. 'Why don't you tell me about this writing of yours, or is it too sacred a thing to talk about?'

The dart went home, and he lowered his eyes. 'Don't say things like that, Janice. I'm not fending you off, I'm not being coy or defensive either. I just don't think it's that important.'

'Well, maybe it isn't,' she returned, making what she deemed a reasonable concession, hoping thereby to put him more at ease as far as his own self-judgement went. 'Maybe you're not yet ready to take on the mantle of Waugh and Priestley and all that starry crew. But it *is* exciting just the same, isn't it? At least it is to me and my small kindergarten mind.'

'Not nearly as important as your singing career,' he countered, adroit, yet without artifice, without giving the impression that he was merely indulging in a conventional gambit with her, to see who would chalk up the highest score. 'You've gone further in that than I'm ever likely to go with my little pastime.'

'I haven't got a singing career,' she said, frowning, making another absentminded halfhearted gesture to pick up the discarded and disparaged sandwich again, and, remembering in time, changing her mind, folding her arms on the table. 'Nothing so grand. We – ' she paused, then went on, deciding it would be both juvenile and arrogant of her to spare whatever feelings he might have on the subject. 'We just go where and when we're asked. Usually to boozy grubby little places, draughty halls and clubs with no acoustics, filling in between the bingo sessions at weekends, singing for our enormous fee plus extravagant travelling expenses at the most sumptuous dosshouses ever imagined by aspiring world entertainers. Talk of Barnum and Bailey.' She realised she was beginning to sound as morose as he had been some moments before, and smiled. 'Still, it's a start, a foot in the door, so to speak, and I love it.' She sipped some more coffee; it had become tepid.

'It sounds a good partnership,' he said after a short silence, his voice neutral, his eyes fixed on the table.

She laughed, rather forced. 'You make us sound like a firm of solicitors or chartered accountants. But it's not so bad,' she mused, playing with some breadcrumbs. 'We get on okay most of the time, in between the hot silly little rows.'

'Clash of artistic temperaments,' he murmured, idly, as if to himself.

'Are you laughing at me, Richard?' she asked, prepared to be amicable and amused.

He looked up guiltily, brushing the hair back from his forehead with a nervous motion. 'Oh, not at all. It was – a silly thing for me to say. I believe,' he continued after a pause, trying to sound detached yet interested, 'he does the songwriting part of things. Is that so?'

She nodded, somewhat distantly. 'Hmm. Quite good he is, too, or so we've kept being told, mostly by people who wouldn't know a modern ballad from a hands-knees-'n-bumps-a-daisy turn at the Pig and Whistle on Saturday night, but it helps the ego.'

'You've finished school, of course?'

'Yes, thank God,' she said, with rather exaggerated fervour. 'I've left that particular madhouse behind. Wasn't even a proper lunatic asylum,' she went on, sweeping back a heavy swath of hair from one shoulder. 'Nothing ever happened. A real damn nunnery. A mixture of moth-ball propriety and giggling guilt.' Her voice assumed, perhaps unknown to her, a lustrous intonation of poised contempt. 'If a little knowledge is a dangerous thing, then I'm the most harmless person on earth.'

'It was that bad, was it?'

She smiled, shaking her head. 'No, not really. Just in retrospect it seems worse than it was, but what I learned all seems so useless now, or maybe it was me, not being blessed with a studious or enquiring mind. God, doesn't that sound pompous!' She became reflective. 'I suppose I ought really to get some kind of steady job while I'm waiting to be discovered and plotting my first golden disc. A waitress or something of that sort.' She looked round to make sure she was not likely to be overheard, and laughed. 'Without being vain I think I could do better than what we've seen of the staff in this respectable establishment.'

He regarded her fully now, returning her smile. 'Somehow I can't see you in a frilly little apron and cap. It just doesn't strike me as being in the natural course of things, as something ordained by your stars. It seems unholy, an awful sacrilege, just thinking about it.'

'No,' she sighed, 'I can't imagine it either. It's frivolous of me, I suppose, but I keep thinking I'm cut out for better things, a more glamorous sort of degradation, with nothing to do with my life except sip pernod in Nice or Malabar and have dozens of men of all shapes and sizes from sixteen to Methuselah fall passionately in love with me, fight hopelessly outdated duels over me and write endless suicide notes while I calmly contemplate the sea.'

'Sounds a reasonable scenario, I must say.'

'I'll probably be terribly original and end up in a maisonette or high-rise block of flats with swarms of kids under my feet all day while hubby is out gallantly slaving for us and slurping back pints in the local with his mates.'

He joined his hands, in a strangely professorial manner, a remote smile on his face. 'I don't see it quite like that. You want success. That's the difference between us.'

'You mean you don't? You've given up already?'

'Oh, it's not a question of giving anything up. It isn't that. I just don't think I'd be worried one way or the other if I stayed as I am for the rest of my life. You would. You'd be furious with yourself, you'd hate yourself.'

She smiled, but again it was with an effort. 'I don't think I like the sound of that. It sounds grotesquely vain.'

'No, it's just the way you are, the way you're made,' he answered calmly. 'It isn't anything other than that.'

She was gloomy, unsure what way to take him. '*Merci*. That's just what I was afraid of – the perils of fame. The all-consuming ambition syndrome and all that. Ruthless, voracious for recognition, letting nobody, nothing stand in my way as I claw my way to the top. Sounds like a very bad movie.'

His voice, soft, had a muted sardonic edge to it. 'Does it matter what it sounds like? Bad movies sometimes have quite a bit of truth in them.'

She gave another profound sigh. 'I don't know too much about anything. I only know that at this stage anyway to be successful in what I'm doing seems more of a challenge than to be actually happy with my life.'

'You don't think the two go together, that having one is useless without having the other?'

'I don't know, I tell you,' she said crossly, her face clouded. 'I suppose you're right, but – well, honestly, you sound so sure, so positive, like a bloody mandarin! Sorry,' she added almost instantly. 'Didn't mean that.'

He remained looking at her in the same reflective way. 'That's all right. I probably do sound insufferable.' He smiled, arms folded on table. 'Speaking as I do from vast experience, you know.'

She found herself marvelling at the change in him; he was still hesitant about himself, still unsure, but now it was as if he were merely waiting, getting his directions right, not indifferent to the opinions and attitudes of others, but no longer intimidated by them, no longer timorous of investigating and finding things out for himself, in his own time, his own way, at his own pace. She envied him; he seemed about to start on a journey that he had carefully planned and mapped out beforehand, not with cold-blooded calculation, rather with slow studied care, with steadfast clarity, wanting to make certain of the journey, its possible twists and turns, before committing himself, before embarking upon it, for she felt once he had started upon it he would not easily abandon it or be deflected from pursuing it to its end, its intended destination as he saw it. The awkward, groping, slow-moving boy was still there, the boy she had met at the dance hall two years ago, being baited and badgered and tormented by the bunch of grinning dolts who had followed in his shambling steps like professional clowns; that boy was still there, glimmering behind his slow thoughtful smile, but it was no longer laughable, no longer something to be pitied; it was instead a growing root, a promise, a foreshadowing of something strong and unbreakable, possessing an oblivious bravery that moved and subdued her. It hurt her to think he was already set apart from her, from any real knowledge she might seek to have of him, rooted in his certainty, moving further away from her, yet her hurt was compounded too of pride and admiration, and a slow deep fear of never finding anyone quite like him.

Again they fell silent, finding words of little use once the ritual of coffee drinking was over; the small café was becoming more and more like a stable, filling up as the night advanced, steam rising from the damp customers like heat from huddled animals, stamping their feet and blowing on their hands as they formed a lengthening queue at the counter, those who had been served from the service hatch that now replaced the waitress looking round for tables, a palpable impatience fuming in the air. It was one of those shutaway insignificant places that enjoyed a certain local notoriety and clientele of its own, doing a brisk business at specified hours. The youth behind the counter no longer lolled, transformed into a smooth-running automaton of efficiency above the staccato clip of the cash register. It was time to go; he forged a polite but firm path through the crowds, paid the bill, came back for her and then they were outside.

It had grown darker, windier, the air heavy with threat, as if the rain had paused only to take a second breath before coming down in earnest. And very soon down it came, almost before they had reached the intersection at the end of the street, making people run and scramble for shelter, the bright shopfronts whizzing past; they laughed as they ran, holding on to one another for support as the wind-driven rain pelted against them, their soles slipping on wet pavements, blundering into veering throngs of pedestrians looming out of the teeming gregarious neon-slashed dark, dozens of ineffectual umbrellas blown inside out like small up-ended black-skirted spinsters twirling about in some sort of mad dervish waltz. They finally

84

found an empty doorway of a newsagents, tight, cramped but sufficient, and gratefully squeezed into it, exhausted and exultant out of the fierce fusillade of rain and slicing wind.

'The time we picked to leave!' she panted, catching her breath and swallowing, lowering the hood of her jacket, excited as a child in its first thunderstorm. 'Poor Richard,' she said, remembering he had had no head covering at all. 'You must be drenched.' He shook his head, smiling. 'I'm all right. At least we're out of it now.'

From their niche they watched people hurrying past, crooked against the wind, the rain lashing down in great grey slants, making the gutters gurgle, beating like soiled white poppies upon the gleaming crown of the road, obscuring the streetlights, flowing down the glowing shop windows like a gauze, distorting everything; traffic slid and slowed, cars and buses lumbering past like stunned overburdened beasts emitting strangled noises, spluttering forth thick dragon-jets of smoke and fumes, groaning and wheezing in the snarled rain-swept labyrinths of streets. Soon the rain teeming down, hitting upon glass and pavement, made almost a musical sound, a tinkling playful rhythm, like a clash of muffled cymbals, booming remotely through the air, lifted aloft by a prancing wind that whistled now rather than howled, enjoying the turmoil it was causing, blowing hats awry and sweeping up skirts and dresses, twisting everything loose and making canopies flat like hideskins.

'Marooned,' she said happily, hugging his arm, 'we're marooned.' He did not answer, staring out into the rain, his angular face lit by the passing traffic, strands of hair plastered to his forehead, giving him a closed, inaccessible expression, the lids sliding over his eyes like shutters. She felt an obscure jealousy of his mood, left out, excluded, forgotten, as if he was unaware of her then, of her arm linked through his, not sharing her excitement, her girlish gaiety, making her seem silly in her own eyes, giddy and cheaply flirtatious, of no consequence beside his inward brooding intelligence, his quiet self-possession that was already over-reaching his years. Silent, she slid her arm out of the crook of his and moved slightly apart, her spirits dampened, chastened, yet rebellious, resenting his absorbed vigil of the passing scene and knowing he probably saw nothing of it whatever, making her own emotions all the more extravagant and frivolous.

Gradually the rain lessened, thinned, its staccato beat fading to a slow receding tip-tap dripping sound; the wind, too, grew less wilful and scurried off over the rooftops as if tiring of its antics; the air grew sharp again, vibrant, cleansed, the pavements steamed, a rinsed invigorating odour rising from the ground in the aftermath of the deluge; the streets that had been almost deserted before save for traffic began humming and filling up again as people shook themselves and streamed out of doorways and alleyways, walking it seemed with a new liveliness and purpose, some glancing about and looking up as if half expecting to see the buildings somehow magically changed; traffic picked up speed, gathered competitive momentum once more, tyres squelching, brakes screeching as commerce and camaraderie and the bristling night life of the city got into its metallic breakneck stride again, the swarm of lights more brilliant and blatant than ever.

'Time for my bus,' she said, stepping out on to the sidewalk, putting her hands in the deep pockets of her jacket.

'I'll walk with you to the stop,' he murmured, his shadow emerging beside her.

'If you like.'

They reached the stop, where a few intending passengers stood loitering about, and to while away the time till the arrival of the bus she strolled up to a shop window bedecked and beckoning with the latest designs in feminine fashion, the plastic models simpering and posing in their imbecile perfection, the rosebud mouths, chiselled noses, lustrous eyelashes, the curved flower-stem waists and tiny bosoms; it all made her sad, too real and large and aching for the world, and her melancholy deepened, grew heavy and round inside her like an unwanted child, raw and squirming inside her.

She turned from the window of empty temptation as her bus came clanking and puffing to a halt. She stayed behind as the other passengers climbed aboard, groping for something to say and knowing it was futile, feeling somehow that their meeting had been a waste, a bright trinket now discarded in the gutter, flowing out of reach with the receding rain, and not knowing why she should feel like this; they had met, after all, had spent an hour or so in each other's company, a minor adventure, surely, in an otherwise trim and uneventful day; it was wrong and stupid to go about in circles searching for hidden meanings, looking for clues, portents, looking for something that was not there, something that did not belong to them and that basically, intuitively, she did not want. There should be no need to look beyond the moment that had brought them briefly together, no obligation on either side to seek an extension, a continuation of the moment; it should end rightly, cleanly, before it grew murky, complicated, undefined, a vague indefinite ache lingering because a word had not been spoken, a gesture made, an understanding forged; that was wrong and muddleheaded and of no benefit to either of them. The bus would take her back to her own life again, the life she was choosing and shaping for herself, and he would go back to his, and it was right that it should be so; she was absolutely convinced of that. They would not forget each other, they would probably, perhaps inevitably meet again, whether often or only infrequently, and this again was as it should be, and must surely be enough. She knew that it was enough, that anything else would be forced and untrue, hurtful to both of them, a gross exaggeration, a sad and pitiful mistake, and that as soon as she was back in her own world again all would be right, all would fall into due and proper perspective, as it would with him also. She was merely being selfish.

She held out her hand. 'Goodbye, Richard.'

In the light from the bus he looked strikingly ordinary and sensible and she felt rather foolish at all her wishful pondering and pretentious suppositions about him.

'Goodbye,' he said, holding her hand and pressing it. The bus conductor was standing on the platform, a jolly-looking paternal man, but he was growing impatient. 'You'd better get on,' said Richard, squeezing her hand tightly and letting it go, stepping back.

'Yes.' She stepped on to the platform and turned. 'Will you send me some of your writing?'

He smiled. 'Yes, yes.' She waved, and he waved back, then turned round and started walking quickly away, merging with the crowds, not looking back once.

She stood a moment on the swaying platform, looking after him, disappointed that he had gone so suddenly, so completely, without looking back. Then she found a seat next to the window and sat down, realising he did not have her address.

PART III
Two Years Elapse

6

'Don't be silly,' said Art, shoving her gently by the shoulders into the dim narrow hallway that smelt of old clothes and linoleum and a faint tang of tobacco. 'They won't bite you, you know.' His voice was brash, jovial, but a little too loud, as if he too was nervous though feeling it necessary to hide it and take command of the situation. 'I could do with a cup of tea, I can tell you,' he said heartily, rubbing his hands and chuckling, 'and maybe a drop of something in it.'

She stumbled over something that jutted out from under the stairs, and saw it was a child's bicycle; domestic debris cluttered the hallway, she brushed against coats hanging thick and heavy from the stair rails, and from the back of the house came the muted crackle of a television set. She hung back, feeling like an intruder, while Art strode on ahead of her into the front room that served as living and dining room, shouted greetings in the same loud cocksure voice, leaving her stranded in her confusion, as if he had forgotten about her. A moment later he came back, laughing and wondering why she was still standing there, and led her in.

'Well,' he said jauntily, stepping aside and grinning, still extravagant and nervous, 'here she is – the missus!'

She felt her cheeks flush furiously as he said this, and she wished to God she was anywhere but where she was, in a strange house and with Art acting in such an idiotic way; she hated him for a moment, hated the way he was both grinning and smirking and rubbing his hands together like a kid who had just won some sort of spot prize at a dance or carnival. She had no time to nurse this grievance, though, for just then a heavy-set man in his harassed middle thirties rose from an armchair by the fire and stepped forward irresolutely, taking an unlit pipe from his mouth and holding it in front of him, indecisive, as if about to offer it to her as a gift. He wore a dull grey cardigan with buttons down the front, what some people often referred to with a certain amount of derision as a 'smoking jacket', as if it were a symbol of domestic enslavement and dull conformity, reddish brown slacks and frayed slippers on his sockless feet, his whole appearance somewhat rumpled and decently shabby; his eyes, pale blue and crinkled, wore an anxious expression that seemed permanent, as if he were forever trying to devise ways of pleasing people or trying to squeeze out of tight corners; his thin mouth was set in rather grim preoccupied lines, a slight rut or indentation at the corner where he habitually held the pipe clamped between his teeth. His sandy hair was spread sparsely, like pale ash or flake, with patches of scalp showing through; a chunky signet ring glinted on the little finger of one hand, and his smile, though hesitant, was unforced in its welcome as he held out his free hand.

'I'm Gerry,' he said, clearing his throat, his handshake firm. 'You are very welcome.'

His appearance somehow complemented that of the room; small, over-stuffed with cosy sagging furniture, a coal fire burning in the grate, a heavy dark old-fashioned sideboard laden with tiny gilt mirrors that gave off rainbow refractions of light, crammed with framed family pictures and small china figures of dogs and portly drinking gentlemen holding jugs; the floor was covered with dull oilcloth, with a frayed length of carpet before the fireplace, and the flowering baskets of the pink wallpaper had long ago faded to a comfortable blur, as of summers past. A long sofa strewn with cushions obviously placed to conceal glimpses of coiled springs and not altogether succeeding was pushed up against one wall on one side of the range, in a corner of which squatted a forlorn rag doll, pop-eyed and scarlet-mouthed, its head hanging half off; a clock encased in mahogany ticked away on the mantelshelf, along with further family pictures in cheap brass frames, snaps of seaside outings, children grinning cheekily into the camera while the adults looked embarrassed and self-conscious in swimming gear, squinting down at their toes or laughing at one another so as not to be snapped full faced. The single front window was draped with dusty heavy green velveteen, shutting out the immediate wet night street outside and deepening the sense of crowded human warmth and enclosed living that pervaded the room.

'Big brother,' announced Art, taking off his crash helmet, putting his motor-cycle gloves in it and placing them on the sideboard. 'Rock of Gibraltar, salt of the earth, heart of oak, the strong and silent type – that's Gerry. Eh, captain? And where's Gwen – where's the little woman herself?'

'Oh, she's – '

'Done a bunk with Albert the milkman or gone on the tear?' Art went on, laughing, not letting the older man finish. 'Family secret, you know,' he whispered aside, making a comic face. 'Gwen's hooked on port-'n-lemon. Been in and out of port-'n-lemon hospitals for years seeking a cure, but all to no avail, alas. Now Gerry here's strictly a real ale man – eh, Horatio?' He winked and clamped an arm round his brother's shoulder in exaggerated bonhomie; it was obvious to Janice, looking on at the spectacle, that he knew he was trying too hard, knew that he was talking too much and making an ass of himself, for he kept stealing anxious, surreptitious glances at her as though for support and reassurance, yet he seemed unable to stop himself, hopping about the room with greater agitation than any hen that ever danced on a hot griddle, making them all uncomfortable, himself most of all, by trying to put them at their ease with his barrage of banter and nervous raillery. He moved about, fidgeting, picking things up and putting them back down without looking at them, warming himself at the fire, plucking at his beard, acting like a prisoner waiting for sentence to be passed and have it over with. 'The old homestead hasn't changed. The bloody houses still haven't decided whether to stay up or fall down. Just like the people, eh?' He put his hand before his mouth and coughed. 'Kids in bed, are they? What the hell's the time, anyway?' he said, swivelling round to peer at the clock. 'Gone nine. Didn't think it was that hour.'

Gerry left off examining his pipe, as he had been doing for some moments past, as if seeing it for the first time, and nodded towards the back part of the house. 'Gwen's in with them. It's a job getting them away from the telly.' He turned back to studying the pipe again, as though for relief.

Art left them. Gerry came forward, unsure. 'Would you like me to hang it up outside in the hall?'

'Oh, it's fine, thanks.'

'Oh – good.' He blinked, seeking out the best place for her to sit. 'Er – sit down, won't you? Here – ' he pulled the most promising looking leather chair over near the fire. 'Is that all right, or would you rather – '

'That's fine, thanks.'

She accepted the offer and sat down, rubbing her palms on the smooth shiny knees of her jeans while he stood hovering opposite her on the other side of the hearth, sucking on his pipe; she felt terribly vulnerable and young before his large ponderous solidity, his slow slippered weight and rooted mass, like a child in front of a ruminative school-teacher who was sizing her up in his own cautious, tentative, unerring way, marking her potential points good and bad, not in any way offensive or intrusive, but observing her from his own impregnable smoking-jacketed distance, much as he might study a young animal newly brought to his attention. His scrutiny was kind, unthreatening, and probably unintentional, but she grew restless under it and concentrated intently on the coloured flame leaping in the grate, wondering what in God's name was keeping Art.

To her irritation she found herself clearing her throat, a mannerism she had always found amusing and vaguely off-putting in others. 'This is a nice comfortable house,' she said, diving headlong into the first cliché that came to her. 'So warm and cosy.'

He pondered this a moment, then nodded, smiling, seeming to appreciate the effort she was making at conversation. 'Yes, I suppose you could say that,' he agreed, looking contentedly around the room, taking the pipe out of his mouth. His eyes finally rested on the low ceiling, criss-crossed with tiny continents of smudges and plaster cracks, as if he found particular interest and pride there. 'Yes, not bad, I suppose.' He frowned, his gaze coming back to the fire. 'A bit cramped, though. Yes,' he said, as if finally making up his mind. 'A bit cramped. The five of us, you know, and just the two bedrooms.' He brightened. 'Still, we manage. Yes, we manage.'

He bent down and inspected the fire, which was burning perfectly well. 'Excuse me.' He shovelled on more coal from the battered brass scuttle, his normally pasty cheeks made ruddy by the increased volume of flames leaping and hissing up the blackened walls of the chimney as he prodded the blazing little pyramid with the poker. 'Ah,' he said, satisfied, straightening up. 'That's the job. Nothing like a healthy fire, I always say.' He replaced the poker inside the hooked rim of the coal scuttle, dusting his hands on the back and side of his trousers. 'Warm enough?'

'Oh, yes, thank you,' she said, edging away a little from the added heat, 'fine.'

He contemplated the frazzled patch of rug on which he stood; her hands were clammy on her lap; there came again the ritual clearing of his throat.

'You don't – er – come from these parts, do you?'

'No,' she replied, 'Surrey, I'm afraid.' She made it sound an involuntary apology, and bit her lip, annoyed with herself.

'Surrey, eh?' He thought a moment, then shook his head. 'Don't know it very well. Don't know it at all, to tell you the truth,' he added, obviously deciding that honesty was the only honourable course to take. 'Might have passed through once or twice, but that's about it.'

'Oh, it's not very exciting,' she said, strangely touched and liking him more. 'Just another place to live.'

'I'm sure it's very nice,' he said, as if gently contradicting her for her own benefit. 'Woods and rivers and that, I suppose.'

She could not stop herself from laughing outright. 'Good God, no! I mean,' she said more restrainedly, 'it's just another sub-city sort of place, miles of roads and houses all looking alike, shops and supermarkets – the usual mess.'

His frown came back. 'But you've got trees, haven't you?' he insisted, almost with truculence, as if wanting to retain an ideal. 'You've got trees and parks and open spaces, haven't you?'

'It's not Devon –' she began, then stopped, aware of the sarcastic edge that was creeping into her tone. 'Yes, we do have a few trees, I suppose, and one or two parks scattered here and there, but nothing like what you've got in London –'

His mouth settled into its grim set lines. 'Not here, not in this part. Hardly ever think of here as London. London's a place you travel to at holiday time.' He looked up at the ceiling again, as if consulting a friend, an oracle, a crystal ball. 'Hyde Park, Regent's Park, The Mall, Kew Gardens . . . that's London.' He gave a peculiar tremulous sort of sigh; he might have been someone browsing through travel brochures of far away exotic places and daydreaming of going there one unforeseeable day. His eyes returned to her, smiling, friendly. 'Still, we're snug enough here, I must say. Nothing to complain of, really.'

She sat mute and rather ashamed, taking refuge in watching the flames; it was hard to think of this heavy-shouldered slow-moving methodical man anchored firmly in his grey toiling thirties to his wife and family, who almost certainly comprised the whole of his existence, having dreams roaming in his head of wooded slopes and birdsong and red-bramble hawthorn-heavy country lanes and cottage smoke curling in the sky; and yet it was clear he had such dreams, he had romance buried somewhere within him, and the thing that stirred her most and made the poignancy sharper was not that he had as much right to dreams as anyone else, but that he should have them at all – that to her was the mystery, the obscure miracle, that the deadening cement-grey monotony and featureless regularity of his life had not quite defeated these visions, which were no more absurd than most visions; that life had not blunted his simple need to believe in things beyond the fading rose-papered walls and crammed little hutches of the terrace house that was his ship in life, the only vessel of voyage and discovery he was ever likely to know. She knew that she should not have been surprised, since even her own limited knowledge had taught her that dreams and dreamers can crop up and prosper in the most unlikely of places and flower in the most barren and unpromising soil; yet she could not deny that she was surprised and moved deeper than she knew to have come upon such a thing entirely unsuspected and, as it were, all by herself. She felt both chastened and elated, and stretched her hands out gladly towards the spiralling flames making such musical furore in the grate.

He looked vaguely towards the door. 'Maybe I should go and rustle them up. They're probably yapping their heads off – haven't seen Art in over a year, I think.' He shuffled a little, seeming to wait for her guidance.

'Oh, there's no great hurry,' she said, and meant it. 'I suppose you were surprised at the news.'

'News? Oh – ' he knocked the empty pipe on the edge of the mantelshelf, plainly adrift in waters which he deemed to be exclusively feminine and out of his depth. 'You and Art, you mean?'

She smiled. 'Yes.' And when he did not answer she went on probing gently. 'Were you surprised?'

'A bit, I suppose. No,' he said, with the same dogged insistence as before on being honest with himself and his questioner. 'More than a bit. Flabbergasted, you might say, the both of us, Gwen and me. Never thought of Art as the marrying type. Mind you,' he added, as if the thought had just then struck him, 'he's young.' He put the pipe into a pocket of his cardigan, then looked down at her, as if a second and complementary thought had occurred to him. 'So are you, of course.'

'Yes, we're both young, there's no denying that.'

He became bluff, back to fire, feet spread. 'No harm in that, of course,' he said, hands clasped behind back, his voice almost jaunty.

'Gwen and me married young ourselves. Green as anything, we were.' He made a rough male harruping noise in his throat, straddling the hearth like a captain on the foredeck. 'Could be the best thing that ever happened to him. Settle him down, you know. Art's all right – one of the best, really – but he never seemed, well, responsible, a bit wild and reckless, you know. Never could hold down a proper job. Him and music.' He teetered back and forth on his feet, nodding to himself, satisfied that he had made a just and accurate assessment.

'I'm what you might call musical myself,' she said, stretching out her feet towards the fire, hands relaxed in her lap. 'That's what brought us together, in a way.'

He became a bit flustered, aware that he had made some sort of gaffe without quite understanding its nature. 'Er – yes. You sing, don't you?'

She smiled lazily, oddly content in his company. 'I try to. So far nobody's thrown tomatoes or rotten eggs, and we actually get paid now and then, incredible as it seems.'

'Yes, that's it,' he said, as if catching the drift of things at last, giving several sombre nods. 'You've teamed up, haven't you, formed some sort of – er – act, on stage, you know, going here and there – yes, he did write and tell us about that, of course.' He stopped and again studied the balding rug at his feet, meditative. 'Must say I don't understand it myself.'

'You mean the wandering minstrel bit?'

He turned to her, giving her a grateful smile. 'Well – yes, I suppose I do. Seems an odd way of earning a few bob.'

'It is,' she agreed, amused to discern that it would never occur to him to ascribe to it the status of earning a living. 'But we both enjoy it.'

'Well, that's good. Yes, that's good.' He looked up as the door was pushed inwards. 'Ah – '

'Sorry I was so long,' said Art, coming in with a parcelled bottle under each arm and another brown-papered bundle held between his hands, a cigar hanging nonchalantly from the side of his mouth. 'I nipped down to the off-licence on the corner – '

He was followed almost at once by a plump matronly young woman carrying a tray with glasses and sandwiches on it, which she set down on the small table by the sofa; the tray also carried steaming hot scones and freshly baked biscuits that gave off a delicious aroma,

94

like being in a baker's shop. She brushed strands of hair back from her forehead and turned to Janice, smiling and holding out her hand after first wiping it in her apron to make sure there was no trace of flour on it.

'Hello, I'm Gwen,' she said in a low, girlish, rather breathless voice, her round pretty face apple-cheeked and flushed from the heat of the oven. 'You must think me awful not coming in to say hello before now, but I was up to my elbows in flour and dough. You're very welcome. I hope Gerry's been looking after you – no, don't get up! Stay just where you are, Janice – that's right, it *is* Janice, isn't it? Yes, of course it is. Have something to eat, won't you – I promise they won't poison you – or would you rather have a drink first? Yes, of course you would. Gerry dear, do draw the sofa nearer the fire so we can all sit together and be comfortable – there, that's better, isn't it?'

She spoke in a rush, never quite staying still, possessed of continual animation, the flurry of her hands keeping pace with the gay inconsequential patter of her words, which were never directed at anyone in particular or had any specific intent; she was simply one of life's talkers, disdaining the habit of talking only when one had something to say, and after only a short time in her company this compulsion of hers to talk ceased to be eccentric and came to be accepted as something absolutely natural to her, the essence of her person, as much a part of her as an arm or leg and without which she would be incomplete. So even in the brief time between her entering the room with the tray and sitting down beside her on the sofa that had been pulled closer to the fire, Janice had formed an opinion of this lively dark-haired little woman, whom she noted was well into another pregnancy. She gave the impression that whatever pleasure others might receive from her chirpy ministrations was meagre compared to her own happiness in seeing that they were warm and fed and comfortably seated and in the best possible health and state of mind. Her round face shone with a berry-brown gloss, already inclined to fullness and a double chin that somehow only enhanced her light air of girlishness, her coming pregnancy adding to her infectious, loquacious wellbeing and jollity; she sat among them crisp and housewifely and pert, alert as a bird on a branch, darting quick dark smiling looks at each of them in turn, irrepressible and delighted to find herself in their midst.

Like a precocious recruit promoted to generalship, leapfrogging the ranks, hoodwinking his elders with no effort at all, Art moved up and down the room, glass in hand, drinking in an adroit way, like a beer-stained gin-soaked sawdusted veteran of innumerable sprees and unmentionable hangovers, the braggart cigar dangling in his mouth, tossing off wisecracks, telling imaginary anecdotes, describing with great fidelity adventures that almost befell them 'on the road', a phrase he kept flinging about with profligate casualness, heightening both their hardships and their miniature victories with a fine contempt for accuracy, making the 'digs' they stayed in even more horrific than they were in reality, the very occasional hotel they stopped in overnight quite unforgettable in its opulence and the exquisiteness of its cuisine; the songs he had written with either excessive ease or excessive anguish, the way that they had performed on stage, the peculiar twists and turns of composition, the nuances of creativity, the enormous burdensome joy of it all: he was in his element, sparing them no detail however mythical, begrudging them not a morsel of his own raptures in the sweat and scent of his trade, bedecking every sentence with superlatives, seeking and easily catching the awe and full-hearted attention of his brother and his twinkling merry-eyed wife. He was absurd; yet there was about the whole of his pantomimic performance a lurking innocence, a harmless though urgent need to be accepted and believed, so that in her heart Janice forgave him utterly and loved him all the more, finding his arrogance irresistible and as potent as an aphrodisiac of unusual strength and lethalness. There was, after all, something of the nursery about it, an infuriating but bewitching brat strutting about with his arms full of the most envied and treasured toys, showing them off with an insolent fervour that quite disarmed the beholders and made rancour redundant and unthinkable. It was such a primitive display of vanity that to object to it would be akin to taking umbrage at the antics of tribesmen dancing round a totem pole at a tribal feast; there would simply be no sense in being angry or resentful; it would merely amount to blaming him for what he was, that which drew her to him so powerfully and made her love him.

She contrasted the bleakness, the almost ascetic rigidity of her own home background to the marvellous intimacy into which she was now drawn, and a sharp sadness that was intensely inarticulate overtook her; her short past stretched behind her like a desert, bare of any real growth, denuded of meaning, marked only by her own lonely footfalls; apart from her grandmother, she had found no haven there, no striving understanding, no attempt at bridges. Her parents had rarely emerged as anything but solicitous strangers to her, scrupulous though stern guardians arching over her childhood and brief adolescence like marble pillars, giving her food and shelter and little else; her sisters and her one young brother she had scarcely known before her time with them was over and she had wandered out into the world, a little dazed by its voluptuous freedom, its blithe off-hand acceptance of her as a person who might perhaps have something intrinsically her own to offer but without imposing any pre-conditions, without setting cold tablets of law before her and bidding her observe and obey. Had her Gran not been there, that other world would have been completely dead, inhabited by conscientious ghosts passing distantly before her, immersed in their own shadows, shrouded in their own skins, passing through each other, never touching.

Art interrupted her reverie, rumpling her hair and grinning. 'I'll just pop in before she puts the brood in the sack. Long-lost uncle and all that – won't be a sec.'

To her dismay he then turned and followed Gwen out of the room, leaving her alone with this balding, puzzled, prematurely middle-aged, kindly stranger, who had gone back to his sentinel post by the fire, sticking the lifeless pipe back into its cubbyhole in the corner of his mouth, chewing on the stem, his friendly if uncertain eyes on her in furtive, abashed glances.

'He's nervous,' he said at last, giving her a quick consoling smile.

'Yes.'

She stood silent, hopeless and lost, still wrapped in her heavy fur-lined jacket, cursing Art for his thoughtless abandonment of her, turning so heedlessly away and dumping her in the middle of this hospitable but painfully awkward silence, as if she had known these relatives of his all of her life. She fumed inwardly; was this how newly married people behaved? Where was all that bliss she should be feeling, all that new-as-morning happiness that should be washing over her like surf, that secret inner certainty of having the world at one's feet and in the palm of one's hand which should have warmed her like wine? She only knew that right then she could cheerfully have trussed and throttled her new husband and shoved him down the nearest manhole, not just with equanimity but perfect glee, and she resented him all the more furiously because she felt herself not very far from tears. She thought of that mad afternoon somewhere in the middle of the country when they had committed the unthinkable folly of signing the marriage register with numb fingers and blind ecstatic faces, and felt appalled, standing in this queer little cluttered-up room facing this homely perplexed stranger chewing so intent and ineffectual on an unlit pipe, trying to be kind to her. What was it all supposed to mean?

'Sorry,' said the man at that moment, making her jump a little, so unexpectedly he spoke. 'I'm blocking the heat from you.' He moved quickly to one side, allowing the heat of the glowing coals to lick at her.

'Not at all,' she answered automatically, forcing a smile and at the same time thinking what a ghastly imitation it must appear. 'I'm quite warm, thank you.'

'Ah, but it must be freezing outside,' said Gerry shrewdly, as if making a sound judgement. He looked at her, hesitant once more. 'Er – won't you take your coat off? Might be a bit more comfortable, don't you think?'

'Thanks, I will, if you don't mind.' She took it off and looked round. 'I'll just leave it here, if I may,' she said, laying it on the back of a chair.

Gerry, sunk in slippered ease and gentle subjection by the fire, followed the restless striding of his brother, who had returned to the room with Gwen, with tolerant eyes, not grasping everything he said, not catching every gilded syllable leaping like sleek salmon from that bearded mouth, but believing all he heard, never for a moment pausing to wonder if all these bizarre escapades and adventures had really happened, not bothering to worry himself over anything as staid and irrelevant as the truth; he was hearing of a world he had never known, and though buried in acceptance of his own, his willingness and need to believe in that world was at least as imperative as Art's, and being wordless, perhaps went deeper. He reclined in one of the ancient armchairs, his glass resting on its shiny arm, feet crossed, high temples glistening from the unaccustomed alcohol and heat from the fire, the stem of his talisman the pipe protruding from a pocket of his cardigan; he was perhaps already becoming slightly drunk, Janice imagined, becoming almost old-maidenish as he relaxed and fell under the influence of the whisky, giving maudlin little sniffs from time to time and pressing his wife's hand as if to reassure her of his presence and of his grave docile devotion, and Gwen in turn would give him one of her bright darting looks and pat his knee in a soft maternal way, making him eat another sandwich or sample another scone, fussing over him as over a lackadaisical child; any minute he could have been expected to lean over and rest his head in her lap. The fire danced, the clock ticked, glasses were filled again; Janice felt herself enveloped in lovely ease, cosseted, cocooned, the rightness of being where she was stealing over her, seeing everything in its place, in its own dusty nook and niche, everything belonging, nothing inapt or jarring, and just by closing her eyes or gazing dreamily into the flames she had no difficulty at all in believing that life had never been anything else than it was at that moment.

At length, his monologue of heroic hardship, comic misadventure and inevitable silver linings becoming more rambling and ragged, Art lapsed into a series of moody silences, his eyes bleary with drink and fatigue, gazing morosely into space. After a while he started to put on his helmet and gloves, his fingers fumbling, muttering it was time they were making tracks, and was briefly adamant when his sister-in-law said they must stay the night, but then Gwen, heaving herself laboriously up from the sofa, took things gently, firmly in hand, taking the bicycle gear from him and putting them back on the sideboard, her whole manner vibrant now with maternal tyranny, charming but invincible.

'Nonsense – you're going nowhere tonight except straight to bed! Not another word – not a single one! Never you mind where to sleep – there's the box room at the back, isn't there? You and Gerry can bunk together in there – take him along, Gerry, and do stop mooning – you look so silly. There, get along, the two of you, like good boys – '

'But Janice,' mumbled Art, holding back, trying to be masterful and not making a very good impression of it, finding it hard to focus on where she was standing. 'My wife – must see after her – '

Gwen gave a rippling laugh, casting her eyes up at the ceiling, taking firmer hold of his arm. 'Listen to that now – lord of the manor already! Never you mind about Janice – we'll take care of ourselves. Oh, aren't men silly! Think we can't get on without them. Do get along, the pair of you, do get along!'

With calm, unanswerable efficiency Gwen shepherded the two shambling men out of the room and down the narrow passage to the little box bedroom at the back that had a large bed in it and little else, their feet and voices stumbling and mumbling in clumsy incoherent camaraderie amid much hiccuping. Gwen returned presently, smiling a proud, rueful smile, blowing back wisps of hair from her eyes, flushed and triumphant.

'Men!' she exclaimed, lowering herself into an armchair, filling it with her soft swollen girth. 'Aren't they the very limit, though? Helpless as newborn lambs after a few drinks. Lordy-lord, what would they do if they had to look after themselves?' She chuckled quietly to herself as she considered this dire circumstance, wiping her moist eyes on a corner of her apron. 'Mind you, it's ages since poor Gerry had more than a few pints down at the Quill and Feather on a Saturday night, playing darts with the lads. Not that I make any excuses for him, mind – gets quite silly in drink, does Gerry – like a mooncalf, he is, just wanting to be petted and fed and put to bed all wrapped up and snug . . .'

Her voice was low and drowsy with unemphatic love; ripeness rose from her like pollen, deep, mellow, languid; she was languorous with caring, tranquil in the abundance of her concern, smoothing the rumpled landscape of other lives, alive with tender conspiracies and sly oblique tricks to ease confusion and alarm and to mantle with her warmth of heart those weak and wounded by predicament. Her eyes cleared and she smiled across at Janice, mischievous as a schoolgirl eager to share a confidence.

'I'll tell you what, my dear,' she said, her voice dropping to an unintentional whisper, drawing herself up in the chair. 'Let's you and me have one more drink and then we'll toddle off to bed – what do you say?'

'I'd say that was a good idea, Gwen.'

Janice rose from the sofa and poured for them both. She handed Gwen her glass, and stood smiling down at her, enjoying the secretiveness of the late hour, the look of anticipation on the pert upturned face before her.

'And now, Gwen – am I wrong? – you'd like to hear how I met Art and why we got married so out of the blue.'

Gwen managed to look placid and expectant at once. 'Well, my dear, if you think you really want to tell me . . .'

Janice put down her glass and heaped more coal on the fire, bringing it alive and making it dance again, the clock ticking away unnoticed on the mantelshelf, then she came back to the sofa and sat down.

7

SHE remembered her last visit. Her mother's long dry fingers twitched like mice in her brown-tweeded lap, her angular face with its habitual indoor pallor quite devoid of emotion, her whole frame cloaked in remote and impenetrable apathy, save for the movement of her fingers, jerking in little spasms, plucking absently at the heavy fabric of her skirts. Her greying hair, still thick, was neatly tied back, a thin furrow of scalp showing down the middle; a vague mauvish hue hovered about her austere mouth, suggestive of fatigue, though above it her forehead was placid, a scroll of smooth unrumpled parchment. There was about her a scent of faded lavender and camphor, and if her dark deepset eyes held hints of puzzled pain, it was as if she were struggling to unravel some enigma rooted in the past and hardly related to the present moment. She sat upright in the wide-winged green leather armchair, the magazine she had been reading lying open at her feet.

'Your father will be –' her mother had paused, searching about in her mind for the apt phrase, as if it were of the utmost importance that she should be precise. 'Shocked. Yes,' she reiterated, pursing her lips, satisfied; 'shocked. That is the only word one can use. Shocked to be informed at this late date that his eldest child is now a married woman, utterly without a word from you to either of us. Not a word, not as much as a casual reference to your plans in all those months you've been away from home. He will be shocked.' She spoke in a calm, delibrate monotone, almost without inflection, blinking her pale lashes from time to time, eyes fixed steadily on the dusky window beyond where her daughter sat at the table. 'No doubt he will take the news quietly, as is his way, but as for his feelings, his true feelings –'

Her mother's voice trailed off, as if she had lost the drift of what she had been saying. Outside the evening had deepened, a late bird somewhere sang a few clear meditative notes before twittering away into silence; lights began showing in the front parlour windows of the houses on the other side of the avenue. A dog barked, and was answered by another.

Janice added another spoonful of sugar to her tea, her single suitcase still unopened at her feet. 'We knew you'd both disapprove,' she said, pensive rather than contrite, slowly stirring her tea. 'Knowing that, it seemed a bit pointless telling you. I thought it better to come and tell you myself. After all,' she said, 'it was only two weeks ago.'

Her mother blinked rapidly once more and made a small preparatory sound in her throat before speaking. 'A phone call or telegram – you could have sent one or the other on your' – she swallowed, as if getting rid of a bone that had lodged in her throat – 'on your wedding day. Surely you could have made at least that small concession to our feelings.'

Janice sipped her tea carefully, unhurriedly, relishing its comforting warmth. 'We did it on impulse, Mom, when the time came. We both had it at the back of our minds for some time, without talking about it or bringing it out into the open.'

'Seems an extraordinary way to get married.'

Janice nodded, smiling. 'Yes, I suppose it does, really. One day we just stopped and looked at each other, you know, in the middle of whatever we were doing – talking, or reading, or eating – I don't know – and smiled and – well, we just *knew*. Knew there was no point in waiting, so we went off and got married. It was a Thursday,' she explained dreamily. 'In a registry office somewhere in the Midlands. It was raining.'

'That young man,' said her mother, wrinkling her thin nose in some distaste; 'I can't even remember his name.'

'His name is Art, Mother,' retorted Janice, using the more formal tone she always adopted when angry or resentful. 'Arthur Devlin, to be precise. He comes from the East End.' There was an unmistakable touch of glad malice in her voice as she thus peremptorily outlined her husband's antecedents.

'Your poor father will be deeply hurt.'

'That Art comes from the East End?'

Her mother flushed. 'Don't be facetious, Janice. He will be hurt that you show up on his doorstep, without a word of warning, and your marriage already a *fait accompli*. What else do you expect him to be?'

'And you, Mom,' said Janice quietly, watching closely. 'Are *you* hurt?'

'I? Why, of course,' said her mother quickly, after some hesitancy, as if taken off-guard. 'How can you ask? I am merely more in control of my feelings than your father.'

'Yes.' Janice put down her cup. 'I didn't mean to hurt either of you, Mom. Please believe that. It just happened the way I've told you. We couldn't let you know because we didn't know ourselves until it happened, and then – well, time just rushed by. We were in a spin and didn't know where we were, until –' she shrugged. 'Here I am. And I'm not expecting a baby, by the way. Thought I'd put your mind at rest on that point, at least.' She heard once more the hard edge of irony in her voice, but did not try to disguise it.

Again her mother flushed, this time more deeply, as if a gross indiscretion had been committed before her eyes. 'No, of course not. I mean, I never for a moment –' She quickly regained her detachment. 'Why, then, may I ask, were you in such an unseemly hurry?'

Janice's fingers tightened a little on her cup. 'I told you. I can't put it in a more convincing way. It was what we both wanted, so we went ahead and did it.' Seeing the cup was empty, she stood up. 'I'm going to have another cup of tea, Mom – will you have some now?'

'What? Oh, yes, all right. Two sugars.'

While Janice busied herself pouring tea, buttering a thin slice of bread for herself, relieved in these slight ministrations from the rigours of futile explanations, her mother sat immobile in the chair, her face a blank glimmer in the gathering dusk of evening inside the room. After some time she stirred and, bending down, retrieved a magazine from where it had slipped to the floor, finding at once the page she had been reading before her daughter arrived, a detailed knitting pattern and diagram for a wool smoking jacket which she thought Douglas might like when his birthday came around before Christmas; it would take her a few months perhaps to finish it, but it would please him to know she was doing it for him. It took so little, really, to please poor Douglas. She gave almost a small start of surprise when Janice handed her the cup of tea.

'Oh – thank you,' she said, quite formal, as if in someone else's parlour. As if with an effort, she focused her attention once more on her daughter, holding the teacup delicately and sipping. 'Now had you taken that secretarial course your father and I were so set on for you, this would never have happened. I'm quite convinced of that, quite.'

Janice sat down again, suddenly tired. 'How can you be so sure, Mom?' She felt anger seething inside her, but forced herself not to show it.

'It would have steadied you,' said her mother, nodding in the same complacent self-satisfied manner as before, pleased with her choice of phrase. 'Yes, it would have steadied you, a good solid job like that.'

Janice gave a tight smile. 'Steadied me? I don't think I was ever what you'd call a wildcat, Mom.'

'You had every prospect of getting a position with your father's firm,' her mother continued, ignoring or unaware of this attempt at irony from her daughter. 'Mr Soames himself said so in private to your father – did you know that?'

'Yes, Mom,' said Janice mechanically. 'Sorry I let the firm down.'

'And it would have come in quite useful now, I daresay, a nice steady secretarial job. Quite useful, now that you've gone and got yourself married.'

'We do earn a living, Mom. Not a great living, no champagne and caviar yet, but a living. Enough to be going on with for the time being, at least.' She brought her eyes back to the face that told her nothing, her anger increasing. 'Or don't you remember, Mom?'

'Remember? I don't quite understand –'

'We sing and play together.'

Her mother's eyes went expressionless again. 'Oh, that. Of course I remember that.'

'Yes, Mom – *that*. It's our life now, our livelihood. It's what we've been doing for almost a year now,' said Janice, her eyes hard and flashing, '*and* living off it. We work damn hard, up and down the country –'

Her mother winced. 'Please don't swear, Janice.'

'Well then, why do you dismiss it like you do, as if it were nothing, as if we were merely amusing ourselves?'

Her mother closed her eyes as from an unpleasant spectacle. 'I cannot help thinking it is all terribly precarious. It was all quite foolish enough before, this' – she opened her eyes and gazed solemnly up at the ceiling – 'this singing craze of yours. But now that you're married –' She stopped, bereft of words, and frowned at the cup in her hand.

'You just don't understand, do you, Mother?'

'No, I'm afraid I don't.'

'It's what we want to do, the one thing on earth we can do well,' Janice cried, rising to her feet. 'To go on to anything else now would mean nothing to us – we'd be throwing away all our hopes and settling for second best, and we're not prepared to do that – not yet we're not, and I hope we never are!'

'All very romantic, I'm sure,' said her mother stolidly, finishing her tea and putting the cup on the table. 'But how will you *live*?' Her voice was neutral, that of someone speaking out of obligatory duty rather than actual apprehension.

For the first time since she had entered the house, Janice appeared excited. 'We met this man last month – Simon Sandford – a sort of record producer, very big in the business. He heard our act and, guess what, he wants us to cut a demo –' She paused in her eagerness and laughed – 'Sorry, Mom – that means making a tape, to see if we come across okay, and if we do this Sandford man will arrange for us to make a proper disc – you know, a single record for the commercial market, so people can go in and buy it in the shops, and if *that* goes well –' She threw back her hair, her face shining. 'Isn't that exciting, Mom? Usually most people have to wait God knows how many years for this to happen –'

'Your father's late,' her mother interjected flatly, going to the window and staring out. 'He's usually home by now.'

The detached, unemphatic brutality of the interruption made Janice shrink back as if from a physical blow. She felt cold and lifeless, as if some essential spark at her very quick had been extracted from her, leaving her inert. She sat down again at the table, her foot striking against the suitcase. It had grown quite dark outside; a car went by, its headlights stabbing along the road; voices of people on their way home from work filtered in, brief snatches of talk, a laugh, a cough; across the way a front doorbell rang, a child's voice lifted in greeting, a gate swinging back on its hinges.

Mother and daughter inhabited their separate solitudes, like two strangers on a train obliged to share the same compartment while headed for different destinations, exchanging the usual undemanding pleasantries, enduring each other's presence and personality with hardihood, since they could not circumvent their enforced intimacy and might as well make the best of it until the journey ended. Janice was dismally certain that the journey had ended long before that evening; she just had not been aware of it until, like a train jolting to a halt, she had been shaken out of her torpor and flung into full consciousness of the reality that had awaited her all along.

Her mother stood by the window, hand placid on curtain, staring out into the darkness, not really seeing anything, and from the mantelpiece the large old-fashioned china clock seemed to toll rather than tick gently over, loud in the familiar silence . . .

Later her father came in and, seemingly oblivious of her, sat down, solid-boned ash-grey head bent over large spread accounts ledger, harsh arc of reading lamp casting his lower frame into shadow, causing his face and sturdy shoulders to seem disembodied, chiselled out of granite, static as an old daguerrotype print.

Struck as always by a tremor of pity and rage at his snail-like burrowing insular industry isolating him from the larger perceptions and discernments of life, she watched him silently, knowing if she stood there an hour he would remain in perfect ignorance of her presence. She moved further into the room, and it was like disturbing an anchorite at prayer in the desert, violating his solitude with her clumsy brash citified intrusion, though she took great care to move quietly and not brush against things. He lifted his face, blind in the cleaving circle of light, peering out into the darkness beyond his desk as if an enemy were lying in wait there. He twisted the flexible column of the lampshade around and out from him, turning the light full upon her, making her blink and throw a hand across her eyes.

'Janice,' he said, then again, interrogatively, 'Janice?'

'How do you do, Dad?' She put out her hand, feeling for a chair or some other thing to steady herself as the glaring light played upon her. 'The light, Dad –'

'What? Oh.' He returned the lampstand to its former position, putting the pen unwillingly aside and slowly rising, coming round to the front of the desk, brushing back his thin hair nervously, shoulders held at a stiff, awkward, defensive angle. 'Your mother told me you had come.' He moistened his lips, leaning with one hand on the desk, his face once more obscured as he stood between her and the light. He looked round vaguely. 'There's a chair somewhere, I think.'

She stepped close and kissed him on the cheek, the gesture taking him by surprise, adding to his confusion. 'How are you, Dad? Not disturbing you, am I?'

'Er – no. Good gracious, no. Just doing the books, you know.' He stood back, scratching his blunt chin, as if wondering what to say next, not quite looking at her. 'Well, now –'

'I'll just sit here.' She sat gingerly down on the edge of the slim bunk-bed in the corner, making sure not to disturb the prim coverlet, waiting until he had retreated once more behind the desk and had resumed his seat before proceeding further. 'Are you well, Dad? Mother wrote some time back, saying you had a touch of – was it lumbago?'

He picked up the pen again, as if for reassurance. 'It was arthritis, as a matter of fact, but it's cleared up now. Yes, it's cleared up now.' He fell silent, turning the pen round and round in his hand, as though it were the only thing in the room he could relate to with any certainty.

She saw his bloodless pallor, the haggard lines on his cheeks and forehead, the large blunt-fingered hands oddly useless and inept now that he was no longer busy with his endless mathematical litanies; she felt a surge of sympathy for him, making it hard for her to speak in the precise unemotional way she knew he expected of her.

'I suppose Mom has told you?' She folded one hand over the other as she spoke, hiding her wedding ring, not wanting to offend him by what might seem hurtful ostentation.

He lifted his eyes and gazed at her, frowning, as if the matter demanded measured concentration. 'About you being married? Yes, she told me. Yes.' His attention returned to the pen, turning it up and down, tapping it against the palm of his other hand, the light falling on his lowered lids, making them seem plump and strangely unhealthy, protuberant, like someone who was being ever so slightly throttled.

'You're not annoyed, Dad, are you, not too disappointed?' She knew she sounded like a nurse asking a sick person about his symptoms, using tact and solicitude so as not to alarm or intensify any awareness of pain. 'I suppose it seemed a bit sudden.'

'I was naturally –' He paused, selecting the word with care. 'Surprised. Yes, surprised, naturally. You're still quite young, for one thing, though today I don't suppose that matters a great deal.' He leaned forward a little, drawing his shoulders together. 'Still – it is done, it is a fact, and I can only wish you well.' He looked at her, quizzical. 'I don't believe we – your mother and I, that is – have met this young man of yours – have we?' He seemed to be trying to remember.

She smiled. 'No, Dad, not yet. I'll bring him some weekend, soon.'

He nodded, his eyes moving away from her to the dull-papered wall behind. 'Yes, very well. It is of no great significance, after all, and I daresay in time . . .'

His voice did not so much trail off into indistinctiveness as come to an abrupt, automatic halt, almost with a metallic click, like a telephone being put down.

'I'm very happy indeed, Dad.'

He looked at her squarely for a moment. 'Then that makes me happy too, Janice.'

He at last put down the pen, placing it carefully between the open pages of the ledger, got up and moved slowly to the window, where he stood gazing out across dark neighbouring backyards, hands in pockets of his thick-corded wool cardigan.

'Yes, it makes me very happy to know that, Janice.' He hesitated, reluctant to tread on unfamiliar ground. 'Your mother especially was a bit upset – naturally, I think. Not hearing from you very often, and then – this news.' He half turned his head, looking at her over his shoulder. 'You will admit, Janice, won't you, that it all seemed rather – odd?'

She measured her reply, knowing it always pleased him to have her ponder and weigh her words, and feeling it was a small enough concession. 'Yes, I suppose it did seem like that, at least to other people, but not to us – not to me and Art. To us it seemed the only logical thing to do, knowing how we felt for each other.'

He stood at the window, a blurred, bulky, amorphous shape on the far side of the desklight, his shoulders sloping forward, hands held tightly in his cardigan pockets, staring out, as if keeping a private, static vigil.

'I daresay, but my dear Janice,' he remonstrated mildly, 'we are hardly "other people". We are, after all, your parents. That, surely, amounts to something, even today.'

'I meant no disrespect, Dad.'

'Oh, I'm sure of that, Janice, quite sure of that.' He sounded relieved, apologetic, as if feeling duty-bound to correct an otherwise diligent and apt pupil on a relatively minor point. 'It is – just life, I suppose. Grandmother is nearing the end, however,' he continued, straightening and flexing his shoulders, 'and at such times a little stocktaking, a little inventory is inevitable.'

'I suppose it is,' said Janice, trying to mimic his dry factual tone. 'Credit and debit, loss and gain.'

'Yes.' He left the window and came back to the desk, sitting down. 'I hope we made things fairly tolerable for her here, your mother and I. We have tried, over the years, and I like to think we haven't been entirely unsuccessful, but your grandmother is of such a strong-willed, independent disposition . . .' He folded his hands and sat staring patiently, blankly ahead, as if abandoning all further pretence of knowing how to continue the conversation, waiting for her to direct and give it impetus, if that was what she wished.

She rose, brushing her hands down her jeans. 'I won't keep you any further, Dad.' Her voice at that moment was remarkably like his own, flat, dispassionate, disembodied, a wintry breath issuing from her mouth, but she chose not to hear. 'I can see you're quite busy.'

She had reached the door before he looked up from his abstracted gazing, as if surprised that she was still in the room. 'Hmm? Oh – yes, as a matter of fact, I am rather busy. You know how I like to do the accounts at home.' A thin imitation of a smile appeared. 'Force of habit.'

She nodded, standing in the doorway. 'Yes. Goodnight, Dad.' She went out, and then came briefly back, pushing her head in. 'I go back tomorrow, Dad.'

'Back?' he repeated, uncomprehending.

'Back to where we live now.'

He stared, obviously feeling some sort of final gesture was called for, but unable to think of any, groping about in his mind for words, picking up the pen. 'Yes. Well, I'll probably be gone by the time you leave. You know how early I set off.'

Janice stood by the door in the gloom, unnoticed, unrequired, watching the bent broad-domed head, the abstracted face and hooded eyes, catching the thin scratch and squeak of the pen moving steadily up and down the page with imperturbable purpose. Nothing had changed.

PART IV
The Present

8

SPRAWLING in a deck chair on the verandah, a tall glass of iced vodka and tonic within reach and that morning's newspapers of singularly no news fluttering at his feet in the slight breeze, Simon Sandford watched with detached sardonic affection his family gathered round the modest swimming pool below him on the rear lawn of the house in Mill Hill, and wondered again why he had ever taken on himself the ritual of paternity when there were so many other rôles he could have enacted with so much more panache and conviction. Each time he returned home it was exactly the same – like entering an over-heated steamroom or reclining in a sauna with the temperature fixed at a torrid tropical level, no matter what the season happened to be. It was quite a large house, like most of its kind in the area, yet there never seemed to be enough space for cool air to circulate, as if along with its other admirable features it had come complete with its own built-in system of claustrophobia. Just by lifting an eye one encountered plenty of open green spaces and rolling lawns and trees that imparted a russet sylvan aspect to the whole surroundings, yet the paradox remained that here he experienced a closed-in locked-cell sensation of confinement and oppression that he had never felt in London's teeming centre, so that he faced each weekend travelling home as grimly as other commuters faced the inevitable Monday morning trek back into the grey dusty clamour and growl of the city. The sight of trees along the quiet avenue leading to the house in the leafy acres of suburbia filled him with the same feeling of doom and impending imprisonment as the grimy rooftops and endless asphalt trails of factories, offices and railway yards inspired in the heart of the traveller returning to the long slow march of another working week in any city in any country in the world. But 'Thank God it's Monday' was not infrequently the thought uppermost in Sandford's mind when another family weekend sojourn had mercifully ground to a halt; setting out for the city's heartland once more was akin to packing one's bags and setting out on safari, with the same tremor of anticipation and excitement making one's hands a little unsteady on the steering wheel, and it was all he could do on these occasions to restrain himself from whistling.

He looked at his family now with the same jaded feeling of familiarity breeding a puzzled resignation rather than contempt, which at least would have jolted him perhaps into a new appraisal of them; his wife Elinor, stretched stomach down on a foam mattress, small face half hidden behind the sunglasses and the latest fat paperback by the latest acclaimed author of improbable and badly written espionage stories, her body all sharp bronzed angles in the bikini that exposed and accentuated her thinness the more keenly, the flat dull lift of her buttocks and her hips and shoulder-blades standing out like whittled sticks; his two sons demurely dipping themselves in the pool, like pilgrims undergoing baptism in the waters of a sacred stream, scarcely submerging their heads – Nathan the eldest, lean as his mother and as solemn, a habitually preoccupied look on his face, in contrast to the younger boy Matthew, tubby and tousled, hesitantly eager to explore and make friends, who laughed, or rather tittered a great deal about nothing in particular, like a puppy unsure either of its welcome or its freedom, afraid of being rebuffed but gamely willing to make the effort; and finally the baby of the litter, Hilary, sitting with knees drawn up to her mother's feet, invariably her favourite position indoors or out, at seven too exquisitely doll-like for comfort, fragile to a formidable degree, causing people to refrain from touching her lest they leave their crude adult imprint on her small vulnerable bones, observing the tepid antics of her two brothers now with grave elderly misgiving, as if they were engaged in the most appalling rowdyism.

Sandford let his eyes travel reluctantly to a fifth figure sitting alone on the far side of the pool, who completed the demure little domestic tableau. This was their German au pair whose name he had cultivated a habit of never remembering, although it was something short, compact, staccato, like the girl herself, an unaccountably sullen creature who gave rasping guttural retorts in lieu of replies to questions and in general behaved as if it were unimaginably demeaning for her to be in their employ or that of anyone else, giving the impression that nothing they said or did or gave her could ever eradicate that immense humiliation. He had long since satisfied himself that the only reason why his wife kept the girl on was simply because she was afraid of her and was dominated by and a little in awe of her mannish misanthropy, preferring to put up with her erratic behaviour and give her a wide berth rather than go to the extreme of exerting her own severely limited initiative by giving her a week's notice. Sandford for his part avoided the odious woman as much as possible, and whenever there were guests in the house he went to extraordinary lengths to put her away out of sight as if she were the family idiot, using the other servants to bribe, cajole or hoodwink her into keeping to her own quarters. Not that he was in the least intimidated by her, for he was by nature a silken bully, an acknowledged master at the delicate tyrannical art of making people move exactly as he wanted them to without seeming to give any thought or effort to the matter; it was simply because he had a genuine dislike of the girl, and looking at her, lolling by the poolside, her breasts like pointed helmets bulging aggressively out of the wet swimsuit, dark cropped hair plastered to her skull, a grotesque parody of an avenging Wagnerian diva gloweringly intent on extracting retribution from the world, he experienced a sharp physical revulsion, like someone already satiated happening upon a feast in progress and being instantly sickened at the spectacle of mounds of glistening uneaten meat wobbling before him waiting to be gorged and devoured. He hiccuped as if gagging on a bone, reached for his glass and took a deep necessary swallow.

His thoughts settled morbidly on his wife and children once more; despite the remote antipathy they aroused in him whenever he thought about them for any appreciable length of time he could not help feeling a certain disgruntled pity for them, which made his general dissatisfaction with them and the whole ethos of his home life all the more pungently felt. They were so damnably lamblike, he thought, fidgeting in his chair, so uncomplainingly sacrificial. Not, he reminded himself sharply, that they had anything to complain about, he provided them with bucket and spade and like pleased children they went about unobtrusively disporting themselves and building their ingenious little sandcastles to their undemanding hearts' content. But now and then it would have relieved the monotony of their glazed amiable complacency had they given tiny voice to a single rebellious sentiment of disagreement or betrayed by a fleeting look that they were at variance or discord with him, any evidence however minute or debatable that somewhere inside their glossy skins they had minds of their own. Far from raising their voices, however, they had never as much as raised their eyebrows; the element of surprise was totally lacking in them, accepting everything he said, whatever plan, suggestion or condition he might place before them, without a murmur of dissent, turning faces rubbed smooth by acquiescence up to him bearing vague obedient smiles, never calling his judgement into question, never once challenging his assertions or his authority, bowing to his despotism, his absolute sway over their destinies. Almost automatically they paid him homage, exactly as one genuflects before a stone idol or intones orisons to a painted ikon; they paid him the obeisance due to an abstract deity or ideal, rendering all the requisite responses and incantations without once showing a trace or flicker of uninhibited spontaneous needful joy.

Joy . . . his thoughts revolved awhile round that small unfamiliar word, touching it tentatively, warily, wondering what portents, what hitherto unexamined possibilities it might hold for him within the context of his family life, which was a little like wandering about a ship one had been travelling aboard a long time and discovering its many hidden recesses and secret places. Theirs had been a singularly joyless little vessel for a very long time now, he reflected, holding the glass delicately between the fingertips of both hands: a sad little barque dipping and rising forlornly upon the placid tide of their existence, never once encountering stormy weather or veering off course into dark exciting uncharted waters. It was like living inside an echoing shell, cocooned from rude contact with the mad milling furious world outside, inhabiting their cloistered little cosmos cotton-woolled against hazard or intrusion, where words floated like tiny inanimate captions in a comic-strip vacuum, tiny bubbles of vapid air that vanished into nothingness as soon as they were exposed to the sharp verbal draught of communication hovering above their heads. They seemed immeasurably incapable of reaching out and touching each other; like shadows they merged sometimes and became one amorphous presence without really intermingling or perceiving one another, colliding without impact and leaving no evidence of the collision behind.

He had once loved his wife, he supposed, though it was now so far off in the confusing yet comfortable haze of distance that he could no longer afford to be dogmatic about it; the one thing he was sure of at this juncture was the knowledge that he no longer loved her, most assuredly not as remotely embodying the person he had once imagined her to be. He gave a small tight rueful smile; 'imagined' was certainly the operative word in this particular process of thought, even if after the first year or so of conjugal rapture he had ceased to practise or prolong the folly of imagining anything whatever about her. As far as the faculty of imagination went, the distance between Elinor and himself had extended and become so wide as to be unbridgeable; it was as if an immense moat had opened up between them, leaving each of them isolated inside their own fortress from the ramparts of which they might direct an occasional impersonal message of mundane significance only before retreating back inside the walls.

It would have been an exaggeration to say that he had actually stopped loving her; nothing had stopped so much as drained away, ebbing slowly, gently, almost apologetically into nonexistence.

Along with the quality of surprise, of wonder, mystification, even common apprehension and perplexity as regards the unwinding of each new day, he had gradually become conscious of something else that Elinor lacked; she was entirely devoid of any sense of anger. She might at times be subject to moments of pique, at rarer times to petulance and vexation that would cause her fine level brows to contract a little and her thin mouth to become even thinner and more parsimonious, but she lacked true ire, that element, mercurial or slow-burning as the case might be, that ignites and flashes sooner or later in any genuine relationship and gives it a potency, point, breath. He longed to convince himself that at least once in her marriage with him his wife had been tempestuously, exquisitely, memorably angry. All he could come up with, however, were timid little vignettes of Elinor sitting in a corner with meekly downcast eyes because of something he had said with unaccustomed vigour or something he had left unsaid with even greater firmness, or else an image would float into his mind of her mooning abstractedly from room to room, holding an unread book in her hand and looking like Ophelia in one of her more drastically retarded moments, briefly restored from her watery doom and trying to puzzle out what it all might have meant. It was not that she was too fine-bred, introverted or fastidious a person to give way to so commonplace and wilful an impulse as anger: it simply had never occurred to her to be angry, and if it ever had she would have been sorely perplexed as to what to do with the anger, how best to get round it and put it out of sight.

He could not be certain, even yet, whether she harboured any suspicions about his other life in the city; she had met Marcie more than once, mostly at some of these boring cocktail parties they had to attend from time to time, or on the rarer occasions when Elinor had visited his office during business hours on one of her infrequent shopping forays into London, when she would always telephone beforehand, like someone seeking an appointment with their dentist or lawyer, and ask if she might drop up for a minute or two if things were not too busy; these indeed were more in the nature of duty calls than anything urgent or pressing she might want to see him about, for she never had anything remotely interesting to impart and soon left after a few pleasant and totally predictable platitudes. It was as if she felt it a matter of etiquette to pop in and say hello, like visiting a friend in hospital when she found herself by chance in the vicinity. At such times the two women got on well enough together, treating each other with bonhomie and goodwill, shaking his hand in both their own, saying the things he wanted to hear, the outrageous flatteries he needed to absorb like food and drink, and he knew even then that they were nothing more than gilded falsehoods wrapped in pretty paper. Something hard and cold and aloof inside him told him so, bade him be on his guard against these false witnesses, and he listened to that clear decisive voice in his head, and did not care, did not declare himself, or betray by flicker of eye or turn of lip that he knew they were lying grossly, excessively, that they were mere panderers to his ego in return for another full glass, another heaped plateful of food. He knew they probably laughed at him, seeing him gauche and eager and bemused, soaking up their praises, and he did not care, did not slink back into the cold comfort of truth, for the words were sweet to his ears, they were as music seeping into him, he wanted to hear them, to savour the sound and taste of them without thinking of their worth, their value or pedigree. A false dawn was, after all, better than no dawn at all, and a spoken word of praise, however bloated with insincerity, was infinitely preferable to cold taut calculating silence.

Maybe later, sometime in the future, in that wide and alien landscape, when he was absurdly older and absurdly wise, he would harden and learn to live without praise, without encouragement and compliment of others, learn to live his life and learn to know his craft in his own lean estimation of both. But that was for the future, it belonged to another day, a person other than the one he was now, something he would have to grow into, something he would have to suffer to attain and deserve. It was mere folly, it was greatly beyond him, to think of that other day, that other person, to imagine himself in that other life hanging obscurely suspended in the uncharted immensity of tomorrow, when he ached now for applause, for acclamation, to hear his name being rolled about on tongues of absolute strangers across the land, to think of himself as someone distinctive, someone people would discuss and analyse and ponder about, like a novel or painting or play or musical composition, someone people would talk about across gaming tables, in railway carriages, hotels, pubs, on the beach, in their beds. As much as the fiery stuff in the bottle swinging now in his indolent hand, hearing his name and his work praised made him drunk with inner revelry, made his head dizzy with glad bedlam noises and his heart thud as in the first wild assaults of love. He played with exuberance the rôle of willing fool lapping up the milk placed at his feet by the hands of wily sycophants giving him the crooked look of approval; dignity, self-respect, integrity, these were the preserves of old people, the hard-won bounties of a plodding meticulous snail-crawling life, and he could dispense with them safely until they caught up with him, like disease or senility or a nagging wife.

The idea of following in his admirable father's footsteps, of burying himself in the small though thriving family business of buying and selling jewellery through a modest little chain of shops, had been firmly implanted in his mind and as firmly he had uprooted it and thrown it aside. To be fair to himself and to please his parents, he had given up one whole year of his brimming ambitious young life trying vainly to adapt himself to this hawker's trade, before laying it aside and relinquishing his position, if not his invested shares, and leaving the day-to-day running of affairs to his younger brother Marcus, a pleasant suitably self-effacing boy, who had a proper huckster's instinct for that kind of thing and a natural aptitude for the unsavoury bustle and din of the market-place, leaving him free to step aside and carve a gentler niche for himself, a young guru growing cunningly old on necessary guile.

Instead he had grown merely gross, in mind, body, circumstance. He had allowed himself to sink ever more deeply into flabbiness seen and unseen until he had now begun to view himself with the same veiled repugnance he had once bestowed upon the family business, a business he had so haughtily dismissed only to swap it for an even grubbier one, where all was elaborate electronic fakery and make-believe of the most sordid and charmless kind, where every standard was sub rather than anti, where people fed daily, hourly, compulsively off each other like rabid voracious animals, and talent was almost exclusively judged on whoever could mouth the loudest most unintelligible and mind-numbing banalities accompanied by the most ingenious combinations of simper and spittle. He had put himself into a bone-crunching airtight box where all was bedlam at full heartless blast, and thrown away the key. He felt a quick lucid disgust at how easily he had duped himself into believing that what he was doing had a certain transitory value and was not entirely a waste of time, calling only for a certain degree of imagination.

A cloud crossed slowly over the sun, cooling its heat for a few moments and bringing a short welcome gloom. On the far side of the pool the German au pair girl lifted her face, leaning back on her hands, shoulders hunched forward in an athletic posture, scowling at the sky for having the impertinence to become momentarily clouded without first asking her permission. Sandford watched with an irresistible morbid curiosity as she spread out her legs in a brazen vee leading to the unimaginable apex, displaying her corded muscular thighs into which the swimsuit sank as into dough, and he fancied how easily a man could be squashed between them before he knew even the faintest stirrings of greed or rapture. He imagined her enfolding a lover in the immense unmapped territory of her flesh, stifling the first gasps of pleasure out of him with the press of her stout sensible teutonic arms as she muttered coarse staccato endearments; at the image he drew back in fastidious alarm, and wished more devoutly than ever that his glass could be replenished without his having to stir. He wondered again why the hell Elinor kept the creature on; as far as his admittedly limited vision could see, she was of no earthly use to the kids, who were by now surely beyond the babysitting stage, and since Elinor, as he knew, never actually went anywhere, the need for a babysitter was superfluous and non-existent in any case. The woman was an ugly appendage they could easily do without, but having once taken her on Elinor seemed powerless to fire her or delegate her duties on to a more responsible level; there she hovered, ponderously, like a grossly overweight albatross about the house, casting her shadow over everything even when she was out of sight, a sort of grotesque curiosity piece, like so many other things both in the house and in his life, giving him greater cause to feel umbrage.

With singular and unabashed naiveté he had set out, too long ago now to be remembered with comfort, to *make* something of his life, contrary to the weary cynicism that had overtaken him in later years; something brilliant, original, daring, a clear sharp deft brilliant statement of intent, loquacious in its broad design, its stunning simplicity, a concise declaration of independence and purpose, to be achieved not so much by anything he might actually do as by the very manner in which he lived and conducted his existence, the way in which he would grandly celebrate the unique fact of his own mortality.

He might as well make the most of this little mid-morning hiatus, he reflected, since the larger part of the afternoon and evening would be taken up by the people he had invited along for drinks to announce the launching, on the following Monday, of the new Clover album, their third within the last two years. He wondered if Art and Janice – who probably thought of themselves most laughably as the two principal guests – would show up, and if they did, which one of them would be the most sober. Their last two albums, he had to admit, had done very well indeed, even to the extent that he had begun to think he might have been wrong in wanting to split them up; it was as if, finding herself under veiled threat, feeling she was being edged out, manoeuvred into a corner, Janice had thrown herself on to the offensive and literally barnstormed her way upwards to impressive stature as a singer, just to show them that she could make herself indispensable to the partnership and to Art's success as a songwriter. Her new-found thrust and impetus seemed to have ignited something in Art, too, for he had begun writing stuff that was undeniably top-class.

Art sat in the shade on the terrace, but his eyes had begun to burn with the reflected glare of the sun, glancing harshly off the greenish pool water and the glass conservatory at the bottom of the garden.

Without having it spelled out, without having it emblazoned upon his every waking thought, without making it the one indisputable and essential emphasis of his life, he knew that Janice had never been unfaithful to him; in thought, perhaps, in word easily flung and as easily taken back, but never, he knew, in deed. How precisely he knew this he could not describe; he merely knew it to be true, as one knows one is alive and must someday die; his conviction was as elemental and final as that. It grew out of an inexorable inner certitude, out of an instinct still strong and unblunted by smug usage; he knew it because he had come to know the secret calligraphy of her every gesture, of her face, hands, eyes, the whole mobile language of her body that he had come to decipher and to map with the exactitude of a cartographer or navigator, and its every line and curve spoke to him with simple eloquence and truth, holding nothing back. This knowledge was total, it precluded doubt and indecision, it surmounted anger and spite and the petty warfare that often raged between them, causing them briefly to inhabit separate islands.

It did not lessen or heighten their awareness of each other as antagonists, as lovers, as persons, it did not at all make living together easier for either of them; it was merely a fact, it was merely how things were, and it alternately warmed and goaded them both, but it could not be denied, it could not be obliterated by any effort of will on the part of either of them. If either had ever been unfaithful, betrayal of that fact would have been immediate and inevitable, they could not have borne or dared to look at each other for a single sustained moment without the pain and misery of that betrayal becoming plain on their faces like searing livid scars. It was not something to be particularly proud of; that would have been as ludicrous and incomprehensible as taking pride in the fact of having been born. Neither was it a conscious credo, a deliberate inclination of will, like a monk pledging himself to a life of celibacy or an anchorite choosing to fast in the desert; it was not a pact between them, the terms of a contract they had both undertaken to observe; it was not any of these things, but something that could not and need not be put into words, which bound them invincibly and would not be broken, however angrily they might strain against it, however much they might resent and oppose it in their private wars with each other, the occasional dreams of escape and freedom away from each other, the meaning of which they could not remotely understand.

The house, the walls, the very rooms Art was now roaming through spoke with mute rhetoric of life gone awry, of the failure of faith and trust, of two people wrapped in the same expensive shroud and never meeting, never touching, never sounding the vital quick of each other, every sterile act of physical congress between them a dry instant duty, a grey obligation, like paying domestic bills, having people to dinner once in a while, checking the stock exchange, obeying the needful observances of convention without conviction, certainly without heat, actors playing a rôle with assurance and aplomb, reading from the same well-thumbed script with rarely a faulty pause or moment of uncertainty, knowing their lines backwards, mumbling them in their sleep. The gilded wreck of Simon's marriage, the orderly ruin of his home-life lay in evidence everywhere, enshrined in impeccable taste, decorously proclaiming diligent survival in a grand misalliance of souls; a spectacle forever on display, a camouflage festooned with success, a hollow but brightly painted hulk kept afloat by social necessity when it should decently have sunk and subsided below the waves long ago; in such a context, marriage was a sick joke, a desecration, a tawdry travesty, a bedraggled second best to honest unpretentious harlotry.

Sometimes idly, at other times with sullen deliberation, he had imagined being unfaithful to Janice; the idea would strike at him with wasp-like belligerence, buzzing round in his head with vicious persistence, stinging him; or else it would steal upon him unawares, like a thief creeping into a tent under cover of night, disturbing his sleep with a mixture of guilt and curiosity, pitching him into confusion and a pained, rueful certainty that he could never do it, however imperative the incentive or inclination. Adultery, he decided, was essentially a retarded emotion, a lesion of the nerve and spirit, not seriously to be recommended as a therapy in any true sense; a sordid last resort where faith was finally dead and buried. Sometimes, looking at other women, being in their company, or observing them merely as strangers, the thought of fornicating with them would come to him with undeniable attraction, for he was young and virile, and had perfectly legitimate fantasies not centred exclusively upon his wife; but soon these ideas would languish and wane into mere abstraction, a joyless concept, vapid in its very nature, and soon the women who had moments before been symbols of desire and lust beyond possession would be restored safely to their ordinary, pleasant, agreeable and quite unremarkable selves, fully clothed, smiling, smoking, sipping drinks, gossiping, talking about holidays, boyfriends, husbands, the latest play or musical, the novel they were reading, the illness they had just got over, the baby they were hoping to have. Ordinary females once more, and Janice even in her absence shining in their midst like Sirius at its most radiant.

Once, in some forgotten town, in some forgotten part of the country, not very long after they were married, an incident occurred which lingered in his memory still, like a miasma that had never quite dissolved, hovering at the back of his mind, on the fringe of his consciousness, something at once half dreamt, farcical, even comical, yet imbued with a vivid reality of its own, too potent to be dismissed, as most dreams are, on returning to wakefulness and the sobering grind of getting on with the business of living out each day. On the strength of a couple of single records that had proved fairly successful, they were by then moderately known, even to the starry extent of people, mostly teenagers, coming up and asking for their autographs. Such recognition was very flattering, but he was young and arrogant enough to think that it was only what they deserved, for he was turning out excellent lyrics and rhythms, and Janice was rapidly becoming the equal of any other female vocalist around, her voice deep, mellow and husky, and capable of reaching a high octave without sounding shrill or strained. They were on the way up, and people were starting to become aware of them.

That particular night, they had come off stage to loud encores and with bursts of appreciative and prolonged applause ringing sweetly in their ears, even if the hall was rather small and the audience not particularly discerning, perhaps, but applause was good to hear at any time and in any place, and like most people of their age, or any age for that matter, of whatever profession or craft, they needed praise and an appreciative audience more than criticism, however constructive and well intended. Janice, flushed and happy, unable to keep her excitement to themselves only, wanted to ring up her parents and tell them the good news, the reception they had just got, and how successful they were becoming. Art frowned at this.

'What do you want to do that for?' he asked, ruffled. 'You know they don't approve of me. They never have. They think I'm some sort of gypsy or nomad, dragging their darling daughter round the country with me like a dog on a leash.'

Although a little exaggerated, this summing up was partly true; her parents did disapprove of Art and the sort of existence they had chosen to lead, and in their sombre, solemn way had been appalled when they got the news of their marriage. Knowing this, Janice rarely mentioned anything concerning their work or, indeed, about their married life, whenever she got in touch with her parents whether in letters or on the telephone, since she knew it would lead nowhere and make Art angry and sullen. On this occasion, however, seeing how her eyes shone with excitement and pride, he smiled, shrugged and told her to go ahead and phone, while he went off to the monastic cell that served as a dressing-room in the lower depths of the building, whistling and with a definite swagger in his walk. It was easy in those early days to tolerate her little vanities, blithely overlooking his own, for she loved him, and he was more than a little smug and cocksure in that knowledge. He had been in the dressing-room for scarcely more than a minute or two, stripped to the waist and drying himself off with a wet towel, there being no such exotic luxury as a shower, when the door opened and, looking in the dusty mirror, he saw a girl enter and kick the door shut with her heel. She had not bothered to knock, and she stood before him, a total stranger, absolutely composed, holding in her hand a bottle of whisky, still in its gaily coloured gift wrapping like a Christmas present. She was probably about eighteen or twenty, quite tall, with a sort of soiled innocence about her, a vicious attractiveness which she wore like an expensive mink coat. She wore a short leather jacket over her blouse, and her dimpled knees showed between her abbreviated skirt and the tops of her high black boots. She suggested not so much the slut or strumpet as someone entering a shop certain of what she wished to purchase and resolved to have it, whatever the price. Her air was at once coarse yet strangely virginal, sure of herself yet furtive, on the defensive even as she faced him boldly, giving the impression of someone trying to hide an unfortunate physical blemish below layers of camouflage, lending to her outward appearance a hard glittering glamour, like a mask. She stood facing him, not saying a word, without any preamble, offering him her breasts that rose brimming like some round silky exotic fruit out of the thin cleaving blouse, like a bird of plump plumage perched there before him, quite still, watching him with dark, insolent, intent eyes, eyes like black marble, blackly staring at him, her long baroque high-booted legs planted apart in a peculiarly martial, aggressive stance, straining the skirt taut about her hips, shaping the smooth slope of her midriff. With a calm slow gesture, as if in mime, she stretched the bottle towards him, smiling now, a sly, naked smile, intimate, knowing, like a former lover ambushing him out of the past, baring her strong purposeful teeth in a stark, animal way.

Like something happening to someone else, detached, impersonal, utterly beyond his wish or volition, something external and unwanted which he regarded with a kind of derisive chagrin, he felt arousal, felt his maleness rising to her, like a slow flame, the stirring of a slumbering serpent uncoiling, rising from its warm hidden nest. Afterwards, in the days, weeks, months that followed, he could clearly remember the slow shock, the throb of sardonic dismay he had experienced, the eerie floating sensation of dream, of unreality that enveloped and held him suspended, rooted where he stood, yet aware of a force propelling him, enormously against his will, towards her, like a sleepwalker, rendering him resistless in spite of the inner calm, the inner disdain he felt for her, this ugly, brazen flaunting of herself, her intolerable audacity, the black greedy intentness of her gaze fixed upon his, spearing his flesh.

Without seeming to move, she took a step closer, and another, until she stood so near he could almost feel the warmth of her breath upon his cheek, touching him like a raw, tangible thing, licking him like a tongue. He saw the pink moist glistening of her bared gums, livid like meat, and suddenly, with a snap of revulsion, with the clash of a bolt slamming back, his trance broke, cracked asunder like a pane of glass struck by a stone from a catapult, and finding voice at last he told her with unfeigned weariness, yet gently, to get the hell out of there, adding with facetious solemnity that if she really wanted to show her appreciation she could by all means leave the bottle behind and his wife and himself would gladly drink a toast to her health and generosity.

For what seemed an infinity she did not move, as if she had not heard him, motionless as a statue; her stillness, her absolute immobility, obscurely terrified and thrilled him, like a too perfect sunset, a too ideal dawn, a carved marvel of menace casting its shadow over him. Then she moved, became animate again, edging away, pointing her breasts at him as if they were missiles, not taking her eyes from him, measuring him up for summary execution. A cold, calculating fury seemed to be working in her, drawing her taut as a bow; her lips curled back slowly, like old pages being turned; her eyes, old and without memory, without depth, stared at him, needling, death-black; for one exhilarating, fear-ridden moment he was certain she was about to bring the bottle crashing down on his head, and to save his life he could not have moved, the image racing through him like the adrenalin of terror; then the ordinary intervened, the commonplace returned, everything became real and normal and absurd again, and still never having uttered a word, she turned and went out, her high-heeled boots clacking out the asterisks of her scorn upon the stone floor of the narrow passageway.

With slow and methodical precision, he went through the routine of changing into his ordinary clothes and putting the things he wore on stage into the suitcase; he performed these actions very carefully, placing the clothes in neat layers upon each other, quite unlike the casual haste with which he normally packed, leaving the whole thing usually to Janice while he loafed and lounged about smoking, having a drink and talking about their stage performance, the mood of the audience, how they should interpret and improve their style, how terrible the acoustics had been, and so on in the same preoccupied, desultory manner. But the incident or non-incident kept returning to his mind.

It was a thing of the utmost unimportance, he told himself, resting his knuckles upon the dresser and regarding himself in the mirror; yes, of the utmost unimportance, nothing out of the ordinary, nothing to get excited or paranoid about. He was reacting as if he had just had a mystical experience, when in reality what it came down to was a dumb randy little bitch with not a word to say for herself, barging in with a bottle of booze and hoping she would find him responsive, a quickfire five-minute coitus behind a bolted door and no questions, no time-consuming foreplay, no pack drill. It happened all the time, these crazy kids with their moronic myopic faces, tier upon tier of them, herded together like sheep and bleating like sheep too, hero-worshipping like mad, prostrating themselves before every personable nonentity that came along with a reasonable stage presence, a passable ability at playing an instrument or jabbering out a song and jumping about the stage in a way that was supposed to arouse the poor slobbering morons beyond the footlights to a shrill pitch of sexual frenzy and emotional hysteria. Yes, it happened all the time, even if it had never happened to him, not yet anyway, he said to himself, grimacing rather than grinning into the mirror, and tonight he had come close to it, tonight he had had a foretaste of what could happen when fame at last caught up with him. Maidenheads galore waiting to be plundered and breached, he pondered, taking refuge in cheap fantasising, staring like an idiot at himself in the mirror, making facial contortions like a particularly unintelligent orang-utan.

At that moment Janice came back.

'What's wrong?' she asked, after starting to tell him about her phone call, seeing his pallor and noting his subdued, abstracted mood. 'You look like you've just seen one of your long-dead ancestors. Are you ill?'

He shrugged off her questions lightly, saying he was just tired and needed a good stiff drink when they got outside. She went on then to tell him all about the conversation she had had with her parents on the phone, and he listened with unaccustomed attention, not hearing a word.

And the things he had cloudily seen in his crystal ball, in that dusty fly-speckled mirror in that dingy dressing-room, turned out to be not entirely false or misleading, for with some inevitable and, at times, rather intriguing variations, as time went on the bizarre little episode, the picaresque little cameo of the mystery girl had been repeated on more than one occasion. The same gaudy enticements had been held out to him, the same colourful lures, at times briskly without coy dalliance, with gloves off, as it were, and the veiled or open promise of other more intimate items of apparel to follow should the invitation be accepted; at other times the approach had been more demure, discreet, eyelash-fluttering little flatteries that aroused in him amusement rather than lust.

In another part of the house, later in the afternoon, the pealing panegyrics and glowing praises still echoing remotely inside his head, like the pounding of distant surf, the hooves of far away steeds galloping over cushiony plains, Art wandered in a morose sombre daze through litanies of rooms, not meeting a soul, walking like a disenchanted ghost amid ostentatious furniture of smooth suspicious modernity, with everything on display, as in a museum or sales room, placed in positions of best advantage; it needed only glass-fronted cases with index cards itemising each object and a guide explaining the history, make and origin of the exhibits to complete the image of cool polished impersonality that permeated each room he passed through. Sometimes he paused to pick up some object, examining it idly and putting it back in its niche, hardly aware of his own movements. Despite the sheen of opulence everywhere in sight, the prevailing atmosphere of the house had an ultimately oppressive and deadening effect upon the senses, a maze of velvet bars and sleek soundless corridors where every luxury was provided except that of fresh open air. The hours lay spaced ahead of him, like empty sacks waiting to be filled with whatever he could find to put into them, roaming from room to room, not hearing his own footfalls, tumbler in one hand, vodka bottle in the other, its contents steadily diminishing.

'What do you think?' Simon had asked, looming large and moist at his side in the early turbulent sway and din of the party, grinning like an obese gargoyle, a vivid carnation in his lapel already beginning to wilt in the heat and clamour of bodies. '*I* think,' Simon had chuckled, chewing his fat lower lip, taking the cigar from between his teeth, '*I* think we can safely say it's been an unqualified success. Now come this way,' the large round glistening man had said, making jocose smoky patterns in the air with his smouldering cigar; 'there's someone I want you to meet, someone quite special in the way of business – '

Art was no fool, he was not nearly so naive as to imagine that all the things people had said to him had been sincere and honestly meant. Even in the giddiness of the hour, even though he wanted with all his heart to believe them, he knew that most of the praise had been false, had been silky exaggerations, blatant spools of hyperbole mouthed easily by people gathered together to partake of free booze and food and entertainment, who felt socially obliged to say these things in thanksgiving to their host, that large lumbering mellow-mooned presence booming loquaciously and glowing in their midst, moving about on his small dainty feet like some genial oversized marionette pulled here and there by the strings of his vanity. People came up to him, all smiles, oozing praise. He was not deceived.

He would be the first to admit, Simon realised, even to boast, that he had continued to take up Art and Janice despite that snub delivered by Art when he refused Simon's attempt to break up their partnership. He did it as one might take up a hobby, as a matter of loose indolent interest, hardly more than that, making himself believe he saw in them a modicum of raw material of which he might make some passable use, just to amuse himself in a remotely creative though desultory way during one of those longueurs of which his life seemed to have had more than its unfair share in recent years. He approached the project with the typical languid passion of a dilettante, careful not to put too much fervour into it, nudged forward by passive curiosity, keeping himself at a discreet distance, hoping for no spectacular results but prepared to be pleasantly surprised if such came. He congratulated himself upon it being the ideal attitude to adopt, and so it had proved for a time; out of the most minimal and casual of enterprises, however, one expects certain returns, not necessarily of a strictly commercial nature, and although it must be admitted that within that context, within the narrow confines of the accounts ledger and the bank balance, the returns had in fact been quite respectable, they had hardly been sufficient to compensate him for the initial effort and the continuing outlay in terms of time, patience, loss of privacy and sheer stamina that had been required to weather all the petulant though wearisome little storms along the way. It had been tough going, but that could have been borne if his heart had really been in it; it had not.

The art of protégé-cultivation was a delicate one and it could be most enjoyable – always on the premise, of course, that one had no other real talent of one's own – and up to now Simon, who could be scrupulously honest with himself, had been content to employ this singular lone talent of his shrewdly, for his own amusement and perhaps profit, since he had so little else to do with his time. The novelty of the exercise, however, was wearing decidedly thin and the practice must soon be abandoned or seriously curtailed if all he got in return for his money and interest was the boorish and exceedingly boring behaviour of ingrates like Art and Janice, who blithely believed that promise was as good as achievement and covered a multitude of petty sins and transgressions which nobody with a tincture of taste and intelligence should be expected to condone.

To entertain agents, managers, PR people of every conceivable type and for every improbable function, and, not least, the 'stars', the 'artistes' themselves, with their grease-glistened skins and doltish whims and the almost perennial aura of stale and powdered sweat that seemed to cocoon them even at their most glittering – he had come to find it all a bone-aching exercise in self-inflicted boredom, trite to the point of insomnia and utterly charmless, arousing in him more and more an irresistible impulse to yawn, smile, close his eyes and reach for another drink. The raw material, the basic stuff of alleged promise that kept being presented to him for approval continually turned out to be no more than a soggy mess of cold porridge already in the process of coagulation; and if, by rare chance, there happened to be a few random raisins and choice sultanas buried somewhere in the mess, these were too few and far between to merit diligent digging out. So he languished in a sort of wishful vacuum as he read and dotted contracts, listened in suppressed pain to aspiring prodigies of imperishable talents strumming, stamping, caterwauling and gyrating away before him in frenzies of hypnotic grotesqueness, and nourished a small secret hope in some as yet unassailed and unbruised part of his mind that someday, somewhere, somehow, something would happen that would make him stop yawning and give him some reason for continuing to devote his still largely untapped energies and ingenuities to the whole wretched business to which he had so rashly hitched his own bright star.

So it was that in Bradford of all the unlikely places on earth he had come to the turning on the Damascus road where lightning had struck him square and true and he had been awarded the Saul-like revelation for which he had waited so long and steadfastly. In that dingy nightclub or tavern or by whatever lurid nom-de-plume it hid its dusty identity, he felt certain Fate had beckoned to him with a kindly countenance, directing his somewhat unbelieving gaze to the two young people harpooned in cruel spotlight on the stage engrossed in their own act of faith, their own magic, uncaring, unaware of the oblivious beer-swilling louts beyond the footlights slurping and snorting in rabid ignorance of the lovely tenuous little spell that was being woven in that smoky hovel. He had sat, drink forgotten, not daring to believe his luck, his eyes and ears, the small fugitive hope that he had nurtured for so long fluttering into winged life, into certainty, excitement beating out a small hesitant fanfare in his temples. Had he ever flirted with belief in destiny – and he had, sometimes, briefly, in a tired desultory vaguely sensuous way – he was prepared to embrace it fervently at that moment and, more, have his palms pierced for his pains. He almost stumbled rising from his table in his haste to get backstage to see them after they had finished their act, afraid it might all have been an illusion, a mirage born of jaded optimism, and that on quitting the luridly lit stage they would have vanished without trace into the smoke-murdered air of that bedlam place fixed so squarely at a point between limbo and nowhere. Miracles, large or small, had to be grasped with split-second urgency if they were to be grasped at all; hesitating was fatal to one seeking a way out of a cul-de-sac. He had been so damnably sure they were the challenge he needed all along, the impetus to shake him out of his lethargy and cause him, for the first time in too many years, to really exert himself and bring him to the pinnacle of the back-slapping knife-flashing loud little cosmos he had chosen to move in, the tight suffocating jungle he had thought to explore, sweep through and subjugate before travelling on to larger wildernesses, larger conquests.

Their very rawness excited and intrigued him; their unsureness, their vulnerability, their blatant innocence had lured him on like a torch in darkness and set him in resolute pursuit. He would work on them as a sculptor with clay, he told himself in those early days, not heeding his own audacity; he would mould and shape their tentative straying talent, put it under a flexible yoke, into a proper harness, move it forward gently one step, one cadence at a time, fondle and flatter it into awakening, into full mature bloom, until it stood strong and upright in its own bright soil, demanding to be admired, to be applauded, envied, imitated, lauded near and abroad as a unique definitive entity, a force to weather all storms and rise above spite and tribulation. His excitement at that time had about it a strange unreal curiously childlike quality; his head swarmed with ideas, he grew dizzy devising ever more grandiose schemes for their advancement, their triumph, never once allowing himself to suspect it might be his own life he was dealing with and dreaming about. He let himself think recklessly, in the gaudiest of romantic clichés, like a hungry child devouring sweets it had never tasted before in all its pampered past. He would be their mentor in all ways pertaining to their success, he alone would be the architect of that success, that storming of staid formless tastes and mediocre standards, he would judge of what particular intensity and brilliance the light of their fame should be when it at last inevitably found them out and fell upon them; not a single nuance of their career would escape his notice or come unbidden or untouched by his hand, his unfaltering knowledge of what was best and right for them. His magnanimity was matched only by his arrogance, marvellous in its own unawareness, and he lived blithely in that tarnished and shoddy light, forgoing the luxury of examining his own motives, since they could safely be put away and dispensed with for another duller day, like something unpleasant put out of sight in a locked cabinet.

And how sadly the radiance had dimmed except for Art's undoubtedly exceptional talent! He pondered now, adjusting his sunglasses; it had sunk until it became little more than a precarious flame forever in danger of being blown out and finally extinguished in the sudden storms that seemed to rise and rage between them of late simply on a look, a word, a gesture, and he grew increasingly despondent and impatient, discerning in them the arrogance and pomposity he had so assiduously avoided seeing in himself. He spent hours now silently railing and cursing them as braggarts, peacocks, loud-mouthed insufferable brats swollen with their own prodigious self-esteem that was slowly but with painful certainty teetering into mutual self-loathing; they strutted about like hardy battle-scarred veterans who had never yet been in a street fight, wearing bright imaginary bemedalled uniforms when they were still in swaddling clothes, acting as if they were burnt out long before they had caught fire.

To add to his sense of injury and disillusion, he had recently begun to harbour the insidious suspicion that he was being laughed at behind his back by friend and foe alike, that he was becoming an object of ridicule and derision, discussed and sneered at over cosy cocktails as the antics of his two precocious protégés rebounded on him, making him look foolish, a false prophet, a bad judge of horseflesh; their fall would be of no consequence, being already so near the ground, but he, having so much greater height from which to topple, would hit earth with greater impact and suffer more damage in the process, the cuts and bruises incurred secondary only to the gross humiliation that would be inflicted. A few broken bones might not be fatal, but neither were they attractive; a nose twisted out of shape was preferable to a splintered image, a shattered ego, but even that unambiguous choice, he felt, was fast slipping out of his grasp. He cursed whatever malignant chance it was that had taken him to Bradford that night; from being the way to Damascus and enlightenment, as it had seemed at the beginning, it was rapidly turning into his own bleak Golgotha, strewn with the bleached bones of his expectations and littered with snares. He had blandly manoeuvred himself into a position from which he could see no way of extricating himself with pride and prestige intact, let alone anything as tenuous and unmarketable as honour, victim of that facile cleverness he alternately admired and loathed in others, the fatal ability to play too many trump cards at once upon that most fallible and unprofessional of assumptions, a hunch, the euphoric feeling of being on a lucky streak; it was tantamount to stargazing, the reading of palms and similar trappings of ancient superstitions, things that up till now had filled him with keen distaste and aversion. Soon, he told himself with grim inner irony, he would be gibbering in a gypsy caravan surrounded by painted trinkets of the occult, reduced to the analysis of the patterns of tea-leaves. Appropriate enough fate for a fool such as he had been.

Bored with the placidly shining sun that seemed to be in the sky only on sufferance, with the sedate little family group, a somnolescent cameo upon the trim laundered lawn, the embellishments of domesticity affronting his eyes wherever he looked, his thirst increasing with his feeling of injustice and betrayal, he heaved himself out of the deckchair, quitting the terrace and stepping through the sliding glass doors into the lounge. It was like stepping into a cool green bower, broadleafed climbing plants dangling in red clay pots from walls and ceiling, flowering blooms glimmering in dark brilliance in shadowy nooks and recesses, his sandals slapping upon the tiles. He refilled his glass with a lot of vodka and very little tonic, not bothering with ice; he flopped down upon a sofa, his back to the window, one foot resting upon a low table. He stared intently at a wispy line-wash drawing of a forest framed on the wall in front of him, not in the least aware of it or of anything else in the room, nourishing his sense of grievance and isolation. He reclined upon the sofa like a defeated emperor, surveying the remnants of his crumbling dynasty, the oaths of fervent allegiance from his subjects echoing mockingly in his ears as they fled and abandoned him. He wanted very badly to get drunk right there and then, drunk beyond recall, beyond this embittered self-absorption that held him in its grip, and knew he would not, could not, with the whole horrible farce of the afternoon still to be faced, the invasion of all those self-opinionated imbeciles, that tawdry army of poseurs and parasites, ponces and paupers, liars and leeches, that array of gilded whores with their fat-jowled and fat-walleted keepers gobbling down the food and drink he would heap upon them, telling him what a dynamic fellow he was, what a capital host, what a reliable friend, and exchanging snide jokes about him as soon as he was out of earshot, regaling each other with tales and instances of his gullibility and incompetence, what a poor fat fool he was, there to be had for the taking. He had in effect rehearsed and arranged his own debacle, paid for others to come along and witness his fall.

Elsewhere: 'Let me run my practised eye over her. Hmm. Not bad-looking, if one goes for that type. Nice tits, not too large, not too small. Nice tight little bum. Good legs. A neat enough package, as far as my none too perfect vision can make out.'

'You're starting to drool and slobber, Wyn. Down, girl.'

'Well, she has to be better than that bleeding Leonora when we're all together in the four-poster in darkest John's Wood. Nearly sliced the flesh off me the other night with her hips. Like bleeding razor blades they are. And no tits to talk of. Still, any port in a storm. Sandeman's preferably.'

'What about you, Frannie – d'you suffer from any delicious aberrations connected with our own tender gender?'

'God, no. Let me screw in the old-fashioned way. But I've got this terrific fixation about the Chink down the hall from my flat, but alas and alack, he's a queer.'

'How d'you know he's a queer?'

'Simple. I walked into his room one night. I was stoned and told him I wanted to fuck him. Turned bleeding green he did, if Chinamen *can* turn green. Told me he was expecting his boyfriend who's an Arab any minute, so would I please quit the premises as said Arab boyfriend got quite violent when jealous.'

'So what happened, for Christ' sake? Did you flee in terror and trepidation?'

'Not exactly. I took off my clothes and danced around him till the poor bugger was reduced to tears and ended up *paying* me to get out of his room. I've still got fantasies about him. Him and me and his Arabian steed, the three of us together in Kingdom Come. Now *there's* a scenario!'

'Intimations of immortality.'

'Oh, let's split this scene, girls. Look at them, I ask you – a load of bleeding zombies who couldn't tell an orgasm from a slight inflammation of the femur. Let's get back to civilisation.'

'I can't, Cess, much as I'd like to. Old Deadprick would throw me back in the fishpond. He's real thick with my lord Simon.'

'Then for God's sake roll another joint, and get more booze before I die of boredom.'

'Maybe I should go to the toilet and roll one – '

'What for? I didn't want to come to this lousy post-mortem in the first place, but now that I'm here fuck them all. Roll one, Wyn, and sod Sandford and all the other pricks – let the good times roll, friend o' mine!'

'I always sin with gin.'

'And I'm prick-merry with sherry.'

'Shades of the prison house begin to close about the growing nymphomaniac.'

'If I don't get high soon compose my epitaph. "Here lieth Cess who once lived, more or less. Amen."'

'Mind you,' said the aging actress inevitably rouged, her mouth a vivid scarlet streak in her creased face, catching the hand of her younger female companion and holding on to it as if it had been a cane to support her. 'Mind you, I shouldn't underestimate him. He does have a certain talent, a certain flair – rather vulgar, if you like, but effective.' She leaned closer to the younger woman, pursing her lips in a conspiratorial pucker. 'He wants to put on Chekhov, you know – O'Neill – Pirandello – that sort of thing – that's his real ambition. To get into the theatre – ' She pronounced the word as though it were a holy incantation. 'The – drama – ' and this time her voice was even more reverential, her free hand fingering the rope of coloured beads around her neck like someone touching an amulet. 'He told me so only the other day – swore me to secrecy – he is heartily sick of this whole sordid pop business or whatever you call it – ' She looked about the room crowded with people of almost indeterminate gender, and frowned. 'Not that I blame him, mind. I can see nothing but flowing manes of hair, some of it quite filthy, and as for the faces underneath all that foliage – well, my dear, how can one tell if one is talking to Paul or Pauline, to Edith or Eddie?' She tightened her grip on the slim wrist of her companion, as if demanding an answer, thin pencilled eyebrows raised.

'It is rather difficult,' murmured the other woman, wincing under the pressure of the claw-like fingers coiled round her wrist. 'As a matter of fact, Charlotte dear, I'm not at all sure what *we* are doing here, at such a weird gathering – '

'Oh, I dare say poor Simon wanted to show us the sort of thing he's trying to wriggle out of,' replied the older woman, nodding her head, serene and knowing. 'How he can *bear* to be surrounded by such grotesque people day after day I don't know. But whether he has the touch, the feel, the instinct for the theatre, for the drama – well, that is quite another matter entirely, is it not?' She let go of her friend's hand, much to the latter's relief, and sipped her dainty glass of sherry. 'It's one thing to pay people to yell and scream and shout yeah yeah yeah over and over again and fling themselves about like demons before thousands of imbecile children, but it's quite another thing to produce a *play*, is it not, to mount a theatrical production in a legitimate theatre before a discerning, discriminating audience. Still,' sighed the woman, studiously averting her mascaraed eyes from the garrulous throng of jeans and sweaters and trendy flaming robes pulsating everywhere about her, 'I do hope poor dear Simon does succeed in breaching the theatrical ramparts, for it will almost certainly mean extra work for me – for us,' she amended patronisingly, once more gripping the younger woman's wrist in a travestied gesture of camaraderie.

'That's true, Charlotte dear,' spoke the other dutifully, barely suppressing a resigned groan.

'And as I said to Simon in Claridges only the other day,' went on the elder Bernhardt implacably, fingering her beads once more in a ruminative fashion, 'nowadays impresarios are made, not born . . .'

In another pocket of the crammed babbling steaming room close to the improvised bar, a couple were engaged in an intense private altercation which they carried on without once looking at each other, both steadily smiling and displaying their neatly capped teeth at friends who greeted them before disappearing into the depths of the crowd concentrated mainly in the middle of the room; both were almost identically dressed in loose-fitting kimono-type robes of a flagrant-flowered pattern, both suntanned, the skin glistening with a suspiciously virile gloss, radiating aggressive bonhomie and health, their hands intertwined at their sides, unwaveringly cheerful, as if forever marvelling in the discovery of each other and wanting to share their good fortune with everyone in sight.

'But he's such a prick, darling,' said the girl, teeth flashing as she waved to a passing friend who waved flamboyantly back. 'Such a fat load of shit, and to see you toady up to him makes me want to spew up all over his lovely frilly silk shirt, no kidding.'

'Shut fucking up for once in your life, my pet,' replied the man, his face beaming as though with adoration, squeezing his partner's hand tighter in his own. 'You know I'm angling for that new contract that's being dangled about like a single fat carrot before a stableful of starving donkeys – '

'Yes, but does that mean you have to lick his bleeding arse?' enquired the girl softly, winsome smile unfaltering, tranquil brown eyes brimming with lustrous welcome for the faces and hands that hailed them out of the crowd, now spilling out into adjoining rooms through connecting doors thrown wide open.

'Yes, my love, it does,' the man assured her brightly, adjusting the neck of his robe with languid grace. 'If it means bagging that contract I'd gladly lick the great man's balls and come back for more.'

'You're disgusting,' she hissed between her perfect teeth gleaming in the heart of her unalterable smile.

'I agree, but then you do like our present standard of living, don't you, my pet? Yes? Then shut that beautiful mouth of yours and keep it fucking shut – if you don't fancy the idea of going out on the streets again.' He pressed her entwined fingers fondly. 'Agreed, my love?'

'You bastard,' she murmured, as though it was an endearment, leaning her shoulder tenderly against his. 'You absolute bastard. I hope you end up being roasted over his charcoal grill, like the pig you are.'

'Ah, darling, and where would that leave you?' he asked, inclining his head towards her as if to nibble her ear. 'Up the dear old Bayswater creek once more, eh, flogging your adorable arse at half the going price for just one more little jab of the holy needle . . .' And triumphantly camouflaging all inward tempests, they continued to smile and regally nod at passing friends and fellow guests, like high priest and priestess, guardians of a sacred temple to which they alone hold the key, shedding harmonious light on all who approached, but admitting no one into the sanctum of their private and inviolate mystery.

A gaggle of bejeaned girls, some wearing vivid red bandanas across their heads, some in fringed leather cowboy jackets and high boots, had gathered near an open window, occupying a little reservation of their own, faces bemused, eyes heavy with gin and marijuana, passing the hospitable and seemingly inexhaustible weed from hand to indolent hand, each looking remarkably like the lost younger sister of her neighbour, their lives flickering fitfully in the smoke weaving about their faces, obscuring minor cruelties, spelling out in cloudy hieroglyphics the uneven anatomy of their abbreviated histories, ponderous with the burden of false mercurial knowledge gobbled up piecemeal and still not digested. Their talk lisped, lulled, fused, a collage, a dialogue limping back and forth like a forlorn tramp, going nowhere.

'Christ, what a drag. What the fuck are we here for, can anyone tell me?'

'Don't you know? To pay homage to Simple Simon's shining new stars and partake of the delicious herb known as Clover.'

'Christ, do you always talk like that, Cess?'

'Only when I'm stoned. I'm a deaf mute when I'm sober and together. Can hardly put a sentence across.'

'Who're you here with, Frannie?'

'Old Deadprick from Notting Hill – who else? You still with What's-his-name from St John's Wood?'

'As long as he pays the rent and keeps the little MG running I'll be with What's-his-name from St John's Wood.'

'Doesn't that sharp-nosed wife of his get in the way – the redundant actress or something? Met her once in a restaurant. All teeth. Snooty bitch.'

'Leonore? Oh no. Doesn't care a shit. Matter of fact we sometimes bunk together, all three of us. Like cows in a manger.'

'Cosy. And do you all –?'

'Sometimes. If we're stoned enough.'

'And who comes out best?'

'All three of us, stupid.'

'You gay, Wyn?'

'Don't know. Can go either way. Whichever way the wind blows.'

'The best of both worlds, huh?'

'Sort of.'

'Don't see the bleeding stars of the show. Maybe they forgot to come.'

'Like old Deadprick last night. Fell fast asleep. Had to finish on my own.'

'That dopey-looking bloke over there who looks as if he's looking for his mother. That's the male part of the act.'

'And I like his male part and all. Stands out a mile in those tight jeans. Wouldn't mind screwing him in a tight corner.'

'The only way to screw, really.'

'Heard some of the shit he wrote on that last album. Weird. Sort of pseudo-simple, y'know? Lewis Carroll with a severe attack of the runs.'

'I heard that too, Cess. Couldn't make out what he was on about half the time. Maybe that's why I dug it.'

'Where's the distaff side of the duo? Does anyone know her?'

'Does anyone fucking care?'

'Over there by the last supper table, beside Simon Peter alias Sandford. The cunt with all the phoney red hair. That's her.'

'You think it's a wig or something, Wyn?'

'Oh, it's real enough. Just *looks* phoney. I remember my kid brother had a pin-up in his room of Rita Hayworth donkey's years ago. Hair all over the place. Just like Delilah over there.'

'Do you think Sandford's screwing her?'

'Not right now he's not. In the still of the night, maybe.'

'He's screwing that black bitch of a secretary of his. Common knowledge in the higher circles of society.'

'Can't say I blame him, with that Minnie Mouse of a wife he's got. Looks as if she's fed on a staple diet of breadcrumbs.'

'I think it's the other way around, girls. I think that black madonna is screwing him.'

'Kinky stuff, you mean, Frannie – whips and black leather, that sort of shit?'

'Maybe. Always felt he was that way inclined. "Please beat me, darling, and the mink's yours." I sort of sense it whenever she's near him.'

'The old black-is-beautiful syndrome, eh?'

'She's not even black – not pure black. Sort of dull shitty-brown, with greyish undertones. Another of Sandford's hybrids.'

'Do I detect a slight note of envy, Wyn old girl?'

'What – me and that fat slob, old drip-dry balls? You're joking, of course. But that refined Amazon, that chocolate-coloured cooness – now she's something else again. Maybe I could work up a flicker of interest in *that* direction on a rainy Saturday night when all else has failed me.'

'That bleeding gay scene's not for me. Met so many boring lesbians in my time, I have. All so fucking heavy and intensive, and they fight like scalded cats most of the time.'

'A popular misconception, dear Cess. Poor bleeding bitches are the same as the rest of us. We're all poor cunts, are we not, opening and shutting our legs, regular as clockwork? Don't be one of the first to throw stones.'

'Oh I'm not, Wyn, honest. To each her own I say. Just can't get into that scene, that's all.'

'More's the pity. You've a lot to recommend you, my girl.'

'Fuck off, Wyn.'

Glasses lifted in slow motion to mouths sullen, sardonic, pouting; still-burning reefer doing the rounds, passing from hand to hand inside an enclosed little circle, a beacon of promise and tranquillity blunting keener needs long ago buried but not unremembered.

'But where's our little starlet got herself to?'

'She's still over there, on the right hand of God Almighty Sandford. Drinking mead, no doubt.'

Simon bitterly regretted not having had Marcie come to this dreadful party; never had he needed her support more, the mere fact of her presence inspiring in him a repose he found nowhere else. But as usual Marcie had been entirely neutral in the matter, at her usual cool distance, neither reluctant nor eager, merely waiting in abeyance, waiting for him to say the word, to say whether he wanted her along or not, and acting for once out of unselfish motives he had decided not to expose her to the undercurrent of subtle and not so subtle insinuations and sly winking innuendoes that invariably rippled in the air whenever they were together in the company of alleged friends, acquaintances and colleagues.

He personally did not give a damn, already loathing his own involvement in such petty internecine mayhem, but he felt at times inordinately protective about Marcie to an almost fatherly degree and detested the thought of her being the object of gutter talk, a piece of sordid salacious gossip bandied about from one gin-stacked table to another in gaudy lounge bars and smoky subterranean gambling dens, as if she were some cheap available harlot out of a scurrilous railway station paperback novel ready to spread her thighs for the right price. Love, or any approximation of it, had nothing to do with these feelings; he thought of it simply as a crude mauling of an item of private property, rough hands groping over something that belonged exclusively to him and nobody else, leaving dirty fingermarks on a smooth exquisite surface. These social scavengers made everything furtive, tainted, befouled, and clandestine as their affair might be, he did not need such vultures to remind him of that fact and make an ugly feast of it.

9

It was beautiful, the night metropolis teeming below, its firefly galaxies spearing the humid dark, flaring like a million candletips laid out for a feast; packed clusters of dim conflagrations wavered and spiralled against the sky, ribboned by miles of illuminated signs flashing on and off, filling the night with asterisks. Through the half-open window came the bronzed labyrinthine growl of the city, the snort and wail of car horns, the crackle of nocturnal animation, the air vibrant with the mute roar of midnight streets serpentined with throngs of seasoned revellers, strolling lovers sequestered in the midst of chaos, lonely people passing like furtive shadows under dripping archways and bridges and limp-leafed trees trapped and rooted in asphalt. The hum of the city came remotely to Marcie, curled in a deep halfmoon-shaped armchair by the window, smoking absently, crunching popcorn from time to time out of a bowl on a nearby table, frail slivers of light reflected in the glass of gin and tonic she held loosely in her other hand.

It was beautiful, and she was bored. She sat in the neon-lit dusk of the apartment, her thoughts stirring slowly, like a cat purring half asleep, lulled by the distant, throaty undertones of the city, the shimmering acres of lights studding the glowing skyline, outwitting the seedling stars, making the moon a pallid insubstantial presence wandering thinly among the lace clouds.

'Christ,' she murmured aloud, crushing out her half-finished cigarette and lighting up another.

She was bored with her life, languidly, indulgently bored with it. Its lush, scented security was becoming irksome, a subtle burden pressing down on her, smothering her in its cunning luxuriance; it was like being gently crushed to death under an avalanche of roses. She felt like slashing the soft satiny surfaces around her with her long curving fingernails just to see if they would yield blood. She visualised herself going on a leisurely rampage through the apartment, room by room, leaving a trail of disciplined destruction in her wake, selecting the things she wished to rip asunder, quite in control of her wildness. It would be like raiding an exclusive birdshop, all the pampered soft-bosomed pets swaying sedated on their perches, and flinging the exquisite cages across the room, from wall to wall, amid a whirling squawking mayhem of svelte ruptured throats, flying feathers and snapped flapping wings. An act of discreet, decorous murder, in fact, such as she felt like committing now, feeling some soft, vulnerable pulse under her fingers, throbbing with throttled piteous life, beating against her palm, supreme with the knowledge that just by a slight tightening of her fingers she could extinguish that pulse completely and forever.

Some things were, after all, eminently qualified to be obliterated and put out of circulation, she thought, inhaling deeply, letting the smoke curl out through her nostrils, wreathing about her head; things that cloyed the senses, ripe to the point of rottenness, clogging the taste buds, running sluggishly through the veins, blocking all grace and celerity of movement, sloughing through the world on bloated appetites, sucking up all smaller prey that lay in their path, ingesting everything into their gigantic gut. She was quite aware that her thoughts in this fashion were turning upon Simon, and she smoked and sipped her drink and smiled to herself in the warm intimate dark, pitiless in her private molestations.

She tossed another handful of popcorn into her mouth, crunching busily, feeling the night air cool on her naked flesh beneath the robe; people had quite an erroneous idea about murder. Most people associated it with hatred, passion, jealousy, revenge, panic or perversion, a frenzied crackling inside the head, exploding with a bang, a blinding roar, like the beginning or end of the universe, apocalyptic in its suddenness and finality. But what most people overlooked in their quest for an understanding of the macabre was boredom – boredom and the potential it possessed for driving one to murder. It could be boredom of the most agreeable and luxurious kind, induced perhaps by too strict and monotonous a regimen of champagne and caviar, lobster and fine wine, and it would serve as well to drive the knife home or press the trigger as the hunger of a tramp, the rage of a cuckolded lover, or the lunacy of an escaped madman transfixed beneath the harpish moon. One need not hate one's victim; that was being melodramatic and self-indulgent, requiring a resounding roll of drums, a clash of cymbals, a whole bloody symphony orchestra in full blast while the wretch was being dispatched into oblivion – as if an act of such mechanical banality deserved such trappings of theatre!

She had often looked on as Simon sat idly paring an apple, seeing the knife glinting in his hand, and the thought would come to her how simple, how undemonstrative it would be to reach over, take the knife out of his hand and, with a brisk downward stroke, plunge it into his exposed throat as he lolled back in the chair, looking up at her, perhaps on the point of politely asking her if she wanted anything. She could see quite clearly the dark blood leaping out of his gashed throat, staining his shirt like blackcurrant, the handle of the knife embedded in the pillowy folded flesh, that look of slightly moronic surprise and enquiry which sometimes came into his eyes whenever she took him unawares by a word or gesture. It took such little dexterity or ingenuity, and hardly anything at all of what most people summarised as 'nerve'; when the moment came, she was sure, it would be as much of a reflex action as yawning or stretching or throwing away the match after lighting a cigarette. There was altogether too much mythology attached to murder, she thought, topping up her drink and rubbing her lower lip pensively along the rim of the glass; it had been romanticised out of its proper context and made into a thing for idiots to drool over.

Not that she wanted to murder Simon, at least not very urgently as yet, though the idea was undeniably tempting and hilarious at times. It would be bound to prove disappointing anyway, a decided anticlimax, like going to all the bother and mess of ripping open a monster teddybear, only to find that it was indeed made only of plain straw after all. In all that ponderous, silk-shirted, lavendered bulk there was so little of him; a bit like searching through mountains of duck feather to come finally upon a small undersized egg nestling at the bottom. She had to delve deep, very deep, to come upon him at all, to find him beneath all that padded protective outer fur, peeling back layer after layer of cushiony camouflage, and when she eventually found him, he was so diminutive, cowering in his puniness and shrinking back from the light, it left her dumb with pity, and furious with herself for her own taloned tenderness towards him. His craven bullying and arrogance to those dependent upon him and too weak or ingenuous to strike back, his suave blustering, his smooth agility at besting an opponent, his chronic megalomania that he presented to the world as serene inoffensive self-assurance, the way he would slink back into a neutral corner when the tempo of debate became too heated or when some incautious competitor or colleague – it was hard sometimes to differentiate between the two species – had trodden on his pet sensibilities, and then to slither out of hiding and deliver the killer blow amid a profusion of handshakes and smiles: these were the things she both despised and envied in Simon, the things that drew forth her barbed admiration, like snake poison being sucked from her bloodstream.

At bottom, if there was such an extremity in so amorphous an entity as Simon, he was a weak man, not because he was prone to self-doubt or indecision, which she knew was not the case, but mainly because of the ravenous way he must feed off other people, usually without their knowing it, in order continually to replenish his ego and keep the momentum of his will driving forward. Yet she knew that, over the years, he had made a citadel out of his weakness, a reservoir of greed and venom that acted as a vital propulsion to his ambition, had made of his weakness a fortress from which he fought off foe and unwanted ally alike; he had not merely hidden behind his weakness and shot off arrows as from behind a shield, rather he had utilised it fully to his own best advantage instead of letting it lie fallow, like a canny farmer making the most of an unpromising crop. He had zealously husbanded those inherent failings and inadequacies that would have debilitated other men, and turned them into power pistons that drove him relentlessly forward, since he knew that to stop and stand still would be to atrophy and be annihilated by the swamp of his own ennui and rampaging nihilism.

Marcie scratched her thigh inside the robe, touching the fine springy pampas of hair nestling there, wiry as young grass, tingling even then under her own indolent fingers; she yawned, dissatisfied and out of patience with herself for allowing her mind to trundle along the same well-worn groove with Simon as the inevitable terminus, plaguing her thoughts when she might have the whole glittering casket of the night-time city to rifle and enjoy, plunder and desecrate, instead of which she now sat alone in a darkened room, drinking and smoking in arid solitude, while he was somewhere out there allegedly negotiating yet another intricate business deal, a very marvel of acumen over brandy and cigars. For the first time in months she felt lonely, irritated by her own company; music would not have helped, and she could not bear to read; a book in her hands then would have been like a fractious child, demanding her whole attention, tugging querulously at her sleeve whenever her thoughts wandered away from it, and music, even the sweetest, would have grated on her nerves like sandpaper. Like moths drawn inexorably round a lighted bulb, swirling in unending circles of futility, her thoughts performed unvarying pirouettes round Sandford, orbiting his obese circumference, a trapped satellite whirling in mutinous obedience to some obscure law of human gravity.

'Christ!' she cried, reaching for the bottle on the table, and then she uncoiled herself, rose from the depths of the chair and, glass in hand, strolled out on to the balcony, the night breeze touching her bare limbs loose and languid beneath the robe. The sky had turned an intense dark blue, almost bereft of cloud now, studded with stars and the moon at last in full dominance, gliding majestic and intimidating in its cold purpose, transforming the babbling city below into an ignominious hamlet lit by flickering tawdry little torches. All about the numerous yellow eyes of adjacent habitations peered at her, veiled, vaguely intrusive, shapes of buildings sensed rather than seen, rising wraith-like in the dark, solid monoliths standing shoulder to shoulder, soaring from the tumultous earth into the bruised lurid air. She leaned on the parapet, looking at the glowing toyland jungle below, crawling with hectic denizens grimly intent on hilarity, its mazes raddled with knife strokes of colour and tinsel, lifting its jangled baying voice, taunting her ivoried seclusion, her brittle useless fidelity to an obese ghost, shut in her opulent cell, bored with her life when it should have been flaring and crackling about her like fireworks. The night and the city condemned her.

'Damn you,' she spoke softly to the brilliant bedlam below, raising the glass to her lips. 'Damn you.'

The shrill clang of the doorbell cut through her like whipcord, though she stayed quite still and unmoving by the parapet, sternly willing her nerves back into their customary state of prepared calm; the buzzer rang a second time, longer, more insistent, and with steady step she returned once more into the lounge, finishing what remained in her glass and putting it on the table. She paused to look in the mirror, her face composed, without makeup, framed by the fuzzy dark aureole of her hair, and tightening the belt of her robe she went out into the vestibule and opened by just a few inches the self-locking door, peering into the faint luminous dusk of the corridor outside.

'Who is it, please?'

A slight, unsteady intake of breath, and someone moved, came closer, overhead light glinting on copperish hair.

'I know it's late, but may I come in?'

Marcie moved aside, surprised, opening the door fully. 'Janice – yes, of course, do come in.' She ushered her visitor in and shut the door, hearing the lock click. 'Come in, come in,' she said, leading the way into the lounge, robe flaring out on either side of her. 'Find somewhere to sit. Are you alone?'

Janice blinked. 'What? Oh, yes – yes, I'm alone.' She looked about her, rather distracted, as if she had never been there before, eyes large, dark and staring. She sat down in the nearest chair, rigid, clutching a large ornate crocodile-leather handbag in her lap, like a mascot. 'Hope I didn't get you out of bed – '

Marcie smiled. 'Despite my state of undress I wasn't in bed.' She went to the liquor cabinet and took out the brandy decanter. 'A drink? You look like you could do with one, if you don't mind my saying so.'

'Thanks.' Janice took the proffered glass, still holding tightly on to the handbag with her other hand. 'I've had a few already. I might even be a little drunk – I don't know.' She took a quick gulp, shutting her eyes, sitting in the same rigid upright position in the chair, moving her lips slowly, painfully, like one coming in out of the cold, though the night was warm and humid. She took another longer sip, without opening her eyes, shuddering slightly.

Marcie moved away and sat on the arm of the sofa, regarding the other girl, seeing her blanched, drawn look, the dark circles round her eyes, the way she gripped the glass and clutched the handbag, the stiff way she held her knees together; it was all very uncharacteristic, and she wondered what had happened to make Janice like this. It was rather ridiculous, Marcie considered, that she should feel so solicitous, so much more senior and adult towards her, since they were roughly about the same age, yet age itself had nothing to do with it, she just felt older than the other girl, more agile at extricating herself from life's sly machinations and unexpected trapdoors springing open abruptly beneath one's feet, plunging down into nerveless, terrifying darkness that seemed never to end; she felt like a veteran confronting a perplexed novice, whom she might have to soothe and talk out of doing something absurd and banal, like jumping off a ledge hundreds of feet above street level, clutching a diary cataloguing her litany of woes, in just such a way as Janice was now gripping that silly ostentatious bloody handbag. Marcie sipped her brandy and braced herself.

'Anything wrong – anything I can do?'

Janice opened her eyes and looked about her, as if only then becoming aware of her surroundings, as if somewhat surprised at finding herself not alone. 'Marcie. No, it's very kind of you, Marcie, but – ' She stopped, looking about her some more, almost in a furtive manner. 'Simon's not here, is he?'

Marcie shook her head. 'No, he's late tonight. One of his high-tempo wheeler-dealer little get-togethers someplace or other.' She looked critically over at her visitor, trying to study her face in the soft-falling light of the lampshade behind her. 'Christ, you look terrible, Janice – what the hell's the matter? Domestic? Did you and Art have a row?' She leaned back on the sofa arm. 'Don't answer if you don't want to.'

'Oh, it's nothing, nothing at all,' said Janice, her voice hoarse, wavering a little; she sat looking down fixedly into her glass, which was by then empty. 'I really shouldn't have come.'

Marcie shrugged. 'That's for you to decide,' she said. 'But you did come, you're here, and your glass is empty.' She rose and refilled both their glasses, resuming her position as before on the arm of the sofa, lighting up a cigarette. 'There are cigarettes on that table beside you – but you don't really smoke, do you?'

'Not much.' Janice gave a tight smile that was more like a grimace. 'Art doesn't approve. Says it'll ruin my voice. Yes, he really does say things like that. "It'll ruin your bloody voice," as if telling a woman to quit smoking because she's going to have a baby.' She drank, a little less rigid and constrained now, her shoulders relaxing, drooping, fingers loose on the handbag, the contracted smile still on her face. 'Not that I'm going to have a baby, of course.'

'Why "of course"?' asked Marcie, blowing smoke rings. 'I should have thought maybe you'd want a baby sometime. Isn't that what most people get married for, or am I hopelessly misinformed and out of date?'

'D'you mind if I take this off?' said Janice, and without waiting for an answer slipped off her short combat-style jacket and let it fall carelessly

146

to the floor. She flopped back down in the chair, unwinding, the brandy working its therapy through her, the contours of her face less stark, colour coming back to her cheeks, the fixed staring expression going out of her eyes. 'Babies. Yes I suppose I'll end up having one or two someday. But not yet,' she went on, speaking in a stilted precise mocking tone, as if into a microphone, spacing her words like someone dictating. 'No, not yet. It would ruin my career, would it not ? To say nothing of my magnificent figure.' She looked over, seeing Marcie quite unmoved and impassive, and her eyes lowered. 'I'm being bloody silly.'

'Yes, you are.'

'Sod it, I'll have a cigarette.' She got to her feet with some effort, the handbag tumbling from her lap, almost tripping her up. She weaved her way to the table where cigarettes lay in a silver case, put one between her lips, lit up from the lighter nearby and made her way back to the chair, tottering like an aerialist on the high wire. 'To hell with my voice,' she said, falling back into the chair, legs awry, hair swinging across her face, puffing inexpertly and spluttering a little. 'Never make the golden disc this way, but who cares?' She reached down and retrieved her glass where she had left it on the floor. 'D'you mind if I get just a little bit more drunk, Marcie – d'you mind?'

'Not in the least. Get as pissed as you like.'

'Yes,' said Janice, voice slurred, drinking, some of it trickling out of the corner of her mouth. 'Yes, I will. I will get bloody pissed – ' she stopped and waved the glass in the air – 'but only if you're sure – quite sure you don't mind – ?'

'Carte blanche, my dear,' replied Marcie, beginning to enjoy herself in a detached, ruminative way, as if it was a show being put on exclusively for her benefit, to amuse and divert her and erase the inertia of the previous hours. 'Help yourself when and as you like. Would you like me to put on some record, or would that be too much to take just now?'

'Too much, much too much.' Janice hiccuped and giggled a little, putting a hand to her mouth, looking like a child caught out in a misdemeanour. 'Really very good of you, Marcie, putting up with me like this – really very good. Glad old Simon's not here, though, damn glad.'

'Are you afraid of him?'

Janice stuck out her chin. 'Afraid? Course not. Afraid of old Simon – me? Course not! Just glad he's not here now, that's all. He'd be what you might call an impediment to speech.'

'If you've come for sisterly advice I'm afraid my stock is pretty low at the moment. But if you just want to talk – fine, go right ahead. My one claim to fame, or notoriety perhaps, is that I always was a good listener.' Marcie exhaled smoke slowly. 'Though whether that's a virtue or sheer lack of initiative on my part, I don't know. So you and the songwriter have fallen out yet again, have you?'

Janice nodded, compliant to the touch of mockery in the other woman's voice. 'Yet again. Me and the songwriter – ' she laughed, a little too readily – 'I like that. I left him doing a demolition job back at the flat. Another one. How we've not been kicked out of there long ago I'll never know. When the landlord does come in answer to complaints from our neighbours, Art puts on the charm – he can ooze charm at the flick of a switch, you know – and off the poor old man goes, almost crying, clutching one of our autographed records, touched to tears by Art's tale of rags to relative riches, the lad from the gutter who made good in the big bad world of pop culture.' She held up her glass, giving it a quizzical look. 'My glass has a funny habit of being empty every time I look at it. May I – ?'

'By all means.'

Janice, seeming to grow steadier and more in command of herself as she drank, went to the table where the decanter stood and poured herself more brandy, then looked over at Marcie.

'Here, let me – yours is empty too.'

'Thanks.'

She splashed brandy into Marcie's held-out glass, spilling some and giggling, then abruptly sat down cross-legged on the carpet, bottle beside her, sweeping back a truant swath of abundant hair from her eyes, grinning.

'Mind if I park myself here – seems such a waste of energy walking back and forth between table and chair.'

'I quite agree. So you left Art in a state of berserkdom, did you, back at the ranch?'

'Yes,' replied Janice, reflective, humorous and at the same time melancholic, shoulders stooped forward, elbows on knees. 'Doing his Samson thing. Wreaking terrible vengeance on tables and chairs but as always not going near the music centre or touching any of our records. He'll simmer down presently and sit in the dark, playing our last disc over and over again and crying into his fine malt whisky, waiting for me to come back.'

'And you will, of course?'

'I suppose so. Yes, of course I will.' Janice tilted the glass gently towards her mouth, sipping. 'Always the same beginning, the same ending. I never know what starts it, how or why. It's weird. One minute there we are, in our warm little nest, all nice and compatible, having a civilised drink, talking about everything and nothing in a wise, funny way, peace, perfect peace. Then next minute or an hour later, I never know which, we're throwing things at one another, screaming and yelling like a pair of crazed orang-utans locked up in the one cage, hating the sight and sound of each other. It's weird.' She sat hunched forward, frowning, as if confronted with some immense intricate enigma; then she sighed, put her glass on the floor, and leaned back on her outspread palms, head falling sideways. 'It's bloody weird.'

'Sounds a fascinating existence, highly charged, never a dull moment, galloping along at a blistering pace.' Marcie looked down at the squatting girl, seeing the smooth arched throat turned golden in the lamplight, the heavy bronze hair alive with glints drawing back the agile neck as if by its soft weight, and felt oddly excited and intrigued, drawn almost against her will out of her sardonic self-absorption into contemplation of another life, another something beyond her own immediate and indeterminate grievances, feeling less certain of her seniority. 'You've been married – what, two years now, isn't it? Not that the time factor matters a great deal, I should imagine. More the texture of the thing, I suppose, the fibre of the relationship. Christ, that sounds like a voice straight out of the agony column. Pure pulp. Forget I said it, won't you? I don't usually slip like that.'

Janice laughed and picked up her glass again, straightening. 'But you're so right. The time you've spent with someone else doesn't matter, it's what you do with that time, that's what matters, that's the only thing that counts in the end. A single day can be as meaningful as a whole year, depending on how you spend it. On the other hand, it can be just as much a waste of time, just as painful and teeth-grinding as a whole lifetime spent in the wrong way.'

'You sound quite old when you talk like that. You almost look old when you talk like that.'

'Well, damn it, I feel old, much too old of late.'

149

'So,' said Marcie, removing a fleck of tobacco clinging to her lower lip, 'you left the songwriter thrashing about in a holy rage, hopped into that nifty little Mini of yours and high-tailed it over here to pour domestic woes into my untutored ear? I'm flattered, of course, but – a little surprised, shall we say?' She blew another expert smoke ring.

'Surprised?'

Marcie nodded. 'Yes, a little. After all, we're not exactly soul sisters, are we? We're not mortal enemies either, of course, nor are we complete strangers. But at the same time we've never been very intimate, have we? Apart from having a mutual connection – or antipathy – in Simon Sandford, we hardly know each other.' Her tone was cool, detached, a little haughty, as if she were trying to regain whatever initiative she seemed to have lost.

Janice regarded her steadily, her face open, somewhat puzzled, sad. 'I didn't think you'd mind about such things.'

'Oh – well, I don't, actually,' countered Marcie, confused in spite of herself, feeling somehow rebuked. 'Not in the least. Friendships have to start somewhere, sometime, and why not here and now? It's just that – well, I'm surprised that you selected me to be your confidante.'

Janice sipped her drink, silent, lost in reverie; she shifted to a new position on the rug, curling sideways on one hip, resting her weight on her outspread hand.

'It wasn't like that. It wasn't that deliberate. You just came to mind. Don't ask me why.' She smiled absently. 'As you say, we're practically if not total strangers. I could've gone walking in Hyde Park, talked to the ducks and swans on the lake, but they don't answer back.'

'Fortunately, perhaps!' laughed Marcie, without much conviction, scratching her shoulder-blade.

'I suppose I needed to listen as much as to talk. I didn't hop into the Mini either. I don't like to drive when I'm – like now. So I got a taxi over. As for leaving Art in one of his "holy rages" . . .' She paused, staring at a framed print on the wall, abstracted. 'His normal creative routine is to sit picking his nose for hours on end, groaning and moaning and telling me for Christ's sake to be quiet, even when I'm curled up in a chair with a book, or soaking in the bathtub – *not* singing, not even humming, not making a single damn sound.'

'A classical case of genius at work. One tiny squeak out of you, and another immortal melody is lost to posterity. That sort of shit?'

'Just about the size of it. I do know one thing – if you want to be brought down from the starry heights with a bang and have your most cherished little illusions demolished in one fell swoop, go and live with someone who's "creative", just for six months, never mind two years.'

'A form of self-torture I've no intention of experimenting with, I assure you.'

'Don't know about self-torture, but it's guaranteed to get rid of those rose-coloured glasses. Like being left in sole charge of a crèche with one oversized squalling infant who won't do a thing you tell him, bangs his head against the wall, throws things about and in general makes a bloody unholy mess of everything. And of course should you leave him alone for a single minute . . .' Janice slowly swirled the amber drink in her glass as might an apothecary preparing an exotic potion. 'That's the creative process. A bit exaggerated, but not much.'

'Portrait of the artist as a bloody bore.'

Marcie got up and began perambulating round and round, stretching her neck back and forward, massaging it with one hand, the robe flowing outwards from her hips, showing glimpses of svelte brown skin. She seemed restless, though her movements were lithe and unhurried.

'I find it hard, though,' she said, pausing to look down at the squatting girl, 'to think of you as the dutiful little wife just sitting by, twiddling your thumbs and waiting to sharpen his pencils and fill the inkstand, like that silly cow Dora in *David Copperfield*, while your lord sits on high communing with the gods. I mean, don't you have a hand in things? Don't you write some of the lyrics, or am I mistaken?'

Janice gave a shrug. 'I help out now and then, yes.'

Marcie began moving about again. 'Just help out?'

'Well, I sort of stand by in case of emergency,' said Janice, studying the pattern of the rug beneath her. 'You know – should the holy stream of inspiration dry up, in I rush, trusty quill at the ready, to do my gallant little bit in the greater cause of Art.' She smiled. 'Poor joke, I'm afraid.'

Marcie drew on her cigarette, its tip glowing red in the dusk. 'You do actually write some of the lyrics, don't you? Then why not claim some of the credit, for Christ's sake? You're not exactly the demure self-effacing sort, so why the silent, suffering stance? How's your drink?' she asked abruptly, going to the decanter and pouring.

'Okay for now, thanks. So that's how you see me, Marcie, is it – wronged, put upon, patient unto death?'

'At the moment, yes, to be quite frank, and so far you've said nothing to disabuse me of the notion. I wish you would. I can't stand that sort of woman.'

'Sorry – it wasn't what I had in mind. A martyr I most definitely am not. I didn't mean to downgrade Art either, by the same token. He has got talent, real talent, which I suppose is a bit unfashionable at the moment, and he works hard at it, damn hard. There's so much to admire in him, and I do admire him, I really do, in so many ways, for so many things. It's just that – ' She fell silent, contemplating the rug.

'It's just that you're a bit pissed off with him at the moment?' Marcie suggested, finishing her cigarette and almost immediately lighting up another.

'Yes. Just as he is with me, I daresay. No genuine argument is ever really one-sided, is it?'

'I suppose not.' Marcie wandered to the window. 'I've often wondered why you two got married in the first place.'

'We wanted to.'

'That simple, was it?'

'At the time, yes. Does it seem such an obvious misalliance?'

Marcie stood silhouetted against the subdued night glow of the city sky, slim and statuesque. 'At times, yes. A case of fools rushing in where angels fear, et cetera. Though I never was much on the side of the angels anyway. But since we're being so confiding and brave and honest and all the rest of it, I must say from the outset it seemed a bit of a disaster.'

Janice pondered awhile, face shadowed from the lamplight behind her. 'Yes,' she nodded finally. 'I guess it does seem a bit like that. We were too young, of course – much too young. We should have waited another two years, at least – that's obvious now. But of course waiting another day was just like death to us then.' She shook her head sadly. 'Now the whole thing reads like a terrible cliché out of a novelette written by a bored suburban housewife hiding behind an improbable alias, like Jane Dark.'

'How old were you in fact, both of you? I don't think I ever quite found out.'

'How old? Barely eighteen – '

'Oh, Christ.' Marcie blew a swift snort of smoke from her nostrils as if in disbelief.

'Exactly. We couldn't see any rhyme or reason for waiting, since we didn't know what on earth we'd be waiting for. We couldn't see a damn thing for love. It seemed so natural at the time, so inevitable. And of course it was – at the time.'

Marcie stretched herself lazily, her throat an ebony marvel in the shimmering light from the window behind, her breasts curving out taut and arrogant. ' "And now?" piped she, dead on cue.'

'And now?' echoed Janice, her voice dull, distant. 'Now we square up to each other at every single imagined insult, like two punch-drunk pugilists who don't know why they're fighting but go through the motions just the same, because they can't help it.'

Marcie glided nearer the open terrace window. 'Sounds absolutely exhausting. A saga of endurance. Both of you must be quite tough to stick it.'

Janice laughed, thoughtful, bitter. 'Oh, it isn't all warfare. There's the occasional ceasefire. Otherwise we'd go bonkers. No, that's not quite true,' she admitted after a pause, frowning at her own flippancy. 'There's more than that, of course. Lots of good times, lots of thrills and quiet interludes, when everything seems perfect, just right, and all the rest incidental. He can be fun to be with, and gentle too, so gentle in his own way, as if he were doing something not quite manly . . .' She bestirred herself, finished her drink and rose none too steadily to her feet, pushing back her hair. 'I'm sorry, Marcie, bloody sorry – '

Marcie turned from the window, back into the room. 'Sorry? Sorry for what, may I ask?'

'Boring you to tears.' She looked round for her jacket. 'I'll be on my merry way.' She found the jacket and started to struggle into it, grappling with some loose lining inside one sleeve. 'This bloody thing – always meaning to get it fixed – '

'Suit yourself, of course,' said Marcie, 'but Simon won't thank me for letting you leave like this.'

'Like what?' asked Janice, a bit aggressive, peeved with the silly wrestling match she was having with the jacket.

'Oh, come on now, don't be coy,' reproved Marcie lightly. 'We're both a bit tight, aren't we, both a bit under the influence, except that I'm not travelling anywhere except to bed, eventually.'

'Bully for you,' retorted Janice, panting with effort and irritation, 'What's my condition or behaviour or state of mind got to do with Mr

Sandford, I'd like to know?' She fought the recalcitrant jacket sleeve as if it were a cobra draped about her arm. 'Why should he even know I've been here? Does he have to know every damn thing that happens under his roof, for God's sake?'

Marcie looked on, cool, sardonic, self-possessed, smiling a little. 'Nothing has happened under his roof, or if it has, it's entirely escaped my attention. Why sneak off like a thief in the night, as if the hound of the Baskervilles was snapping at your ankles? Seems rather pointless to me, that's all, but do exactly as you please, of course.'

'Damn it!' Janice burst out, losing patience and flinging the jacket across the room, cheeks flushed, hair a little wild. 'I just don't see why I should be answerable to Simon bloody Sandford – I'm not his mistress – ' She stopped, embarrassed and confused, chewing her lip.

Marcie inhaled calmly. 'Whereas I am. Point taken. That, in a way, puts a certain liability on me. Unlike wives, mistresses have to be unfailingly polite and discreet if they are not to fall into disfavour and lose that privileged status. Besides,' she said, laconic, 'I like you. Haven't realised till now how much I actually like you. Isn't that odd?'

'Thanks a lot,' grumbled Janice, her resolve to leave waning somewhat when set against the deep-padded intimate warmth of the apartment and the unexpected solicitude of the other girl. 'It's nice to be liked.'

'No, no, I wasn't being sarcastic, and certainly not patronising,' said Marcie, resting her elbow in her hand, hip jutting out, bent smooth knee showing through the fold of her robe. 'I honestly do like you a lot, Janice, and I don't like all that many people. In fact, I don't like people very much. They bore me. You, on the other hand, interest me. I don't quite know why.'

'Tell me when you've made up your mind,' said Janice, sitting down abruptly in the same chair, as if stricken by a sudden disabling malady. 'I'm tired.'

'We've tons of sleeping space here,' said Marcie, crushing out her cigarette in an ashtray. 'If you care to nod off for an hour or two. No problem.'

'Sleep is the last thing I want to do.'

'As you wish. How about coffee, something to eat?'

Janice made a grimace. 'Likewise food. Maybe another drink.'

'Sure.' Marcie hesitated, lifting the brandy decanter, then putting it back down, brows together, as if trying to come to a decision. She tapped her fingers meditatively against her hip. 'Look,' she said finally, 'you can have all the drink you want, but maybe a joint would do you more good.'

Janice wrinkled her nose, amused. 'A joint – hash? You have some here?'

Marcie nodded. 'Sure I have. You look surprised. Why?'

'Doesn't Simon mind?'

'He doesn't approve. He's remarkably conservative in some ways. He knows I like a smoke now and then, and that's that. Well, how about it? Share one with me to celebrate our new-found friendship?' Marcie stood back, smiling, waiting for an answer, a humorous contempt shining in her eyes.

Janice gave a short hard laugh. 'Why not?'

'That's good, then.'

Marcie went into the main bedroom to the left and was gone for some time, then she came back, leisurely rolling a thin brownish cigarette paper between her agile fingers and licking the inside of it with her tongue when she had compacted its contents to her satisfaction. She lit it, slow, careful, and took a drag on it, inhaling deeply, drawing the aromatic smoke into her lungs and holding it there, in no hurry to let it escape, her eyes half closed. She stood there by the low glass-topped table like a priestess performing an ancient esoteric ritual, a delicate muscle in her jaw working, her face remote, purged almost of expression, marked by a beautiful and unnatural vacuity, like the repose of death. Without a word, she handed the raggedly glowing pencil-slim tube to the other girl, as if passing on the holy wafer to a communicant.

Janice held it gingerly, as if afraid she might hurt it if she pressed too hard. She put it to her lips and inhaled, sternly refusing to splutter, closing her eyes as she had seen the other girl do, forcing herself to look calm, lethargic, even a little disillusioned, like a seasoned drinker holding mute dialogue with a bottle of his favourite beverage, wanting and waiting to be transported on to a higher plane of awareness, but experienced enough to expect merely a mediocre muzziness.

'Okay?'

'Okay.' Janice exhaled at length, letting out the smoke with a convincing show of reluctance mingled with enjoyment, trying to disregard the sickly-sweet after-taste it left clinging at the back of her throat. She handed it back. 'Ah, that's good.'

Marcie took it and sank to her knees on the carpet, her attitude prayer-like. 'It almost makes one love the world.'

'Yes,' enthused Janice, accepting the smouldering stem when it was again offered to her. She inhaled, fought off a spasm of revulsion, let the fumes out slowly as before. 'Yes, it does, doesn't it?' She handed it back to the kneeling girl.

'And believe in pots of gold at the end of rainbows. Well – *pot*, anyway,' drawled Marcie dreamily, smiling indulgently at her own culpable pun. Her eyes lifted lazily, enquiring. 'You've had it before, of course?'

'Of course!' retorted Janice, sounding indignant, taking the weed once more. 'Where do you think I've been all this time – in a nunnery?' She took a determined pull, handed it back.

Marcie smiled, the same far away transfixed expression on her face, cloaked in impenetrable serenity. 'I just wondered.' Her sensitive nostrils quivered as she inhaled, her eyelids pulsing minutely.

The cannabis smoke wreathed about their faces, veiling their eyes; their voices when they spoke at leisurely intervals were soft, low, remote, as if they shared a grave and imponderable secret, murmuring like drowsy birds settling snugly down for the night in the same feathery nest, beyond the gruff intrusion of others, letting words rustle like gently turning leaves between them.

'Isn't this good, hmm?'

'Ah, yes, it certainly is.'

'Better than booze, I think, don't you?'

'Oh, yes, much better than booze.'

'I'll roll another when this one's through. Okay?'

'Fine.'

'You look very much at peace now.'

'Don't say that – it sounds as if I'm dead, laid out.'

'I meant you look relaxed, not tense anymore.'

'That's how I feel. Ah, it's almost finished, though.'

'I'll roll another. No panic.'

'Silly to panic over anything really, isn't it?'

'Be right back.'

'I'm not going anywhere.'

Marcie rose like a slim faultless flame, without seeming to move a muscle, vanishing once more into the bedroom, gliding like a ghost, seeming to move through solid objects, noiseless, facile, leaving the subtle gravity of her presence in her wake, vibrant, alive. Janice, left alone, pondered on the gallant, menial little deceit she had practised

156

on her nocturnal hostess; she felt some predictable guilt about it, but she was also slightly amused, since the lie itself had been so unnecessary. True, she had smoked cannabis before, but once only, one dismal night in some equally dismal hotel room, after a particularly uninspiring evening show in the local flesh-pot of whatever more than usually faceless town they had been playing in. Nothing remained of that lifeless evening save the lingering odour of the single joint she and Art had so morosely shared, more out of boredom and frustration than any sense of adventure, a smell that prevailed over the stale mustiness of the walls, floorboards and bedclothes; she no longer recalled how or where they had obtained the stuff, only that the whole experience had turned out to be so disappointing, so much of an anticlimax after all the bloated hyperbole they had heard spouted about the alleged delights of smoking hash, that neither of them had felt any overwhelming urge to repeat it since, though they moved in circles where it was as readily available as an ordinary cigarette or a drink. She supposed it was possible that Art had smoked the odd joint now and then without her knowing it, but she rather doubted it, for he had not mentioned it once, and it was one of his quirks to boast and exaggerate, in his oddly innocent way, about things he had done without her, things that he had chanced upon away from her, around which he would weave intricate and highly improbable tales completely out of proportion to what might or might not have happened.

Tonight, however, holding the slim gritty little tissue between her fingers, putting it to her lips and keeping the cloudy syrupy smoke trapped and reeking inside her for as long as she could, she had to admit that it was all undeniably different, a kind of metamorphosis that edged things almost to the nebulous fringes of magic, mysterious, tantalising, full of clandestine allure, a sense of trespass that excited her as much as the actual narcotic itself. That it was in point of fact an unremarkable and rather pathetic little interlude in the mundane stampede and tedium of things she knew quite clearly if she really wanted to stop and think about it, but she did not choose to, because it was of no consequence, and did not hinder her careless enjoyment of the gradual change that was being wrought in the very air around her. It was now as if several mirrors were placed before her in an endlessly receding sequence, each proportionately smaller than the one in front of it, each containing a precise facsimile of the same separate segment of reality, reproduced in flawless fidelity, and into each mirror she could transpose herself in perfect safety, as snugly as fitting her fingers into a glove, unerring and unfaltering even as she sat entranced and immobile in the chair, eating fire and feeling nothing save a delicious, furtive, almost carnal exhilaration, disturbing, irresistible.

Marcie had come back and was kneeling exactly in the same pose as before, as if she had not stirred, and again the glowing blade of the joint rotated between them, the night sky pulsating the strumming beyond the window. She drew the magic miasma greedily into her now, her pores oozing peace, the blood lyrical in her veins, holding audible concourse with her senses. Fear was not far away, the tremulous, thrilling fear of the initiate, a lurking dread of oblivion poised on the fragile edges of perception waiting to invade and overrun, but it was loud with wonder and enticement for her, a menace she almost ran to meet. Everything was fluid, suspended, illusory; the room that held them was a revolving crystal orb, the objects in it rising in gentle levitation, playful animals doing ingenious parlour games for her amusement, looming, diminishing, assuming comic, grotesque shape, harbouring immense possibilities of surprise and exaltation. It was as if she sat in a cinema, dimly lit, watching jack o'lantern images flickering upon a swaying screen in demure paroxysms of antic bliss, unconnected, out of mundane focus, suffused with a quaint gargoyle existence of their own, cavorting on shimmering cobweb strands like arrogant trapeze artistes scornful of hard dull surfaces. She felt her will, her tenacious resolve to retain a hold on factual things, slip languorously from her, like a rusty anchor sliding beneath the waves; the uniqueness of the moment surged through her, indolent in its conquest, leaving her marooned in a softly teeming vacuum where logic no longer had relevance.

'How do you feel?' asked the crouching girl in dark devout shadow, the live flame hovering in her mouth.

'Odd. Distinctly odd.'

'You feel good, though, don't you?'

'Yes. Scared, but good. I don't want to think about it.'

'Ah yes, it's best not to. Spoils it when you think about it. Relax.'

'Yes.'

From her cloudy, glimmering height she peered down at her companion, a tawny primal presence in the dusk, the almond ovals of her eyes huge, nimbus of hair about her face ennobling her with pagan majesty, a hint of feline violence glinting like dormant lightning through her midnight-mauve skin, rendering her alien, a remote sardonic enigma, pungent as earth assailed and caressed by rain, coiled in self-knowledge, dictating the stellar motions of the universe within the amorphous walls of the room, as near as death and intangible as starlight, solid as marble and elusive as water running through one's fingers, immediate and invulnerable.

'D'you love Simon?' A high involuntary giggle lazily hushed.

'Love Simon . . . ! Only as muth or as little as the ground beneath my feet. Let me ask you an equally obscene question – '

'Go ahead.'

'Are you happy?'

'As much as anyone has the right to be.'

'That's a pretty dismal answer.'

'Yes, it is, isn't it?'

'You talk like a middle-aged trollop with a streetful of kids trailing after her. No offence.'

'Don't you sometimes feel a bit of a parasite, living on Simon's lordly sufferance?'

'Oh, frequently. Most mistresses do, I suppose, if they're not too hardboiled. I can live with the feeling.'

'I feel slightly sick.'

'Want to throw up?'

'Not yet, thank you.'

'It'll pass after a while.'

'Like most things.'

'Getting philosophical? Always a good sign.'

'Of what?'

'God knows.'

'What's it like being a mistress?'

'What's it like being a wife?'

'Point, counter-point. That's no way to conduct an intelligent conversation. We *are* being intelligent, aren't we?'

'Oh, I shouldn't worry about it. Speaking for myself, I haven't had an intelligent conversation for years, so I'm not qualified to judge.'

'I often thought being a mistress was like being a pet animal trained to do special little tricks.'

'Not this one. I scratch, maul, spit. Red in tooth and claw. That's me. I leave no discreetly rumpled pillows behind, no tossed blankets. More like scene of ritual slaughter.'

'You could be describing marriage. Mutual cannibalism. Eat one another alive day by day, night by night.'

'A lean enough diet. Why then do you stay together?'

'Habit, force of. Or maybe it's nice being eaten alive. I don't know. Something between suicide and murder.'

They spoke in dream-like tones, hardly asking questions or expecting answers, each engaged in a private monologue, self-orientated, self-locked, immune to any change of intonation or inflexion in the other's voice, aware of each other as shadows possessed of possible animation, each existing in a companionable void, yet alive with languid discernment of mood rolling like a slow tide between them.

'Before you came, thoughts of murder were running like lice through my head.'

'Simon?'

'He was certainly there, enmeshed in all the lovely gore. I saw the blood spurting out of his neck, his nice soft baby-fat neck, after I plunged the knife in.' The flame glimmered in the unseen mouth, long lascivious intake of breath, cool moonlit sweep of hand passing the tiny beacon. 'Not that I could ever murder him. It would be like murdering a child asleep in your arms. I like to while away the long Simonless hours thinking about it. Just to see that comic look on his face if I ever did . . .'

The cradle-like luminous cloud that enveloped her rose subtly, elevating her and bringing her gently down again, swaying on warm capricious rumours of wind from burnished shores glistening in magical distances glimpsed and never gained.

'You must hate too, sometimes. It is unavoidable, and salubrious into the bargain.'

'Hate. Oh yes, one must hate intensely. It takes the bloody awful sweet nothingness out of things. Sometimes I hate with a passion that thrills me as much as sex, which only thrills temporarily anyway. Hate goes right into the bloodstream, like a narcotic.'

The arrogant strangely noble head, sculpted for battle, rose like a dark exotic bloom out of the musing shadows, eyes glinting like polished daggers. 'Yes, one must hate.'

'I sometimes hate this business we're in. A jungle, a circus, a rat-trap, a gigantic phoney, a den of thieves and pimps . . . use every cliché that's ever been written about it, and it's still true, they each and every one of them apply. At times, in the middle of a recording session, surrounded by all that mechanical junk, enclosed in that little soundproof glass coffin, I panic and break out in a sweat and shake like someone afflicted with the palsy, overcome with shame and disgust at the artificial banality of it all.'

'Alas, pitched too soon into the public arena, into the full glare of the spotlight, given a tab, a manufactured image, a processed persona, seen as a voice and nothing more. My heart truly bleeds for you.'

'Endearingly second-rate, that's me,' said Janice. 'And if that sounds maudlin, it's just because it is maudlin, like most of the truth about ourselves. Hard to be honest with yourself without sounding maudlin. Like talking about something you know really well, game, hobby, profession, without boring the person on the receiving end. I seem to have lost my innocence without really knowing I ever had it. Dispossessed of something you never had. Yet I suppose I must have had it once.'

'Ever read Huxley on mescalin? Like stuffing your mouth full of cottonwool. Says it heightens the perception, does Mr Huxley. Doesn't say what happens if you haven't got any perception.' The benign yet malevolent glow was dwindling, waning, etching frailer arcs in the air as it passed between them. 'Almost finished. Shall I roll another?'

'Simon will need a bloody gas-mask when he comes in.'

Marcie was on her feet, moving about the room, touching things, lingering over surfaces smooth and grainy, soft and sharp; she stepped out on to the balcony, the city drumming and flaring below her, its crackling, swirling mazes blurring into bulbous globes of light, spilling like lava to the farthest limits of the night. She stretched her arms above her head, exultant, seduced by the fable of the world as it found her out at that moment, and did not know if she cried or laughed.

When she came back into the room, a large, huddled, formless bulk stood by the table, round jowel-sagging face perplexed, bemused, sunken eyes peering shortsightedly into the dusk, lamplight dull on sloping sandy temples, looking up and staring at her as though at an apparition.

161

'Why, Simon, darling!' she exclaimed, on a rise of irresistible, hysterical gaiety, rushing forward and almost tripping, clasping his cold glove-holding hand in both her own and shaking it up and down with prodigious verve, her hair wild and tumbling about her face. 'Welcome, welcome!'

10

SHE replaced the telephone in its sleek cradle slowly, face expression-less, devoid of emotion, and moved back to the table where she had left her drink, moving like someone coming out of an anaesthetic and still slightly drugged. A few cheeky sparrows were hopping outside on the windowsill, pecking at the breadcrumbs she had placed there for their breakfast, looking impertinently in at her now and then with bright black enquiring eyes, as if asking for more. Art emerged from the bedroom, bedraggled in his pyjamas, yawning, scratching under his armpits, his toes curling as they touched the bare floorboards.

'Who was that?' he asked between yawns.

She took up her glass, then put it down again without touching its contents. 'That was my mother.'

Art stifled another yawn, taken by surprise. 'Your mother? What catastrophe made *her* call us?'

'Not us. Me.' She moved to the window, the sparrows not at all frightened by her approach, busily finishing off what remained of their slender repast.

Art scowled. 'I forgot I'm still in purdah. After nearly three bleeding years! Anyway, what did she want, if I may be permitted to ask? When are you going to have a baby, dear – was that it?' he mimicked imperfectly, moving over to the rug and hugging himself as if for warmth, though the day shone brightly outside and the flat itself was comfortably heated. Seeing she did not stir or make any reply, his tone changed to one of petulant pleading. 'Oh, come on, Jan – don't stand there like a statue, like bleeding Lot's wife. What's wrong?' He picked up the glass and sniffed it. 'And why are you on this stuff at – ' he looked at his watch – 'three in the afternoon?'

'I've got to go back home.'

He put the glass back down abruptly. 'Home? What the hell – I mean why? What's up? Someone hasn't copped it, have they?' She turned and looked at him, and he looked away, shuffling his feet. 'All right – bad joke, poor taste. You know I don't mean – well, what *has* happened? Don't just stand there like Desdemona, waiting to be strangled any minute.'

'My grandmother died this morning.'

A look of relief came upon his face, and he almost yawned again. 'Oh – your Gran. Sorry to hear that. She had a fairly good innings though, didn't she? Not that that means it isn't – '

'I'll just take a few things along with me.' She went into the bedroom.

He stood open-mouthed for a moment or two, then quickly went in after her. She had got out a small leather red-check suitcase on the bed and was carefully putting some items of clothing into it from the built-in wardrobe in the corner, her movements methodical and efficient. He watched her, stunned.

'You mean you're going now – today?'

'I'll take a train and leave you the car,' she said, not pausing in her preparations, moving from wardrobe to bed, packing the clothes in neat folded layers. 'The funeral's tomorrow.'

'But – but damn it all, you can't leave today!' he spluttered, going round the other side of her, trying to catch her attention. 'We've got to be at the studio by six – '

'Cancel it.'

He stared, as if she had lost either her memory or her reason, or both. He gave a nervous laugh. 'Cancel it? What the hell are you on about? We can't cancel it! It isn't a bleeding dinner date – we're recording an album, for God's sake. There are still six more tracks to do – Janice!' he said in a rising voice, grabbing her arm. 'Are you listening to me? You just don't walk out in the middle of a recording session – I mean you just don't *do* it!'

She shook off his hand and faced him, strangely calm. 'Do what you want. I'm going home to see Gran.' She resumed her packing, turning away from him.

He stood back, knotting his fists. 'It's not what *I* want. We're a team, remember – a partnership. How the hell can I carry on with the album without you? Simon would have apoplexy – they'd have to scrap the whole damn thing, and you know the schedule we're working to. It's got to be finished by Saturday, which gives us exactly two full days to round it off. The sales people are screaming for it and if it's not ready on time, forget it. Is that what you want?'

'I'm going home to see Gran.'

'But she's dead, for Christ's sake!' he exploded, thumping the wall with one fist. 'What difference does it make whether you see her or not? Will *she* know?'

She paused as she was about to fasten the clasps on the suitcase. 'Yes, I think she will.' She pressed the clasps together, pushed the two metal hasps into their sockets, then locked it.

'Spare me the mystical bit,' he said grimly, crossing his arms and leaning against the wall. 'You know, don't you, that if we foul this one up it's curtains for us? Simon won't want to know us. As it is, we're not exactly top billing, people don't know who we are any more, and if Simon boots us back into nowhere, that's exactly where we'll stay. Doesn't that mean anything to you?'

'Not much any more.' She turned round wearily. 'Look, Art, it isn't like you say. I'm not running back to a corpse, back to a frail dead old lady, nor am I walking out on you. Your future is secure. You can get ahead without me – I've known that for a long time now. Musically we've reached a full stop together, which doesn't mean that we can't stay married.'

He went pale, his eyes dark and sunken and a sudden fear creeping into them, dilating the pupils. 'I must say your sense of timing is deplorable,' he muttered, bitter, crabbed. 'You wait till we're in the middle of recording what could well be our make-or-break album to deliver this kind of ultimatum. Marvellous.'

'It isn't an ultimatum – '

'Prophecy of doom, then,' he said, trying to sneer and failing miserably, lunging away from the wall and stamping up and down, mouth working furiously behind the dark apostolic beard, narrow forehead beaded with sweat. 'Call it what you like. It all boils down to one thing – you're fucking everything up. Everything we wanted and worked for – ' he flung up a hand, sweeping it round, indicating the room, the furniture, the rest of the flat beyond – 'this, our plans for the future, our life together – ' he turned on her savagely – 'yes, our life together – that, too! Don't say it'll go on as before, because it won't, it can't. How could it? We've never known anything else, have we, any other kind of life from the time we met, so how can you talk about going on "as before"? Before what? There never was a before, only what we've always had and known. And now – ' he stopped, breathing hard, looking at her as though at a mortal enemy – 'and now you're throwing it all away, kicking everything from under us, taking advantage of a poor old woman dying to walk out without having to feel guilty about it. I call that contemptible!' He stalked into the front room and went immediately to the whisky bottle, filling a glass with a trembling hand and gulping it down to halfway, fingers taut.

She remained standing by the bed, hearing the throttled, angry sounds he was making, pushing things out of his way; she took the suitcase off the bed and stood it upright on the floor. Her limbs felt leaden as she went back into the other room.

'I'll phone Simon,' she said. 'I'll explain. An extra day or two can hardly matter.'

'It can, and it does,' he snapped, his back to her as he stood by the table, gripping his glass. 'Can't you see he's losing interest in us as it is, without springing this on him?'

She went slowly across to the window. 'I think what really matters is that you're afraid.'

'Of the bogeyman?' he rasped.

'Of going out on your own,' she replied, looking down at the trees beginning to blaze in their autumnal splendour once more in the quiet avenue. 'Of branching out without me, without Sandford, without props –'

He swung round. 'Props?'

'Yes, Art, props. That's all anyone else ever really is to you – props, extra padding, protective clothing to keep out the cold. All you need, you see, all you really need is your talent, your talent to write songs and play music, and that's something I think you'll always have. So isn't it time you accepted that and made the most of it, instead of thinking you need others around you to spur you on and keep you up to par?'

'Thanks for the philosophy lesson.' He emptied the glass and plonked it down hard on the table. 'You're making a real song-and-dance out of something you've obviously made up your mind about. Why not come out with it? You're bored with our life and want to get out – that's it, isn't it?'

'That's not it.' She leaned her hands on the windowsill, the birds making a fluttering little commotion at her nearness, but still trusting and unafraid, their feast almost gone. 'You know as well as I do that I can't go on singing much longer. You know my voice is almost gone. It's time to face that fact as well.'

He swallowed. 'Don't talk shit. You're singing as well as you ever did, better at times – '

'Oh Art, stop it!' she said with tired impatience. 'Why can't you admit, even sometimes, that unpleasant things can and do happen, and must be faced?'

He gave a harsh, choked laugh. 'Unpleasant – is that what you call it? Just unpleasant, when what you're proposing would break up our whole damn life? Talk about understatement – '

'Don't dramatise! Why do you run away from things?'

'I'm not running anywhere except up the fucking wall!'

'Oh, for God's sake, Art!' she cried, exasperated. 'It's my voice I'm losing, not my life.'

He was silent for a few moments. 'I feel dead, just thinking about it.'

'There you go again, dramatising – '

He held up a hand, stopping her. 'No. You know as well as I do, I write everything around you. Not *about* you, not that kind of sentimental shit, but around your voice. Your voice is as much of an instrument to me as that bloody guitar there. Every line, every note of music I conceive in terms of your voice. Take that away and I'm left with nothing.'

She twisted the wedding ring about on her finger. 'There are other singers – it just means a change of direction, of emphasis. And why do you have to have lyrics, anyway?' she challenged. 'Why not go in instead for instrumentals? That would open up a whole new field of experiment for you, and you've always said you wanted to experiment, so why not – ?'

He threw up his hands. 'Talk sense! Talk bleeding sense just for once! How many kids today go in for instrumentals? What percentage of the market? Do you expect me to change overnight from ballads to writing screen scores and soundtrack music for films? That area of the business is littered with corpses!'

'Somebody writes that kind of thing – ' she began lamely.

'Oh sure – if you're struck by lightning, or are prepared to sit on your arse in the wings till you're discovered and asked to write the score for the latest James fucking Bond or something out of the Bible! As easy as that. No sweat. No,' he said, walking up and down, a comical figure of fury in his rumpled pyjamas, mouth livid and working like a serpent entangled in the dark bush of his beard. 'I know

167

my limitations, what I can and can't do. I can write a certain kind of music, a certain kind of ballad, with you, your voice, as my medium.' He stopped pacing and looked at her, appealing, puzzled. 'Don't you know that?'

'I listen to myself sometimes,' she said, after being silent for a while, folding her hands in front of her, reflective. 'I stop in the middle of a song, as if listening to someone else, you know. And it's painful. Like a jittery schoolgirl warbling at a garden party or a fête in aid of the local gymnasium. I sound like I'm walking on broken glass in my bare feet.' She regarded him steadily as he stood at the table. 'You've a good ear, Art, an excellent ear. Don't you hear it too, even if you don't want to? I can't believe you don't, it's so obvious.'

He reached for the whisky bottle as though there was nothing else in the world he could do, drinking straight from its neck and dashing a wrist across his moist mouth. 'You're getting neurotic, that's all – neurotic! There's damn all wrong with your voice. I think you're just making excuses to quit. That's dishonest.' He banged the bottle back down on the table, eyes smarting with the harsh intake of liquor. 'That's bleeding dishonest.'

Janice pondered awhile. 'Perhaps it is,' she conceded quietly. 'I'm no paragon and certainly not above being dishonest. But I believe it would be more dishonest to blithely ignore what's happening to my voice and just go on and on, till someone whispered a friendly word of warning in my ear, to the effect that I should stop fooling myself and get out gracefully before too many others started to notice my decline and fall.'

'Christ!' he almost snarled. 'If you were that lousy, do you think Simon would go on putting his money behind us? Whatever else he may be, he's no fucking philanthropist.'

Again she seemed to give his words serious thought. 'I don't know,' she mused. 'Maybe Simon's a much kinder man than we've given him credit for so far.'

He flung up his hands once more. 'A prostitute with a heart of gold I can just about believe in, but the idea of Simon Sandford doing an Ebenezer Scrooge, beating his breast in atonement for past sins and showering everyone in sight with gifts . . .' He laughed, mirthlessly. 'That, my dear, passeth all understanding. Try another gambit.'

She shook her head resignedly. 'I've tried to explain, to make you understand why I must go to Gran now – yes, even though she's dead.

If you don't or won't understand, then I can't help it. I only know I have got to be there with her.'

When next he spoke his voice was low, controlled and intense, with a hard metallic edge. 'All right. So you must go. You're wrecking all our plans, our commitments, but you must go. Fair enough. But what are we really talking about? Death, grief, duty, family feeling? No. What we're really talking about is us, you and me, our life together. This death in the family – it has only brought to a head what you've been thinking for months past. That *we* are finished, concluded, at an end. All the rest is incidental, and I mean no disrespect to your Grandma.' He looked at her, daring her to deny or contradict. 'That's it, isn't it, Janice – you think it's we who are finished, and not just your voice?'

'No,' she answered, calm, meeting the hard interrogative intensity of his gaze. 'Only my voice.'

She moved once more to the window, absently observing the antics of the sparrows hopping about on their spidery legs, forlornly pecking at crevices in the concrete ledge in the hope of teasing out some hidden crumbs of bread.

'How shallow you must think me,' she said, breaking a silence. 'If I thought there was no future together for us, I wouldn't wait for someone to die to act upon that feeling.'

'What the hell else am I to think?' he demanded, fingers roaming about his beard. 'What choice do you give me? If it isn't the death of your grandmother, then it's this nonsense about losing your voice, a spectre you've plucked out of nowhere, like a magician plucking a rabbit out of his hat.'

'Except for one thing,' she said. 'The rabbit was there all the time, hidden somewhere. I'm not feverishly concocting stories in order to vindicate myself, Art.'

'I still say your voice is as good as ever it was – '

'Oh, I dare say I could get by. I can still croak out a fairly good imitation when it comes to the push. But that's not what either of us want, is it? We both knew all along, I think, even from the start, that as far as singing goes my best would last only a short period. We've been lucky, it certainly lasted longer than I thought, at any rate, but now I'm getting rapidly past it, and there's nothing you can do about that. There's no surgery you can undergo to correct that.' She lapsed again into a brief silence, staring out of the window. 'I'm losing interest, Art, and that is irreversible.'

All the fight, the rage, the heroic futile vehemence seemed to go out of him, leaning by the table, shoulders drooping, thin hand irresolute about his mouth. 'So what happens now, to us? Forget about careers and other worthless things for the moment. What about us?'

'I told you,' she said, turning back into the room. 'There's no reason why we can't – '

'I know what you told me,' he interrupted, his voice bleak, dull. 'But you know it wouldn't work. There'd be nothing to cement us, nothing to hold us together any more. We'd be loose, like straws in the wind. This is the only world we know, the music we make together. It's what keeps us going, keeps us in tandem. You know that as well as I.'

'There should be something else,' she said, rather desperately, 'there must be – '

'But there isn't, is there?'

He looked at her, beaten and defiant at once, and she looked away, unable to meet the misery and truth in his eyes.

There was more than one dead person in the house. As Janice lay in her old bed, in her old room, under the sloping ceiling in the small recess by the window, the same macabre thought came to her again and again, absurd and gothic in its implication, yet undeniable, insistent, a shadowy presence that would not be pushed away: more than one dead person in the house.

The old woman laid out so formally in her final mortal raiment retained more life still than the living occupants, retained more spritely sensibility and wise gaiety than would ever flicker in the closed stone-smooth faces of her mourners, observing her obsequies with the same nerveless stoicism as they had observed the placid unwinding of their own lives. There was a spry dignity, a dominant aura almost of celebration about the dead Gran that was completely absent from the life that purported to continue to breathe in the house, as if some bright, elemental, irrepressible force had waned and departed, and left in its place a pallid imitation, cold ash, embers from a fire that had burnt long and strongly and gone out in a merry blaze of leavetaking, frolicking its way out of the world.

Seeing that calm almost unwrinkled face framed in brown cloth, restored by death to childlike delicacy and refinement, it had seemed to Janice somehow obscene to grieve too bitterly, she felt it would have been a mere show of petulance and ostentation, like crying out for more where there had been a whole lifetime's profligate outpouring and abundance of love and companionship. It would have been a profane intrusion to bring her narrow burden of sorrow with her, a desecration of the deep vibrant hush that had finally rounded off the unique covenant with life that her grandmother had enjoyed and honoured so fully throughout her years, even when at last condemned to the indignities of invalidism in her own little quarters that had been built for her at the top of the back garden, and where she held roguish court to her fancies and vivid recollections, fingering each of them lovingly as other people might handle books or tell their beads. The only tears permissible at that hour were those of quiet melancholy that such a life had inevitably to close, tears that totally precluded despair. To give way to excessive grief, looking upon such serenity, would be akin to demanding encores after the dancer had given of her best, bowed and retired; to ask more would amount to blatant ingratitude, as well as spoiling an impeccable dénouement.

Janice felt like one who had been away for many years on hectic unending travels and, on returning to what had once been home base, found everything so utterly changed and turned around that she was instantly lost, stranded, all previous landmarks and directions obliterated, even the memory of them alien and unreal to her. And yet of course nothing had changed; it was as it had always been, and only her awareness of the pervading bleakness that lay like a patina upon everything had sharpened and intensified during her absence, so that the pang of resentment and regret for all the things that she had never known shot through her with even keener poignancy, like a physical pain. Whatever heart the house might once have had was stilled now, wrapped in a brown shroud and laid upon a neatly laundered bed, soon to be consigned along with a bundle of frail bones to the anonymous earth; after that, the house could disintegrate and vanish off the map and she would not miss it or seek out the spot where it had stood. Her last fragile sense of belonging was growing thinner and dwindling with the ticking of the clock; nothing had power or appeal to hold her further, and she wanted only to be gone, back into the confusion, uncertainty and occasional anguish of that larger life, which might indeed bewilder and infuriate her, but in which she at least felt herself alive, needed, vulnerable to hunger and love.

She felt panic rising in her, overcoming her with the old easy triumph, and with all her strength she fought to deny the awful void where her childhood and awakening years should have been; she sought to pluck one bright image, one unspoilt memory out of the past, some small scrap of happy recollection that might make the present bearable and soften the overriding indifference and bleakness of which the house and the room where she now lay spoke with such melancholy eloquence. But such spiritual archaeology was futile; even those brief and perhaps illusory feelings of happiness that she managed to dredge out of the void were obscured by rigid admonitions and reprimand; the prettiest flowers were poisonous, the sunniest streams treacherous with hidden sharp-toothed perils, and picturesque ruins discovered on rare country outings held menaces far from quaint and were under no circumstances to be approached without parental guide and supervision.

11

IT was over, before it had really begun for her, and with a lazy, satisfied grunt he rolled off her and flopped onto his back, gasping a little. He looked sideways at her, a drowsy, uncertain half smile on his face.

'Okay, love?'

She looked away without answering, fixing her eyes on the glimmering curtain, and in a short while he was asleep again, snoring, his mouth slightly ajar, mumbling in a querulous, indistinct way, at odds with whatever dream he was having. She hated him. She hated his bland, unquestioning acceptance of something that was still largely a revelation, a gradual, tentative delight to her, his brief flaring that thrilled and fired her, then the swift descent into ordinariness, the awful complacency that followed, the profound torpor that settled upon him, bearing him away from her; she hated as much as she envied his effortless return to oblivion, lying sated as a breast-fed infant cocooned once more in its warm deep cradle, face flushed in slumber, no longer in need of her. She lay beside him, sunk in bitter lethargy, hands on her slack thighs, feeling the faint wetness there, promise of a tempest that had whimpered and ebbed away into nowhere, and hated him fiercely as the morning began, choosing to ignore the subtle whisper of self-loathing that lay below the surface of her extravagant resentment.

The rain spattered against the windowpane in small urgent flurries, like someone begging admittance out of the cold dank misery of the wakening day. She lingered in bed, inert, tired in mind and limb, fighting her hostility, her sour sense of grievance, trying not very successfully, to shift the blame to herself for expecting too much, seeking always the major moment when the minor was all that could be attained. She closed her eyes; she imagined the anaemic morning light creeping, furtive as a thief, wary as a clandestine lover, over the straggling city, touching gilded domes, spires, cupolas, glinting down through the foliage of trees in the quiet parks, lending lacklustre credence to the new day that was totally devoid of newness. She thought, turning on her side and smiling thinly, of the enduring schizophrenia of the city. One half of it was prim, trim, prudish, sedate, its avenues tree-lined, arboreal, its houses white-stuccoed, half asleep, leaning on solid foundations, gazing across at each other like retired stout-jowled duchesses and elder statesmen. Pin-striped, bowler-hatted, the master of these houses was embroiled in the early ritual of orange juice, coffee and toast, timetables and leisurely departures to the glass pyramids of commerce, mid-day cocktails and cigar-punctuated lunches gilt-edged to induce with the minimum of fuss that fashionable malady of the affluent and industrious, the executive coronary, followed by indolent superannuation in green-belted slippered ease. The other half were scourged by clocks and nomadic barking dogs, coming awake to the hoarse hooting of factory sirens, iron gates clanging open to admit the hordes of human worker ants to which they belonged, shopfront grills snapping wide, radios crackling, car horns snorting like thundering elephants, asthmatic creak of buses, the hangdog morning limping graceless and ragged through echoing canyons of high-rise mausoleums and warrens of faceless carbon-copy dwellings cemented together without being consulted in static uniformity, like partners in unholy matrimony, the wet pavements reflecting back the merciless routine of lives large and small, plodding about in separate bestiaries, hemmed in by the city.

Abandoning finally all pretence of wooing back the comfort of sleep, she got out of bed, feeling with her feet for her slippers and wrapping the nightgown tightly about her. She paused awhile by the bed, looking down at his face corpse-like in its pallid composure, the closed lids red-rimmed, the hollow cheeks and biblical beard giving him the look of a martyred saint. He slept like a child, with the same total absorption, the same utter oblivion and profundity that erased from his features all token of consciousness and mobility and gave to him an aura of impenetrable and somehow repellent insensibility. No one should sleep like that, she thought, as if they were embalmed or already in the grave; it was obscene.

She went into the small neat black-and-white tiled kitchen and set about making a pot of tea. Her mouth felt horrible, with a foul aftertaste lingering at the back of her throat, clinging like fur; she must have been on vodka last night, she decided, or had at any rate started out on it, before switching at some point during the interminable drum-and-cymbal clashing hours of the evening and night to God alone knew what other volatile concoction. It was all a rather familiar fog out of which nothing very clearly emerged; she remembered the club they were in had huge musical notes made of gaudy plaster running up and down the walls, the stage constructed of illuminated blocks that kept changing colour underneath her so that rainbows danced inside her head; the chaotic fog was full of the same faces, the same intimate strangers, the same conversations that came unerringly back to the same point of non-departure, and she remembered being buoyed up by the same savage hilarity that caused others to marvel and exclaim at her stamina and unflagging vivacity when everyone around had had enough and was making the usual fumbling gestures with car keys, handbags, putting on scarves and shambling into topcoats and jackets, moving in a straggling ungainly exodus towards the exits, exchanging weary goodnights between yawns.

When the water had boiled, she poured half of it from the kettle into the pot, spooned in the tea and left it to draw; then she sat down at the table. She wished she could stomach a cigarette – it might help to clear her head, but just the thought of it made her queasy, an obscene act of pollution inflicted on the day before it had properly started. She wished also that she had remained in bed, for she knew she could not go back to sleep now that she had got up, and wondered what the hell she would do to make the morning pass without dragging its heels. She would probably get dressed and go for a walk in the park, if the rain was not too heavy. A new wave of resentment surged through her; he had woken her in an act of quick brutish love, solely for his own satisfaction, and had almost immediately slipped back into unconsciousness once his need had been placated. She felt close to tears, and knew she was being absurd, but did not care. She could always take a couple of sleeping pills and curl up on the sofa, but some kind of deep ingrained prudery worked against that step; alcohol was one thing, a social ritual, as long as it did not get out of hand; likewise a few occasional whiffs of cannabis, but towards sleeping tablets she felt a curious reticence, remembering the beautiful ease with which she had always been able to sink into slumber, putting her thoughts away quietly as she did her clothes in the wardrobe. She regretted the passing of that natural facility, along with so many other things that had gone out of and come into her life in the course of the last few years.

She leaned her elbows on the table, closing her eyes, waiting for the tea to draw, hearing morning sounds beginning down in the street and in the rooms above and below theirs; remote thud of doors, footsteps hurrying along the corridor, subdued murmur of voices, the querulous creak and flush of drains, a child's clear bright laugh uninhibited by the solemnity of early morning. The house, like the street and the city below, was stretching itself and coming awake in the usual begrudging way.

She did not try to excavate the buried ruins of the night before, a futile exercise in any case, since only the usual happened. Going through their now all too slick routine on stage, the obligatory encores and tepid flurries of applause, and the long hours of drinking and haphazard talk afterwards, where everyone seemed to know everyone else, greeting each other with the fervour of long-lost kin and promptly forgetting all about it the next moment as they turned to the newest arrivals on the garrulous scene, wandering up to the overcrowded table, glasses in their hands and vacant smiles on their faces, waiting to be initiated, to be hailed and hugged and asked teasingly about their love life before being jovially ignored in the glazed din and gabble. The row with Art over her going to her grandmother's funeral had petered out. Simon had been tolerant; there had been a postponement of the recording session.

She poured out a mug of tea when it was finally ready and gulped it down avidly, relishing the way it burnt her throat, rinsing away the odious night-before taste that lay on her tongue like scum. She wanted so little from life, from being abroad in the world; she wanted nothing more dramatic than to know some kind of enduring happiness, and that, she reflected with a tight smile, was perhaps the most dramatic thing that could happen to her or to anyone. The forlornness of that seemingly simple expectation chilled her and forced her to take refuge in thinking that there was something basically craven about the common human desire to be happy, happy at all costs and at any price to others or to oneself. Yes, she decided, hardening into stoicism, gripping the mug – there was something hunted about it, defiled, cowering, whining, this terrible yearning after happiness, clawing one's way to the golden ideal like a famished mongrel snarling through whatever dirt and debris to get at a bone, willing to put up with any hurt, insult, humiliation, as long as it closed in on its prey at last and sank its teeth into it. That kind of hunger was so superficial, so functional, as easily appeased as any other bodily imperative; it took a rarer kind of perversity to live without hope, without illusion of sustenance and renewal in loving and being loved by another human being.

A life stripped of hope would not of necessity mean the absence of pain, would not make any lighter the burden and essential loneliness of existence, no, but the pain at least would be one's own responsibility and not cheaply attributable to another, and only strength, solitary and singlehearted, could come from the knowledge that nobody else on earth could be blamed for the failure of one's dreams. She wished she had that strength, that singular bravery that would enable her to fashion her life for herself and not for the fleeting, flippant satisfaction of others. Maybe it would come to her when she was incredibly old, too old to put it to any good cause, shawled and slippered and nibbling soft biscuits.

She shivered, despite the warming tea and the fleecy robe against her skin, and got up from the table, clutching the mug in both hands and wandering back into the bedroom. He had hardly stirred, lying in the tangled wreck of the sheets, his breathing deep and regular, supine with an oblivious, naive repletion that was oddly childlike and pathetic and made it difficult for her to sustain her anger towards him. He lay sprawled like a swimmer who had battled gallantly against adverse currents and, upon gaining the shore, had fallen down in a profound swoon of exhaustion, dead to the world and all its frivolities and distractions. She had seen him often, coming off stage after a performance, walking about like someone in a trance, utterly drained, sweat glistening on his blanched face and staining his shirt, hardly aware of her as she brushed past him in the cramped dressing-room, sitting in the chair as if insensible, beyond speech, staring into space. At first she had regarded this extreme show of depletion on his part as being nothing more than a form of juvenile exhibitionism, as symptomatic of youth as acne or a nervous tic, something that would disappear in due course; but it did not, and it was almost with a shock that she realised it was genuine and unfeigned, leaving her not a little in awe of the total self-absorption he expended on his music. The making of love had the same effect upon him as that of music, and to her chagrin she came to acknowledge that in both acts her own rôle was becoming so subliminal as to be insignificant, a minor chord in an intensely private scenario that he orchestrated and constantly revised, independent of her.

She moved to the window, streaked with rain, and stood there thinking about their life, its abrupt uneven edges and ragged ends, its chronic disarray and crowded emptiness, of which they were both acutely aware but pretended to ignore, fearful of being left for too long to their own resources, knowing the desert that faced them; yet she knew the paradox was that they were too much together and had inhabited the one space for far too long without moving an inch onto neutral ground. Neither could draw a breath without the other knowing it and being somehow, subtly affected by it as by their every gesture, expression, intonation and intent. Neither knew any other life beyond the one they shared, and its inexorable claustrophobia was proving too great a strain to bear, getting them both down and grating on their nerves even – or most of all – when they were silent.

At first, it had been a marvellous novelty to be so much together, a new romantic discovery and adventure day after day, finding out small things about each other that were never mundane in their eyes; likes and dislikes, hopes and habits, foibles and fancies, passions and prejudices, things that deepened the delight they found in each other's presence. It had seemed so wonderfully natural, being together, not wanting for anything else, open to the joy of the world but secure against its harsher intrusions, as if constantly being in each other's sight was the only thing both had been waiting for in order to come alive, the one and only way they could possibly live their lives. It was something that did not have to be given up to the dry stuff of thought, but was only to be felt, experienced, savoured and cherished, like a beautiful painting or a good meal, like an outing to the seaside or a moonlit walk, something that belonged primarily to the senses and knew its keenest ecstasy there.

When or how, least of all why, it had begun to change and be terribly different she could not say; it was one of those things that had no discernible onset and could not be traced back to a definite point in time. It had simply grown, like grass in the city, thusting up through concrete crevices, unstoppable and insidious. It was now a constant irritant, an ordeal, being together so much, a matter that bristled with potential danger, even when they did not end up quarrelling about it. In the beginning it had been rather as if two explorers, pursuing separate paths in the jungle, had somehow stumbled upon each other against all the odds, too surprised and overjoyed by the encounter to question it very deeply; now it was more and more like two prisoners forced to share the same cell, each resenting the confinement and bored to death with the daily knowledge of the other's personal little quirks and mannerisms, the lack of privacy, the absence from their lives of the sheer luxury of being alone.

They had been thrown together by an indulgent but inconsiderate fate long before either of them could possibly know if that was what they really wanted, and they could find no way of extricating themselves from the entanglement. Their singular and spellbound life had become an irascible bondage, had spun rapidly awry into a succession of loud rattling perspiring nights amplified to the point of screaming, and exhausted daylight hours behind drawn curtains in cheap hotel rooms, punctuated by the distant shrill of telephones and trolleys trundling past their door. It was a pallid, unreal, hothouse existence, blinkered, insular, morbidly inward-growing despite the clamour and glare in which it was set. They shuttled along narrow grooves propelled by other hands, doing what was expected of them, sometimes reaching heights of near excellence and depths of positive mediocrity of which more often than not they themselves seemed to be the sole surveyors. They were shifted and moved from one place to the next, up and down and across, like pieces on a chess board; recording sessions were the worst of all, when for hours several times a day they would be locked inside soundproof glass cubicles, at the untender mercy of woodenfaced technicians, sound engineers, floor managers and countless lesser luminaries of the record trade, ensconced behind steel and chromium consoles of intricate dials and instrument panels, impassive and relentless as gods dictating their destiny, masterminding their every move, wheedling and bullying them into retake after retake, rendition after rendition, until they had reached the required pitch of electronic, disembodied perfection, synthesised and modified beyond recognition, until what came out at the other end, the processed finished product, sounded freakish and luridly unreal even to their own ears. Their talent seemed to rest entirely in the hands of others, a mechanical thing, a marvel of gadgetry and slick expertise erasing all trace of the original nervous exuberance. But much as they might resent and rail against such remote efficiency, such robot-like control and management of their basic desire simply to sing and make music, what they both secretly feared most was that the merciless momentum would slow down and one day stop altogether, leaving them standing stockstill and staring aghast at one another, free of the judicious restraint of commitment, unharnessed and at a loss to know what to do to fill up their days.

His talent, tentative as it was, had nonetheless seemed tough and resilient, a wiry growing thing capable of receiving hard knocks and of being buffeted about without wilting, without suffering serious damage. Was it now beginning to falter, to be eroded by doubt and hesitancy, spinning about in little webs of indecision and ending back in the same place, inside the same grey context? He had turned out about a dozen new songs in the last couple of months, new only in terms of time, each a paltry wretched parody of the one before it, full of fashionable, shrill and rather obvious protest, cheap cynicism and dissent, the melodic structure quavering and unemphatic, limp echoes of lines he had written and welded together several times before, weak variations on a theme that never seemed to change gear and remained stationary. Though he was too proud ever to admit it, she knew he craved her approval; she did not deliberately withhold it from him, but he would fall back dismayed and fuming when she felt she could not look him squarely in the face and tell him what he ached to hear, when the actual fruits of his labour were so unripe, so unpruned, the contents derivative and vapid. Seeing her groping for words, her face clouded with doubt, he would sit looking at her, bitter-eyed and trembling, waiting for her to pass sentence; after her first few faltering words he could not restrain his furious disappointment and would break out.

'Is that all you can do – criticise? Is it such a wrench for you to give me a bit of praise now and then? Or is that too much to ask?'

She would lift the hair from her eyes, sitting on the rug in front of the electric fire set in the grate, which they had put in to economise on the cost of the central heating. 'I'm only trying to help. If you want a fan club – '

His mouth settled into a savage grimace, looking down at her from the chair. 'A little praise – that's all I ask. Instead of which you do nothing but sneer.'

She flushed. 'I'm not in the habit of sneering – '

'You do nothing but make petty objections, time after time. My God, you're a great help, a real angel in need!'

'Look,' she would point out patiently, keeping her voice calm, 'if

I'm going to get up there and sing your songs, surely I have some sort of say in the matter?'

'That's it!' he cried, clutching instantly at the straw she had unwittingly held out to him, bending down towards her, harsh and accusing. 'That's just it! Your damn voice, your vocalising, the way you mangle every bloody line I write – that's where the real trouble lies! You trivialise everything!'

She could only stare back, too stunned to make any retort in her own defence. His face and voice became uglier.

'Cole Porter himself would sound like a poor pathetic hack the way you sing lyrics! Your idea of feeling is to croak like a frog with bronchitis – '

She would stare up into his face, numb and chill inside, no longer feeling the steady warmth of the electric bars on her cheeks and hands. He would glare back, defiant, unrepentant, but with the wounded look of an animal that had been brutally cast aside and rejected when it most needed to be flattered and petted and given gentle handling. The pages he had dropped from his lap as he sprang angrily out of the chair would curl up in heat beside her on the rug.

It had gone from bad to worse until all sensible critical discussion became impossible between them, degenerating into a slanging match, his reaction to even her most reasonable, most minor suggestion so vehement that soon she came to dread the times when he would show her his latest compositions and insist upon knowing what she thought of them. He would listen attentively at first, even make some quick scribbled note in the margins, as if resolved to be practical and mature about the whole thing; the façade would crumble, however, and the familiar pattern reassert itself – another heated row, another bout of embittered and absurd recriminations and hurt denials, followed by acrimonious silences that might last for hours or even days, depending upon how serious or how childish the original dispute had been. After such occasions they would be severely, elaborately polite and formal towards each other, going out of their respective ways to show how well-mannered and considerate they could be in attending to innumerable domestic little courtesies they would normally have found rib-tickling and hilarious, standing stiffly on ceremony on the most innocuous and routine of occasions. In work they had of necessity to be in tandem, and thereby found a welcome catharsis and relief of tension, but once back in the staid world beyond the footlights they would revert once more to polite, stolid mono-syllabic exchanges, keeping as far removed as possible, buried in a book or staring unseeing at television in chairs conspicuously wide apart, neither of them willing to make the first move to break the silent hostilities and dissolve into unconditional surrender. Rehearsals were another minefield to be traversed with the utmost caution; he was seldom satisfied with her interpretations, hard though she tried to follow his fervent and sometimes far from succinct leads, and his subsequent tantrums and accusations were so patently unfair that she built up an instinctive and stoical endurance against them, but sometimes, stung into retaliation, she would hit back, and because she so seldom gave vent to her feelings, her words carried a barbed accuracy that seldom failed to find target and make him flinch, taken off guard.

'Thank you,' he would utter grimly, standing stiffly before her; 'thank you so much for your vote of confidence. How can I fail with such a tower of strength behind me?' He would shut his eyes, a muscle jerking furiously in his jaw, as if forcing himself to be calm. 'What exactly do you object to, may I ask?'

She would then try to explain as impartially as she could the changes she thought should be made in either the lyrics or the melody under review, trying to defuse the argument that was brewing beneath the surface of their talk; but as she went on his face would darken, and he would flail the air with the bundle of knotted pages he held gripped in his fist.

'Typical!' he would pant, a hoarse cackle choking his voice. 'You and your bogus middle-class notion of what sort of things the great British public want to hear – oh, typical! D'you want to cut the balls out of everything I write so as to make it acceptable in the local bloody glee club in Tooting Bec?'

She could not help laughing, though she knew it would anger him more. 'Don't be absurd. That's not what I meant – '

He banged the table with his fist. 'That's exactly what you meant! Storm the citadels of Kingston-upon-Thames and nothing shall be denied you! Breach the ramparts of Ealing and victory is yours! Hammer down the stout doors of Ilford and the world is at your feet! Surbiton, here we come!'

'If you're quite finished with your geography lesson – ' She stood back, eyeing him with imposing sarcasm. 'God, you bore me, with your inverted working-class snobbery and self-proclaimed right to be obnoxious. Poor little under-privileged you! Why don't you just wrap yourself in the red flag and have done with it?'

He would shake with even greater wrath under her sardonic appraisal. 'You – you're incapable of objective evaluation, of constructive criticism. You and your delicate preconceived ideas and maxims, your distrust and abhorrence of things outside your neat respectable background – '

'Which would surely include you, don't you think?'

'Me?' he would laugh, shrugging. 'Oh, I was a mere aberration, something you'll correct and discard in time, I'm sure. God, if you only heard yourself at times – !'

'You don't mean to say you do? Never once have you listened to a word I said – '

'And why the hell should I? What you know about music could be put on a pinhead. Scrap what you don't understand or approve – that's your motto, your golden principle. Scrap, scrap, scrap – Christ, you should be in the junk business!'

'I thought that's precisely what we are in.'

'I don't know why in God's name I bother to show you anything at all – '

'Why do you, then? Why in God's name do you?'

For moments they would stand and glare at one another, like implacable adversaries, she with controlled, resolute anger, hands clenched tightly at her sides, he pale, trembling, incoherent, striving for ever more telling, more inventive and resounding invective; then he would twist away and either fling himself on the bed to glower silently at the ceiling, as if all his woes and tribulations were focused there, or else he would dash out of the room with a muttered curse and be gone for hours, finally shambling back dishevelled and half-drunk, struggling to remain silent and wronged, pretending not to notice she was there, taking elaborate care not to bump into things. Then he would break down and in a maudlin torrent tell her what a bastard he was, how miserable he had been going from one faceless bar to the next, how much he loved her and would she for God's sake forgive him before he went completely out of his mind. She would hold back, still smarting, hurt, jealous of the time he had spent away from her, not willing to give up her anger so easily; but hearing the raw wretched self-reproach and anguish in his voice, she would be moved to tears herself, and turning to him would take him in her arms, sharing his misery and glad capitulation, overwhelmed by the renewed intensity of their love for each other, convinced all over again that nothing else mattered as long as they loved and were together. They would cling, kissing as though for the first or last time, fumbling with their clothes, laughing, crying, vowing, pleading, and tottering together like two drunks, would fall upon the bed, riven with need, and feast upon their love, lightheaded and insatiable after too long a fast.

The windowpane was striped and stippled with tiny zig-zag rivulets of rain, turning the world outside to a kaleidoscope of broken, quivering images; in the street below the garbage truck had arrived lumbering its way from house and shop, collecting brimming bins left outside on wet pavements like grotesque offerings. She saw the yellow-oilskinned workmen slouching about, hoisting the bins shoulder-high, tipping the rubbish into the mechanical chute of the truck to be churned and crushed by the rapacious steel jaws of the machine and carted away to incinerators and municipal dumping sites, just as the devious industrious denizens of the catacombed city would one day be disposed of in much the same manner, their bones deposited in the earth under useless stone monuments engraved with their brief histories or burned to insignificant ash.

She raised the mug to her lips, and made a face: the tea had gone cold and tepid. In the bed behind her he had begun to snore again.

12

ONCE again, they had met entirely by chance. Now they strolled through the park, not saying much, constrained, diffident, each well aware that they were now on a new and very different footing, and looked to the other for the help and understanding in coping with it that, obscurely, neither of them could give. Soon after they had met that morning, she had told him about her career and her marriage. He had looked at her steadily.

She tried to meet his gaze, but could not, and felt angry with him and herself. 'Oh, I just don't know about happiness. Not at this stage anyway.' Then she went on, 'It's much too nice a day to stand here discussing things that might never happen. We're wasting all that sunshine, and it's a sin.' And impetuously she had slipped her arm through his and they had started off through the still quiet and relatively traffic-free Sunday morning streets, he with a sort of studious steadfast dejection manfully borne, and she determined to talk of other things and not being very successful.

So they walked slowly in the park now, catching occasional glimpses through the trees of groups of riders strung out in a line, all togged out in equestrian finery, moving at a leisurely canter, the coats of their steeds shining like burnished leather in the morning sun.

She felt embarrased as they walked along arm in arm, like figures from a bygone age, but since it was she who had first made the gesture she could not very well withdraw her arm now without needlessly offending him. After a while, however, and much to her relief, he seemed to become aware of her unease and quietly took his arm away, walking beside her with hands clasped behind him and his eyes on the ground, like someone on his way to an appointment he did not want to keep, until they found a bench on which to sit.

'What a gorgeous day!' she exclaimed, unable to contain any longer her inner joy and her pleasure in the scene around her. She drew a deep breath, drawing in the sharp clear air greedily as if it were wine. 'Isn't it just lovely, this time of year?'

'Yes,' he answered slowly, lifting his eyes and looking about him with obvious lack of interest. 'Yes, it is.' He lapsed back into silence.

'Tell you what, Richard,' she said, swinging back her hair from the side of her face, 'let's go down by the river – shall we?' She made it sound like an invitation, an enticement that no healthy male could reasonably decline.

He shrugged. 'All right, if you like.'

She glanced sideways at him, his gloom communicating itself to her, and made a new effort to steer both of them away from the hazards and potent dangers of remaining silent for too long.

'You've hardly spoken a word about what you're doing now,' she said, putting her hands under her knees on the bench and swinging her feet. 'Have you by any chance entered the Trappist order since I saw you last?'

He smiled. 'Hardly. I'm afraid that would be against my religion anyway – not that I'm very sure what that is.'

'In one of your letters you said something about getting a job on a newspaper. Is that still on?'

'You mean you not only receive my letters but actually read them?' he said, trying to make a joke of it but unable to keep a note of irony from creeping into his voice. He looked down, abashed. 'I'm sorry. That was childish of me.' He looked out at the river, where a few sedate little family cabin cruisers had begun to chug along, raising a soft milky spray in their wake. 'Yes, one of the small local papers. I do odd jobs, teaboy and occasional cub reporter rolled into one. I still have the job at the garage, of course. It brings in the pennies.'

'But the writing – you haven't given that up?' she asked quickly, studying his face.

'It gives you up sometimes,' he replied, 'rather than the other way round. I'm still dabbling in it. It isn't so easy to give up.'

'Won't you let me read something?' she asked, aggrieved. 'I did ask you before.'

'Surely you wouldn't have the time?'

She looked at him to see if he was mocking her, but his face was solemn.

'I'd make the time,' she replied quietly. 'You mustn't think it's all one mad hectic scramble up and down the country, you know. It gets really rather boring at times, and I do have lots of moments to myself. So there's no real or valid reason why you shouldn't send me on something.'

'If you like.'

'I do like!' she flung back hotly, then relented. 'You know I'd love to read anything you've written.'

'I doubt that very much.'

He was silent, gazing out at the bustle that was beginning to take place up and down the river, small braggart boats veering away from their moorings, low din of engines, thin blare of horns rising in the air.

'All right,' he announced, as if coming to a carefully thought-out decision. 'I will send you on something – don't know what – as long as it's on the clear understanding that you brought it on yourself.'

'Done!' She held out her hand, palm upwards; he looked at it a moment, grinned and smacked his own palm down gently.

'But what about addresses?' he asked. 'Don't you flit about rather a lot, even if it's not a mad scramble?'

'We always leave a forwarding address,' she said. 'Not that we are exactly inundated by fan mail, of course,' she laughed, 'but we haven't lost touch with the outside world.'She looked at him, happy. 'I wonder what you'll send me to read?'

'God knows. Bits and pieces,' he added vaguely, and smiled. 'You will then see how truly bad I am.'

'I'll take that chance.'

'I had no idea you were so brave.'

She poked a funny face at him. 'Oh, in my business you soon develop a very thick skin.' She looked steadily at him, trying to discern his mood. 'But you will send me something, Richard, won't you?'

He nodded. 'Yes, I will.'

And on that, because in spite of everything she had a date with Art, they parted.

187

13

SHE heard the bedsprings creak behind her as he stirred and sat up, giving several loud yawns

'What time is it?' he asked sleepily.

'About twelve,' she replied, not turning around as she stood by the window, the empty mug in her hand.

'What's it doing outside?' He threw the quilt to one side and swung his legs over the edge of the bed, his feet just touching the floor; he rubbed his eyes and looked about him, as if not quite knowing where he was.

'The rain's cleared,' she announced.

'Ah, good.' He passed a hand over his mouth. 'God, I'm parched. Made tea, did you?'

'Yes, but that was hours ago. It's stewed by now.'

'What were you doing, up so early?'

'Couldn't sleep.'

'Didn't you take a sleeper or something?'

'I suppose I must have.'

He chuckled. 'You mean you don't remember?'

'I mean it doesn't matter. I just couldn't sleep, that's all.'

He saw the irritable movement of her shoulders as she stood still with her back to him, draped in the nightgown. 'All right – don't snap my head off.' He sank back against the pillows. 'I only asked.' He looked across at her for a few moments. 'Are you coming back to bed, love?'

'No.'

'Well, that's the end of that conversation.' He smoothed out the pillow behind him with his fist. 'What exactly do you plan to do for the next couple of hours – just stand there like Lot's wife? At least *she* turned to salt, which was tasty enough, when all's said and done.'

She made no response, framed in the weak light of the window, and he continued his silent appraisal of her, seeing how her hair hung loose, reaching almost to her waist, the outline of her jaw sharp, poignant, vulnerable; he wanted to touch it, very gently, and trace with his thumb and forefinger its thin, delicate contour, as he had done so often before, sometimes as she slept. He wanted to perform so many small, tender, unostentatious ministrations, to delight in small flatteries and homage that she might find pleasing, apart from the grander and grosser imperatives of love; yet it made him sad and angry to realise how blithely unaware she most often was of his rapt and silent observations, of how avidly he followed her every movement and gestures with his eyes; it was galling to him to have to give mere utterance to his feelings and clothe them raggedly in words before she could become aware of them or even realise that he had them, for transmuted and altered by language they became staid and banal, like precious and piquant essences corked and labelled in a bottle, robbed of their unique and indefinable freshness. For days at a time, or so it seemed to him, she went about oblivious of him, acknowledging the commonplace observances of everyday and nothing more, as if she inhabited a separate space, a separate world that only marginally included him, cast in the rôle of an unavoidable stranger, an inessential piece of furniture in a very private living-room of her own, that pleased her vaguely whenever she chanced or chose to notice it, but which most of the time made little impression upon her. He smiled at his own exaggerations, however, and turned on his side, still watching her.

'And what have you been thinking about all this time – anarchy and murder?'

'You wouldn't be interested.'

'Oh, but I would!' he exclaimed stoutly. 'How can you say that? Nothing you do is alien to me, to pinch a phrase from some old Roman or other who had nothing better to do with himself than think up clever things to say.'

She remained enclosed in thought by the window, staring down into the street already well into its midday bustling stride and clamour; wan shafts of sunlight were trying ineffectually to break through the leaden clouds, making the raindrops that still clung to the windowpane glisten and flare with minute brilliancy. Then she turned her head slightly, looking over her shoulder at him as he lolled in bed, smiling serenely across at her.

'Do you remember making love?'

Her voice was low, calm, conversational, yet the question struck him like a blow aimed and delivered with expert timing, catching him offguard, jolting him; before he could counter or put his thoughts into any semblance of order he had babbled forth the fatal rejoinder:

'When?'

The smile on his face still lingered like a ghastly mask as she turned about and looked at him fully, her fingers gripping the mug; even in her mute anger, in the swarming midst of her resentment and barbed sense of betrayal, she could not help thinking how comical he looked in his string vest and bedraggled under-shorts, his thin hairy legs and the few squiggly hairs on his bony chest, so that she felt like laughing and crying out in rage and ridicule. She turned and went into the kitchen, leaving him staring stupidly after her; soon he heard the babble of rock music as she snapped the transistor radio on, then the slam of the bathroom door.

'Christ,' he muttered, feeling the skin on his face tighten and grow taut as the transfixed smile left it.

He remembered, of course, almost as soon as she had asked him, and certainly long before she had left the room; he recalled the hot pulsing need of her that had pervaded his torpor, rousing him to fumble for her nearness half in dream and half awake, the fantasy flaring livid and alive against him, lyrical and filling him utterly; he remembered, but it was by then too late, the unforgivable sin had been committed and he was unequivocally condemned.

He lay back and stared balefully at the ceiling, cursing himself, feeling like a mutant, a criminal, a rapist almost, found guilty of an act of abject and obscene depravity and defilement so that he would never be able to look her straight in the eye again. All he wanted now was to somehow squirm and burrow his way out of the net of existence and escape into nothingness; the knowledge of his own brute callousness pressed down upon him like chains, oppressive and insupportable. Then other more amenable thoughts came to his rescue and relief, ameliorating the anguish somewhat, making his fall from grace less absolute, less precipitous and horrific to his mind; he began to feel aggrieved. After all, he reasoned, he was surely not the first in the history of humankind to nod off to sleep during a feast, however lavish and sumptuous, and stumble into oblivion while the party was at its loudest and most profligate. Men and women had been making love, he assured the ceiling and unanswering walls, in various states of derangement and delirium ever since the human form evolved and crawled out of the primeval slime, dreaming as they made love and making love as they dreamt, sustained and impelled by one narcotic or another, real or imagined. So what the hell did it matter if whisky softened and obscured the sharper edges of love's remembrance; was he supposed to recall every damn sign, landmark and milestone of the journey on the way to the summit? And anyway, were her own feelings so fastidious, so refined and exquisite, and of such an aesthetic tone as to be irreparably blunted and plunged into abysmal disarray by so ordinary an aberration as that which had overtaken him? He climbed sourly out of bed, pulled a robe round him and stalked into the kitchen, ready to be as strident as he had to be in his own defence.

The muted bedlam of the radio came from the bathroom above the splash of the shower; he tried the door, but found it locked from the inside. He called out, loud and angry, and, receiving no reply, rattled the handle; then realising the futility of it, he gradually overcame an almost irresistible urge to smash every cup and saucer in sight, put on some water to make tea, sat down at the table and tried heroically to organise his thoughts.

They needed to get away, abscond for a while from the whole killing scene of playing one-night stands, fulfilling dates at half-empty halls, travelling half the night from one nameless place to another, dropping into bed exhausted at all hours, stumbling about like automatons; the whole business was getting to them in the worst possible way, until now they had had practically no real say in the running of their own lives. They needed to get right away, down to the country perhaps, a countryside that remained largely unknown and invisible to them as often as they had traversed it in their nomadic pursuit of recognition and livelihood, rattling and trundling along in the creaking almost decade-old estate car that ferried them from one engagement to the next, through half the night or early dawn, passing through market towns and villages large and small, through some of the loveliest natural scenery in the land, as if blindfolded, muffled, sealed in their skins, too tense and expectant on the way to a stage performance, too depleted and insensitised on the way back, thinking of nothing save journey's end, one more stiff drink, and bed, sleep, forgetfulness. They shuttled and scurried through the countryside like soulless hawkers anxious to sell their wares to the highest bidder, ignorant of the wonders they passed, minds parcelled and crimped by commerce, with always an impersonal, imperative voice telling them what to do, carving up their days and nights into precise compartments, bullying their existence with shrewd and alluring tyranny.

They needed to apply the brakes, halt, come to a full and uncompromising stop and gather together their few remaining wits before they spun headlong into still deeper chaos and uncertainty. They needed to cast everything aside for a fortnight or so, escape to some place the mapmakers had blessedly overlooked, to say nothing of those other myth-makers, the ingenious practical pranksters who devised and distributed their catalogue of glittering deceptions, the glossy holiday hymnbooks that annually inundated the land with their gross fantasies of sylvan tranquillity and vistas of Eden-like glory. The scene, the scenario unfolded slowly and clearly in his mind . . . a ramshackle country inn of beguiling decrepitude, watched over by a couple of elderly guardians of the peace, deep in a sleepy hamlet of crooked runaway streets and granite-faced aged cottages, with little bright gardens and lace-fringed windows, where the most dramatic thing to happen would be the spectacle of the local scholar, the schoolmaster, a cadaverous, melancholic bachelor, of course, rambling home of a twilight Saturday evening moist-eyed and bardic with ale to his desolate monkish abode, quoting Shakespeare and Donne to the hedges and cobblestones and the faithful stray dog that never left him, lyrical in his cups, lifting his ruinous countenance to the flying moon beseechingly; or again, the local red-jowled pot-bellied bobby being fetched to talk sense to the sinewy, choleric blacksmith spitting fire and marvellous venom in his smoky forge over some immemorial insult to the family name uttered in hazy times by some long-dwelling inhabitant of the local churchyard, ritually recalled by an incautious intake of rum . . . It was all so clear and real to him, he wanted to go and relate it to her there and then, certain that she would be as fired as he was by the image, and as eager to turn it into reality.

It would not be anything as banal and mundane as a holiday, he decided; it would, in fact, be the honeymoon that they had never had, an interlude of idyllic idleness that would not in the least be idle, full as it would surely be of small happy discoveries about each other which they had never been able to make before because of the pace of their lives; it would be a time to take slow, grateful stock of their world, a leisurely inventory of the good things in it, sifting and casting out the dross, in no hurry to speed the process of finding one another again. They would be free of sly, iniquitous intrusions and demands, released from the false euphoria and security of work, its daily deadening tedium, its fraying tensions and insinuations; free from hyperbole, facile praise, the murderous rotation of flattery and promise that kept them running, that buoyed them up as much as the meretricious stimulation of alcohol, that store of suspect bottled blessings, the unending round of fatuous, unrecollected parties singularly devoid of celebration, the awful compulsion to surround themselves with near strangers, with human and emotional bric-à-brac, and when they were at last alone, deafened by the silence of each other, with hardly a word, thought or coherent, genuine feeling to share and explore, passing in remote orbit, obliquely, veering away at the least imminent point of contact. Their conflict was not insignificant, was not shallow or unsubstantial, and certainly did not exclude real pain, yet at root it originated out of their basic inability to sit quietly together in a room and not want anything other than that small magical circumstance; it was as simple, as sad, as comic and terrifying as that, and with a sense of panic he wondered what either of them could do about it before the estrangement became unbreakable.

He was jerked out of reverie as the kettle began to hiss on the stove; he got up and poured most of the boiling water into the smaller pot, putting in the tea; turning to sit back down to wait while the tea drew, he gave another slight start, seeing her in the bathroom doorway, her hair a damp amber cloud about her face, the robe clinging to her wet body; he became aware of the profound stillness, the radio no longer blaring; breadcrumbs on the checkered tablecloth, the thin hum of the refrigerator, faint grease marks on the wall above the stove; he stood rooted, tremulous, his mind held by a sudden intense piercing conception of her disconsolate beauty, hearing his own heart.

'I'm making some tea,' he managed to say at last, feeling his throat dry; he drew out a chair for her at the table. 'Fancy a cup?'

'Please.' She came forward, leaving wet footprints on the linoleum, and sat down, drawing the front of the robe more tightly about her. 'Are you hungry?'

'Er – no, not very,' he answered, his voice still unsteady.

'I can make you a omelette if you like, or there's some meatloaf left in the fridge – '

'No, thanks, not just yet.'

He picked up the enamel tea-caddy, adorned with a Victorian engraving of a royal procession in plumed carriage-and-pair, and toyed with it idly, standing on the other side of the table, his fingers tapping out a thin rhythm, not looking at her now and hoping his face bore a suitably grave and preoccupied expression to mask the strange turmoil he felt within.

She joined her fingers together on the table in front of her, eyes lowered. 'I'm sorry I made such a fuss just now. It was very silly of me.'

'No, it wasn't,' he countered, as if rushing hastily to her defence against a crass outsider who was accusing her of some heinous transgression. 'It wasn't silly at all.' He frowned. 'It was boorish of me – not to remember, I mean,' he amended, embarrassed, but determined to square up to his own lack of grace. 'A man shouldn't forget something like that so easily.'

She smiled faintly. 'Neither should a woman, don't you think?' She raised her eyes.

'Er – no, I suppose not,' he uttered, slightly nonplussed, putting the tea-caddy down on the table. 'But it's usually the man who does the forgetting, if we are to believe the best novelists.' He sat down. 'I'm sorry too. It wasn't like the way it sounded, believe me.'

'Oh, it doesn't signal the end of the world, either way, whether we remember or forget.' Her voice sounded tired.

'But isn't it better that we should remember? I mean,' he said, leaning earnestly forward, frowning again, 'if we forget so easily something that's supposed to be so meaningful – well, where's the magic and mystery of it, then?'

She pressed her joined fingers more closely together. 'Perhaps there's no magic or mystery in it. Maybe it should all be quite functional, like food or sleep or going to the supermarket at weekends.'

'You don't really believe that, though, do you?'

'Right now I'm quite ready to believe almost anything.'

He studied his neatly pared fingernails, noting the way his right thumb and forefinger were calloused from guitar playing. 'I've been thinking, Jan.' He paused, hoping for some murmur of encouragement from her, but she remained silent. 'How do you feel about getting away for a while?'

'Away from what?'

He looked at her, baffled and hurt. 'From what? Why, the whole bloody scene, the whole grind and slog. We need to get away from it for a while.'

'Together?'

His eyebrows positively shot up. 'Together? Of course – do you have to ask?'

'I wanted to make sure I knew what you meant.'

'For God's sake, do you think I'd want to go haring off somewhere on my own, without you?' She regarded him steadily, as if on the point of saying something, but stayed silent. 'Well, what do you think?'

Her face was pale, impassive, brows dark and level over lowered eyes. 'What do I think about what?'

He drew the corners of his mouth tightly, exasperated. 'About what I've just been saying. Chucking everything aside for a while, getting away, out of bloody London, leaving the whole damn thing behind – Simon, work, people – everything.'

Her voice when it came was distant, polite. 'Oh, that.'

He waited, staring at her. 'Is that all you can say?' he pressed when she still did not speak.

'If I knew what it was you wanted me to say, then maybe I could say it, with a little effort.'

'And why should it be with an effort? Can't you try to understand what I'm trying to say?'

'I don't. I don't understand at all.'

There was a certain calm finality in her voice, completely devoid of artifice, that made it the more strange and disconcerting for him to hear, and her face told him nothing.

'Look,' he continued patiently, 'all I'm saying is, we need – '

'I think the tea should be ready by now.'

His face darkened. 'Oh, to hell with the bloody tea!'

He glared at her, then sprang up, almost knocking over the chair. He visibly steadied himself and went about pouring out the two cups of tea, sugaring then and adding milk with grim precision, placed the pot back on the stove, flicked the off switch, and sat down again, crossing his arms.

'Let's start again.' He looked at her over the steam rising from his cup. 'I think we both need a break.'

'And I must ask you again – a break from what?'

'Don't you think you're being a bitch?'

She held the cup delicately in both hands and lifted it to her lips, sipping. 'Possibly, though that wasn't my intention.'

'Then what the hell is your intention? Can't you just say what you think of the idea, instead of sitting there looking like a dispossessed sphinx?'

'You know as well as I do,' she said slowly, her voice not rising above a whisper intimate and clear, 'that we both want to hear the right thing from each other, only the right thing, all the time, though not necessarily in the same context, or even in the same room.'

He picked up his cup and noisily gulped down tea. 'When you're finished with your second-hand aphorisms and kindergarten riddles, I'd still like to hear what you think. I'm being serious, believe it or not, but it's not easy with you in your present frame of mind.'

'I don't think I'm in any particular frame of mind, and I know you're being serious. So am I, except I think perhaps we're being serious about different things, and certainly in quite different ways.'

He studied her for a while, the lines of his face hard, fingers of one hand stroking his beard. 'All right,' he said at length, measuring her mood, at once probing and incurious; 'so we inhabit separate rooms, do we? Fair enough. Now tell me – ' he bent forward again – 'is there a communicating door in between?'

She put down her cup. 'That's something we should try to find out by degrees, don't you think?'

He spread out his hands in mocking ingenuous fashion. 'You mean you want to know what *I* think? I didn't think that was of the least importance to you.'

'Which shows again your uncanny penchant for being wrong.'

He got up abruptly and began pacing up and down, no longer willing to be intimidated by her fresh newly-washed proximity, the awareness of her nakedness beneath the robe flowing over him in small sharp brilliant eddies of muted need, swaying his resolution to remain distanced and on an even keel. He went to the small kitchen window and paused, looking out over neighbouring rooftops and the far glitter of glass towers.

'It must be marvellous to be so self-sufficient,' he said, 'if a little daunting at times.' He dropped the print-patterned chintz curtain and resumed his pacing. 'I mean, it must make you feel – well, isolated from your fellow-man, from the majority of ordinary mortals.'

'And you think that's what I am, self-sufficient?'

He stopped, hands clasped behind back, and looked at her. 'Well, aren't you? I mean, isn't it obvious? If you're not, then all I can say is, you give a brilliant imitation of it.'

'You're wrong, you know, quite wrong.'

He shrugged and went on moving about the room. 'Perhaps, since I seem to be wrong about most things, according to you. I think I'm just about right this time, however.' He looked across at her again, shrewd, hawk-like. 'You need nobody. Did you know that? Nobody. Your life is something you can handle quite well on your own. Other people are a mere interference, a nuisance, something you've learnt to tolerate and put up with over the years, but which you could happily do without tomorrow. Sufficient unto yourself, over and above all else. That's you.'

Her eyes took on a wistful humour as she followed his perambulations around the kitchen. 'You make me out to be a real repository of wisdom, Methuselah's wife with shades of Cleopatra, a mixture of Lolita and the old woman who lived in a shoe.'

'That places you in rather choice company, then.'

'And hopelessly out of my depth. You mightn't choose to believe it, but I'm just as confused as you are. I feel like screaming my head off at times for no reason, or for the strongest reason of all – I'm scared.'

'You, scared? Oh, don't give me that!' He tugged fiercely at the tufted point of his beard. 'Your life is a solo that needs no accompaniment. You play it best on your own.'

She sat sombre and remote in the chair. 'If only that were true,' she murmured, half to herself, then she laughed lightly. 'But I wouldn't want it to be true anyway. I'd be at a loss to know what to do with all that wisdom, and no one to share it with.'

They both fell silent, and it seemed a long while before either spoke again; in the early afternoon hush, with city sounds muted, the electric whirr of the squat refrigerator in the corner by the sink almost grated; the sun had finally ousted the clouds and shone bright and new, throwing patterns on the floor from the window, and casting reflections on the ceiling from some water that remained in the sink. When she did speak once more her voice could have belonged to someone else, so neutral and estranged it sounded from everything she was feeling.

'Would a baby help, do you think, or would it only complicate matters still further?'

He turned slowly about to face her. 'A baby?'

'Yes.' She reached both hands behind her, lifting the heavy wet rope of hair from her neck and twisting it into several sleek coils to hang down her back. 'I'm asking you if you think we ought to have a child.'

He sat down. 'I never thought of a child.'

'You mean it never occurred to you that I might get pregnant one day?'

He crossed his arms again, his face sulky. 'Oh, don't think me a complete bloody fool. Of course it occurred to me. But we've always been careful, haven't we?'

'Yes, of course, but has it never occurred to you that I might not *want* to be careful, one day?'

He stared at her, his eyes seeming to be very far back in his head. 'You mean you want a baby?'

'I mean it's possible that I might, one day.'

He looked at her almost with dismay, unbelieving. 'But don't you know what that would mean? It would destroy everything we've been building up.'

'Our singing, you mean?'

'Our career, yes. Our whole career. Having a kid would put an end to all that.'

'No, it wouldn't, Art,' she said quietly. 'It would only mean that I would give up singing.'

'Well, yes, isn't that what I mean? We'd end up in the middle of nowhere, like millions of other couples, saddled with a family, and after that mortgages and building society loans and all that kind of shit is only a matter of time. Why throw up our career for all that? There must be easier ways of committing suicide.'

'I wouldn't be throwing up a career, Art, since it's my firm belief that I don't have one.'

He gave an exaggerated groan. 'Oh, Christ, not that again! We've been through all that before – '

'That's just the point, Art. We haven't. It's something we never really talk about. We sidestep it each time. We walk around it, look at it out of the corner of our eye, but we never talk about it. Don't you think it's time we did?'

'What's the damn use?' You know my views on it. We'd only be going round in circles, coming back to the same point. You just seem intent on wrecking our career. Before it was because you thought your voice was going. Now it's because all of a sudden you want to be a mother.' He gave a dour mirthless laugh. 'What will it be tomorrow, I wonder? Maybe you'll have a sudden overwhelming desire to be a lady parachutist or take a sudden all-consuming interest in the social habits of earwigs. It's just one bloody caprice after another with you.'

She smiled. 'It's the first time I've ever been accused of being capricious. The idea appeals to me, though I'm afraid I wouldn't be able to live up to it. The thing is, Art, I know I'll never be anything other than average, whereas I'm convinced you can go on and really achieve something as a songwriter without having to make your songs tailor-made for me. I really do feel that's the crux of the situation.'

He smiled sourly. 'Thanks for the vote of confidence, and your honesty does you credit, but where exactly does that leave us? Do you think I can just forget everything we've managed to do together and start from scratch all over again? Just turn about and start off in a new direction, like getting into a new suit of clothes, or moving to another part of town?'

'I'm sorry, Art, but I can't put it any better than how I've already tried. I never stopped believing that you'd do much better working on your own, and I still believe that, perhaps more than ever now.'

He stood behind a kitchen chair, gripping the back of it. 'And you're not pregnant?'

She laughed. 'God, no. I'm not pregnant. It has very little to do with that, anyway. I feel I just can't contribute very much any more to our work together, to the music, which from now on, I think, should be *your* music. That being the case, the idea, if not the fact, of my having a baby appears less horrendous or destructive, since it wouldn't interfere with anything – at least not in a professional way.'

'You think not? I've been writing crap now for the last couple of months – we both know that – and so you think I'd work better with a squalling infant in the background?'

'Oh, if there was a child I'd keep it well out of earshot, though I've heard it said some people do work better under duress.'

'Not me – not bloody me, I can tell you. Put a gun to my head, and in next to no time I'd be begging you to pull the trigger.' He looked at her with dark, troubled eyes, fingers abstractedly rubbing his beard, perplexed and pensive at once; he crossed to her side of the table, pulled out a chair and sat down, taking her hand. 'You're not just being maternal, are you, love?'

'That wouldn't be so awful, would it, so unusual? But no, I'm not. I don't think I'm a particularly maternal person, on the whole. Maybe I could grow into one, but I really don't think we should be asking ourselves that kind of question at this moment. It's not the issue, is it?'

He sighed, stroking her hand, determined to be gentle, patient, considerate. 'What is the issue, then? Is it that you want to – sorry, but I can't think of any better way of putting it – is it that you want to "normalise" our life a bit more – is it by having a kid you think I'd become more responsible – something along those lines?'

She looked steadily into his face. 'Nothing was further from my mind. I'm afraid I'm a much more selfish person than perhaps you might already think.'

He ceased stroking her hand. 'What do you mean?'

She saw the hurt, the puzzled suspicion in his eyes, and hated it, but felt she had no option save to go on. 'I mean that whatever reasons I might have for wanting a baby, or for wanting or doing anything else for that matter, would first and foremost have to be my own. The decision would have to be mine, as well as the consequences. To do anything merely to please or interest someone else nearly always turns out a disaster, or at the very least a sad mistake.'

He pushed away his chair and stood up. 'I see. And so I don't enter into your calculations, is that it – I don't figure in your neat little list of priorities?'

'I'm not saying that at all. Not in the least. You have something to do with everything in my life, with most of what I feel and think and do. But don't you see, Art, it is *my* life, just as your life should belong to you before it can even remotely belong to anyone else or include other people in it – don't you see that? Isn't that the only way it can be?'

He shrugged, looking down at her. 'It seems to me we're not only talking at cross purposes – we're thinking at cross purposes, too, and there's no bloody future in that.' He went towards the door, shaking his head. 'No bloody future at all.' He stopped at the door and turned. 'I'm going to have a drink, which just happens to be one of *my* priorities right now. What about you?'

'Must you always run away?'

'Run away? Oh, for Christ's sake don't be so melodramatic.'

'Can't you for once stay put and talk things out, even if we don't reach anything as spectacular as conclusions?'

'What's the point? As you said earlier, all either of us want is to hear the right thing from each other, the thing that satisfies us most, and as of this moment the only thing that will afford me any satisfaction, of however sordid a kind, is a drink.' He paused once more. 'Sure I can't tempt you with one?'

'No, thank you. I need no temptation in that direction. We must be ready to leave by six at the latest, remember.'

He nodded. 'Ah yes – for Brighton, its Regency charm and bracing air. You could say it's just down the road.'

'Except that it isn't, and it's your turn to do the driving.'

He waved gaily. 'Oh, don't worry your adorable little head, my sweet. By six o'clock I will have drunk myself into a state of disgusting sobriety.'

He went on into the bedroom, not closing the door, and presently she heard the clink of glass and bottle, then the strains of a jazz solo as he put on a record, making small private comments and exclamations of pleasure at certain favourite passages. She caught glimpses of him through the door, padding about, glass in hand, eyes closed, nodding his head emphatically as he listened to the music. She stretched out on the table, resting her head on her arms wearily, wishing the day would get on with its dull progress of becoming night again, and feeling that they had hardly uttered or exchanged a single word.

14

THE ticking of a clock had always appealed to him; it was a companionable sound, a soporific accompaniment to the gradual easing of the senses into slumber, a friendly murmur of reassurance in the loneliest hour, in the loneliest room, that even the worst conflicts and aggravations of the day could last only so long and, like everything else upon earth, must diminish and subside with the inexorable passage of time. He remembered how, as a child, he would wander about in his father's first jewellery shop, fascinated by all the glittering treasures laid out on little beds of velvet and in display cases, exquisite watches and miniature clocks of meticulous craftsmanship, and pausing he would bend an ear to listen to their mechanical heartbeats, some louder or softer than others and all in their distinct, modulating and changing tone as he slowly turned his head above them, listening first with one ear, then with the other. Sometimes, when trade was quiet and in the doldrums, and there were few people coming and going, he would stand still and listen intently to the busy chatter of the clocks and watches, setting up a decorous concourse from every nook and corner of the shop, looming and receding as he moved his head; often he fancied he was standing on some desolate shore hearing the distant rhythm of waves, infinitely soothing and persuasive, leaving small tranquil echoes trembling in the air, and hated the harsh clanging of the doorbell when at last a potential customer entered.

Tonight, however, the beat of the clock on the bedside table reminded him more and more of a time-bomb, primed and ready to explode at any second, ticking with even louder menace, booming, filling the room with commotion, jangling his tight-strung nerves, creating trapped havoc. The nocturnal stillness throughout the house was intrusive, permeated with threat, so that unwillingly he found himself straining to catch the least sound, the least punctuation or interruption of that ordinary silence, like one keeping a death vigil and morbidly aware of the erratic breathing of the dying person, wondering when the end would come.

He felt his skin beginning to cloy with sweat. Seldom did he find any difficulty in getting off to sleep, at times boasting that sleep came to him as it would to an innocent child; rarely did he have to resort to sleeping tablets or tranquillisers, to which he had in any case a superstitious aversion, a peculiarly old-fashioned distrust. An hour earlier, though, tossing and turning, strangely restless and agitated, he had broken the pattern and taken two pills, washed down with a generous glass of port, and had settled back on the pillows to wait for the expected languid slide into welcome oblivion.

To his chagrin, the potion had somehow merely heightened his edgy alertness, so that to his senses the faintest creak, the faintest shadow or rustle became magnified, alien, brooding; to remain as he was, clamped between the sheets, prey to absurd and hideous fancies, became suddenly intolerable, a meaningless act of self-torture; it was like embracing celibacy and abstinence simply because he was alone and all opportunity of pandering to his sensual nature momentarily out of reach.

Flinging aside the quilt, he sat up, switched on the table lamp and reached for the book he had been reading, only to discover he had finished it the night before; he swore under his breath as the culprit clock told him it had gone a quarter to one in the morning. The lamp threw a warm soft penumbra around the bed, cocooning him, but beyond stealthy shadows seemed to move and sway, the curtains stirred as if concealing peering intruders; he told himself repeatedly he was being foolish, boyish, absurd, but to no avail; the imagined dervishes would not be driven away by mere logic. He was scarcely what he himself would have described as gregarious, or inclined in any real sense to unburden himself to others, but at that moment Sandford felt a keen urge – amounting almost to panic – to talk to someone, even if he had little or nothing at all to say or communicate. He at once thought of ringing up Marcie, if only to hear her voice, then he remembered with flagging spirit that she had told him she would be spending the weekend down in the country somewhere with some close relatives who had recently returned from a sojourn in Canada with enough money to re-establish themselves in their native land. He knew his wife was in the next bedroom, just down the hallway, but she was most probably asleep by now, and he realised that in any event he would simply not be able to talk to Elinor, no matter how obediently she might listen; it would be akin to invading the hushed privacy of a perennial invalid on the flimsy pretext of finding out if she was feeling any better. He decided he would go downstairs to the library, find some ponderous tome of suitably esoteric content more or less guaranteed to induce coma, and armed with a full glass of brandy perhaps, return to bed and quick unconsciousness.

He threw a nightrobe loosely over his pyjamas and, finding his slippers, left the room and made his way carefully down the corridor that led to the staircase, making as little noise as possible; he had always been as scrupulous about the privacy of others as he was about his own, and for that reason did not switch on any lights. At the same time he detected a faint glow at the end of the hallway that drew him, and somewhat to his surprise found that it came from his wife's bedroom, a thin yellow streak leaking from under her door. Reaching it, he paused outside, puzzled that she might still be awake at that hour, wondering if she was all right or if she needed anything, yet reluctant to disturb or in any other way intrude upon her. He remained listening for a while, hearing nothing, and judging that she had simply fallen asleep over a book and left the light burning, he turned to continue on his way to the staircase. Then a sound did reach him, coming from Elinor's room, subdued, inarticulate, as of someone murmuring or weeping in their sleep. He stood on the landing, mystified, intrigued, and making up his mind at last, turned the handle gently and paused on the threshold peering into the dim-lit room.

His wife lay in a semi-reclining position, her face turned to the wall, resting on the velvet headboard of the bed, apparently asleep; a book lay open on the eiderdown. He moved softly forward and stood close to the bed, bending over slightly to get a better view; her eyes were closed, the lids shadowed, faint traces of tears upon her cheeks; the sharp facial bones were skeletal, the skin taut and pallid, lending to her whole countenance all the semblance and delineament of a death-mask. He shivered, hearing the strange pattern of her breathing, not at all ragged, but low, regular, intense, as if she were absorbed in some kind of earnest inward dialogue, her fingers tapping slightly, not twitching, as though in emphasis. It was the first time in many years that he had looked at her like that, without subterfuge, without any sort of defence between them, and he felt a little ignoble, ashamed, as if spying surreptitiously upon her, meanly subjecting her to scurrilous scrutiny when she was at her most vulnerable, bereft of all necessary camouflage, exposed to his erstwhile and perhaps merciless interpretations and helpless to shield herself. He might well have been gazing upon a total stranger instead of the woman he had been married to for almost eighteen years; he could not have experienced a keener sense of distance alloyed with guilt. In a small dilemma whether to switch off the bedside lamp or leave things as they were lest he should wake her, he debated awhile within himself, decided the latter course was best, and was about to turn and leave when, without preamble, as though she had been awake all the time, she turned her head and looked up at him, the habitual faintly apologetic smile upon her face.

'Is that you, Simon?'

For some reason he could not fathom the very ordinariness of her voice unnerved him; he stood, hesitant, fingering his chin.

'I couldn't sleep,' he said, and to his own ears it sounded as if he were groping for an excuse. 'I was going down to get a book and noticed the light on in your room.'

'Oh dear, how silly of me.' She picked up the book and placed it on the bedside table. 'Strange, I almost never drop off like that.'

'I know. I just came in to see if you wanted anything, since I was on my way downstairs anyway.'

She smiled more fully at him, grateful and surprised. 'That was very kind of you, dear. Very kind indeed.'

'Not at all,' he answered, becoming quite formal. 'Is there anything I can get you before I go?'

'Oh, I don't think so, dear – no, I'm quite sure there isn't, thank you, Simon.'

'Well, in that case I'll be on my way. Good night, Elinor.'

'Good night, Simon.'

He moved towards the door, stopped, and came back a few paces. 'I'm probably mistaken, but I thought I heard you crying in your sleep.'

She felt her cheeks with her fingers. 'Oh, was I? Just some silly dream, I expect. I seem to be having quite a lot of silly dreams lately – isn't that odd?' She looked at him, a small worried shadow between her brows. 'I'm sorry you couldn't go to sleep, dear. Now I know you don't approve, but perhaps if you were to borrow one of my tablets – '

'I've taken two already, but they didn't help.' He drew nearer the bed, hands in pockets of nightrobe, looking rather gloomily down at her. 'You're not ill in any way, are you, Elinor?'

She regarded him placidly. 'Ill? Why – no. No, I don't think so. Why do you ask, Simon?'

He chewed his lip. 'No reason. It just occurred to me you've been looking rather pale lately.'

'I was always pale, Simon,' she said quietly, the faintest hint of irony and reproach in her voice. 'Even as a girl. But you've probably forgotten that.'

'No, of course not,' he replied curtly, looking away. 'I meant you looked paler than usual, off-colour. I thought perhaps there might be something the matter with you that you didn't want me to know about.' He gave a short laugh. 'Women are sometimes foolish like that. Mock heroics, most of the time.'

'There's nothing the matter with me, Simon.'

'Well, as long as you're sure.' He bent forward a little, studying her almost with suspicion. 'Now that I think about it, you don't look at all well to me. Maybe I should phone Dr Rubens in the morning and have him look at you. A check-up would do no harm. No harm at all.'

'Only if you think so, Simon, though I'm feeling quite well, really I am.'

'Nevertheless, I think I'll get Rubens over sometime tomorrow and look you over thoroughly. Always best to make sure.'

She sank back upon the pillows, content as ever to let him take command and submit without question to his wisdom. 'I dare say you're quite right, dear.'

'Well, of course. I don't want you being carted off in the middle of the night or any of that nonsense. It would be inconvenient, to say the least.'

'Inconvenient, dear?' she queried, mildly reproving.

'Of course, and since in the long run the actual expense would be the same –' His eyes shifted over her, then veered away. 'I'm sorry, my dear. I don't mean to sound harsh or unsympathetic. Not in the least. It is not my way.'

'I know that, Simon,' she murmured soothingly, seeing that he waited as if for her to confirm his own estimation of his admirable lack of rancour. 'You are kindness itself.'

He looked suitably vindicated and pleased, in a refined, discreet way. 'One tries. It's just that there are so many things I have to think of and take into account, and everything, naturally, falls to me.'

'You are very patient, dear.' Her eyes, no longer timorous, rested calmly and fully upon his, but he did not notice. 'The last thing I would ever want to do, Simon,' she went steadily on, 'is cause you any fuss or bother. In anything.'

'Oh, quite, quite,' he muttered, with a certain underlying flippancy, as if annoyed that such a sentiment should ever be expressed, since it was only fitting and entirely appropriate that she should indeed feel that way. He sat gingerly down on the very edge of the bed, large soft hands held loosely between his knees. 'We seem to have got out of the habit of talking to one another, Elinor. Or haven't you noticed?'

'Oh, dear,' she said, glancing guiltily at him, automatically assuming the fault to be hers. 'It's been so long, really, since we talked together on any regular basis, dear, that I must confess I had hardly noticed that we no longer seem to confide any more in each other.' She rested her head back on the pillow, plainly hopeful that he was satisfied with her response.

He frowned, staring down at the carpet. 'Confide is a strange word, and it isn't at all what I had in mind. It implies, does it not, a great store of dark and hidden knowledge which people feel impelled to impart to each other, preferably in whispers or hushed tones, and of course that is quite ludicrous in our case. We almost certainly have nothing to confide in each other, then, in the strict confessional sense, but that doesn't mean we can't talk, surely?'

'I suppose not, dear, if only I was sure what it was you wanted to talk about.'

'Try not to be obtuse, Elinor. It is really quite simple. We seem to have nothing whatever to say to each other, beyond the merest commonplace exchanges, and personally I find that rather sad.' Again he appeared to await her reply before proceeding further.

'Yes,' she agreed, becoming aware of his expectant attitude, dreamily rubbing the side of one nostril with her forefinger. 'I daresay it *is* sad, in a way.'

'I find it very sad,' he reiterated with some force, irritated. 'Very sad indeed.' He pursed his round moist lips, waiting sternly for her to defend herself against the implied, unspoken charge.

'If there was something I could do about it, dear, then of course I would,' she said, unable to suppress a sigh; 'but it seems there is never anything you wish to discuss with me when you are home. At least nothing important.'

'It need not be important,' he said sharply. 'I do not ask for anything exotic or unreasonable. We would not necessarily have to have deep philosophical discourses or arguments of a high intellectual content in order to pass a pleasant hour or two in each other's company. Home-life does not consist of such things, as far as I have been able to make out.'

Her fingers roved absently along the fringes of the eiderdown, her face wistful, eyes clouded with obscure longing. 'It would be rather nice if we were to come together a little more when you're at home, Simon, to talk and share things a little more.'

He looked uncomfortable. 'Well, yes, perhaps. It is only civilised behaviour, after all, when two people find themselves obliged to more or less live under the same roof.'

She laughed softly in a peculiarly girlish fashion. 'As long as you don't expect me to talk about business matters. I never could understand business, as you well know, dear. I'm a deplorable dunce in that respect.'

'You never tried to understand, did you?' he muttered, grim-faced. 'But never mind – it is not my intention to reproach you, Elinor. There are times when I want to speak of things that have nothing at all to do with my business ventures, believe it or not. Still, I must not complain. You have your own life, I know, and I'm glad of that, at least.'

'Yes,' she reflected after a pause, her voice very low; 'I do have my own life, as you call it, small though it is, and I'm grateful. But sometimes I wish – ' She smoothed out some wrinkles in the eiderdown. 'Sometimes I wish you could enter into it a little more, Simon, though of course I know you're almost always tremendously busy.'

'You should really make an effort, Elinor, to enlarge your life, get out and about more, get to know people, make friends.' He shifted impatiently on the bed, clasping his hands together. 'I can't be expected to be in two places at the same time. I can't be expected to provide everything, all the trappings of family life as well as running a highly complex and competitive business in which one lapse, one slip of concentration and purpose could prove fatal. You really have no conception of the demands made upon my time and energy day in, day out. Why else do you think I spend so much time away from home, living up there in the clatter and smoke of London? If you think I enjoy it you're mistaken, but I do get to meet people, even those I don't particularly want to meet, and that is what you must do, Elinor. Meet people, even if you have to force yourself to do it. You can't just sit back and be a wallflower all your life. The world won't come to you,' he finished brusquely; 'you must make an effort to meet it halfway.'

'I never was much good at meeting the world,' she said, placid and remote, hands quiet now on the quilt. 'I only wish it were possible for you to come a little more into mine.'

He raised his hands and brought them down on his knees, rising stiffly. 'Yes. Well, we can't waste our lives away wishing things were this, that or the other, can we? Things just are, and we either take them as they are, or we go round in a daze daydreaming ourselves into the grave. It would be a strange world,' he added pedantically, drawing himself upright, 'if we had everything trimmed and cut and fitted to our wishes and desires, and I'm not at all sure it wouldn't be an unhealthy one into the bargain.' He went towards the door. 'Sure there isn't anything that I can get you while I'm up and about?'

'No, nothing, Simon, thank you.'

'I'll make that call to Rubens first thing in the morning, and get him over to look at you.'

'You haven't forgotten tomorrow is Sunday?'

'What does that matter? Rubens is a businessman, the same as myself. He's getting paid for his services.'

'I just thought he might be off somewhere for the weekend.'

He shrugged. 'There are other doctors in the immediate vicinity, as I recollect. Samuelson has a good reputation. Or would you prefer a non-ethnic opinion?' he added, with a faint sneer, touching the doorhandle.

'I'm happy to do as you please.'

'I thought so. Well, I'll say good night, Elinor.'

'Good night, Simon. I do hope you get back to sleep.'

He loitered on the threshold. 'I still think I'll go and find a book.'

She picked up the volume she had placed on the bedside table. 'I don't suppose you'd be interested in this, would you?'

'What is it?'

'A biography of Lord Tennyson, by a rather clever young woman who used to write book reviews and now appears to have rather a lot of children, poor thing.'

He grimaced. 'A case of the biter being bit. No, thanks. I find very few people deserve full biographies anyway, and I always found Tennyson extremely tedious. Well, good night.'

'Good night, dear.' Her voice sounded very small and distant from the bed.

He stepped out, carefully closing the door behind him, and waited until the tell-tale slit of light had been extinguished; then he moved swiftly along the hallway, reached the staircase and descended, fingers lightly flitting along the sleek curve of the banister as he went.

He felt so relieved, ebullient almost, after leaving her that he had to restrain himself from breaking into a soft jaunty whistle as he went downstairs into the faintly glimmering depths of the broad vestibule. It was as if he had escaped from a stuffy claustrophobic hospital ward after paying one of those boring duty calls, glad to be out in the open air again; he had sometimes gone on such a pious errand, to see a sick relative, friend or colleague, and however much he might sympathise with the patient, he had always felt on leaving an immense gratitude that he was not back there in the sickbed with immaculate nurses hurrying past with trays full of syringes or enema pots, or standing guard over him like stone angels, the smell of flowers and disinfectant mingling uneasily and sickeningly in his nostrils. He had hardly ever been really sick in his life, apart from everyday hazards like colds or toothache or the usually monthly visitation of a hangover, and in common with most people who are possessed of robust good health he had a certain awe and suspicion, mingled with distaste, for those less fortunate, the habitual semi-invalids of the world who spent the greater part of their mortality in a morbid embrace with frail, persistent, undiagnosed illnesses, wishing them well, of course, and a speedy recovery, and even on occasions sending them get-well cards or bunches of flowers, but not really relishing the prospect of spending any more time than he had to in their company. Their game good spirits and forlorn cheerfulness always wore him down and depressed him, and he normally ended up feeling guilty and in worse shape than they whom he had so valiantly come to encourage and console.

Not that Elinor ever actually complained; she had no need to, for she had the innate quality of simply *looking* unwell nearly all of the time, and in a way that was not even physical; it manifested itself not in any outward, ostensible way, but just by her very presence, so that whenever she was in a room all talk, all conversation would sooner or later revolve gently around her, the voices lowered and murmuring concernedly, as if some kind of subtle emanation flowed out from her and set off equally subtle vibrations in the people about her, making them more solicitous towards her, as though they feared a sudden incautious raising of their voices would trigger off in her excruciating headaches or fearful palpitations. So, even though she might sit down at table and eat and drink as well as, if not better than anyone else there, the impression was formed indelibly in the minds of all those present that Mrs Sandford was of an exquisitely delicate not to say precarious state of health of the kind that, while it commanded compassion and respect, invariably kept people at bay, however willing they might be to be friends with her. Thus, Elinor preserved her privacy whilst gaining the warm sympathy and admiration of nearly all who came in touch with her for her gallantry of heart and lightness of spirit in the face of adversity so bravely borne. As much as he distrusted the word 'psychic' and its ill-informed profligate use, a word that of late seemed doomed to be applied indiscriminately to practically every human ailment under the sun, there was none that could more aptly convey the peculiar nature of Elinor's condition, that odd intractable languor that enveloped her like an aura and that eventually became stifling and overpowering.

He almost never looked back upon the past, something he regarded as a sheer waste of time, an act of culpable self-indulgence, in the main distracting the backward glance that so easily distorted things; nostalgia was perfectly all right in its own way, as long as it was kept sternly in check and not allowed to blur the realities by which one must live. Yet he could still quite distinctly remember being attracted, when he first got to know Elinor, by her air of superb disengagement from the world, thinking it a quality in her, an indisputable mark of good breeding, of her superior indifference to the opinions and pursuits of her peers, a happy counterbalance to his own callow impatience and the cloudy ambitions that filled him and drove him impetuously forward like an explorer into each new day. To him, at that remote rosy time, this disarming listlessness of hers represented chic, cool poise and discernment, as much as did her boyish slim-hipped wispy good looks, and offered him peace from the jagged spur of his vague disquieting dreams of avarice and self-aggrandisement. That was long before it had begun to cloy, when he still had hopes of the enchanting chrysalis transforming overnight into a bewitching butterfly, a metamorphosis that had become aborted at some indeterminate stage and turned into a pitiable parody of that early promise.

Suffused with this sudden inexplicable sense of freedom, he wanted then merely to roam at will through the house, a house that he had never really thought of as his own, but rather as the place where his wife and family lived, as a barren weekend retreat which held the few loose threads of his other life. He wanted nothing more at that moment than to amble from room to room at his own pace, his own tempo, and become gradually reacquainted with the house, free of the lurking presences of others slyly vigilant of his movements, nibbling insidiously away at the edges of his life, accepting his support, his munificence, but not really needing him, unaffected in any deep sense by whether he would live another ten or twenty years or drop down dead in the street the very next day, gaping grotesquely at the sky. It was strange to imagine those other lives continuing within these very walls, breathing, growing, maturing around him as he moved so stealthily through the house now, almost as an intruder or burglar; lives he had helped to create out of a single act of passion that seemed now to belong to a long-dead person, necrophiliac in bleak retrospect, loathsome even to contemplate let alone try to reconstruct. The estrangement he felt from those living testimonies to himself, from his own flesh and blood, was as keen and poignant as it had ever been, or at least as he had allowed it to be; fortunately, though, it was tempered with a sense of inevitability, of almost rueful relief, like looking back in cosy reminiscence on a group of inmates one had once shared the same prison cell with, glad to be free of their inescapable company now and able to regard them with wary, watchful affection, from a clearly defined distance. To permit himself to crave their belated attention or concern would be nothing more than a maudlin exercise, an absurd piece of fantasising, expecting pleasurable plants to sprout on soil where nothing had ever grown before, soil that had never been tended or prepared for such a yield. It would be as futile as trying to hail someone who had long passed out of earshot and almost out of sight, and he was in the last instance immensely disinclined to make the effort.

He reached the bottom of the staircase, and paused, entranced by a blue blaze of moonlight streaming in through the pointed mullioned oriel window above the heavy panelled front door. A little dazed, almost without his knowledge, he found himself in the library, a long wide room with a single cathedral-type window and where again moonlight predominated, bookshelves rising in serried rows to the dim vaulted ceiling, resonant as the deep belly of a ship; without any great urgency he began searching for a book. At last and at random, he took down a volume, reassured by its ponderous weight, brought it across to the coldly fiery window to decipher its title, gave a satisfied grunt, seeing it matched his mood, and putting it under his arm left and made his way down the hallway to the dining room, in indolent need of a drink.

Pouring himself a brandy, he lingered by the ornate cocktail cabinet taking long meditative sips and dreamily topping the glass up again each time, lost in a strangely troubled reverie that was yet peaceful, only half felt; after a time he wandered out into the hall, pressing his fat moist lips lusciously together like someone chewing on a grape, and went on into the lounge, which he reflected was just about his favourite room in the whole house.

He thought of his wife, and felt sorry for her. She was such a desperately pathetic figure, marooned in her cluttered emptiness, her life sapless, bone-dry, loud with insignificance. He lifted his glass abstractedly to his lips; he was not totally inhumane or insensitive, he assured himself, not by any manner of means; he had a heart, after all, he had a capacity for pity that few people suspected or were allowed to glimpse, and certainly he pitied poor Elinor – dispassionately, though, as he would view a desiccated moth in a glass case or specimen jar, a vague comfortable pity, devoutly thankful that his mercy was not strained or burdened by anything as daunting or as crushingly tedious as day-to-day hourly contact with her; that kind of cohabitation would be insufferable at this stage in his life, if it had ever really existed before. He hardly knew her, which might sound absurd after having been married to her for eighteen years, but it was nonetheless true; he hardly knew his own wife, except on the surface, and even there, he acknowledged, there were things he knew nothing about, areas and aspects of herself and her life that remained unseen and invisible to him. Nothing hidden so much as – well, merely absent, nonexistent, at least as far as he was concerned.

He had long ago ceased to wonder why he had ever married her, for it only perplexed and exasperated him and filled his mind with alarming doubts about his own faculties of judgement and discernment. He did not shut her out or exclude her, it was nothing as definite as that; no, he reasoned, it was simply how things had fallen and settled between them, the form their life together had assumed. It was unreal and most inconceivable to him now that he had once spent whole periods and portions of his life with her and her alone, whole consecutive uninterrupted days and – yes – nights with her, as a matter of course, without thinking it odd or ludicrous or slipping into fathomless dementia; it was like looking back on a quiescent nightmare that no longer held any potent threat, but that never really faded and kept creeping back to gnaw at strands of memory with small sharp mice-teeth; disguised as a thin snigger in a curtained corner, a smirk of mean triumph on a veiled face glimpsed at dusk, as if a subtle form of revenge was being invoked upon him for he knew not what tangled reasons, out of malignant inchoate spite.

The night heat was oppressive; he loosened the cloth of the pyjama top away from his skin, feeling the clammy sweat ooze and trickle down his chest and over the folds of his belly. He leaned across and unlatched a window, pushing it outwards, but not a breeze stirred; the air hung heavy and drooping, layered with heat, thick with distant sullen threat. He listened intently, and imagined he caught a low sound, inaudible almost, far off in the night, like muffled hooves or the slow desultory beat of drums, no more than a murmur that insinuated itself into the stillness, strangely exciting and menacing. As he watched, expectant, alert, craning forward as though in a theatre or cinema at some important point in the drama, a coil of lightning lifted through the invisible horizon and writhed almost lazily across the sky, opening and spreading outwards slowly like the gnarled fingers of a clenched fist; it licked the tree-tops and fell with a cold brilliant flare upon the earth, bruised and lurid, glancing icily across the surface of the water in the swimming-pool; it flickered and streaked away into the distance, then came flashing back once more, running up and down the sky, still with the same sultry, indolent momentum; it hovered for some moments, a stark gleaming blade etched vividly into the firmament, and abruptly vanished, leaving the sky once more a dense black slate dotted with pinpoints of stars. The remote sound drew nearer upon the vanishing spurs of lightning, the hooves, the drumbeats clattering across the desolate prairies of space, a distant gigantic bronzed bellowing, as of barrels rolling and rumbling from end to end of the sky, emitting sharp staccato barks, growling and grumbling indistinctly into nowhere, leaving a silence more profound than before, no longer torpid, no longer laden and padded with heat, but exquisitely attuned and susceptible to the faintest breath, the faintest stir or fall of leaf, in which he could hear the loud strumming of his blood.

He sat for interminable moments at the window, hardly stirring, not wanting to break the spell, but inevitably it broke, the night lost its mystery, its veiled romance, its pretensions of magic. The hard glare of the moonlight hurt his eyes, making them water, and he shut them tight, picked up the glass and emptied it in one gulp, throwing the brandy down his throat as if impatient to be rid of it, to get at least that wearisome pretence out of the way, his guts remaining icy, unaffected by the assault of raw liquor. The apathy that he hated in his wife wrapped itself round him now as snug as a shroud, tight as a skull-cap, hemming him in; he was as much victim, or slave, to the same mummifying insularity as she, and the more to be despised, since he was free in so many more ways, ways that she could never begin to grasp, let alone desire. His choice of freedom was panoramic in comparison with her own.

Elinor's life, on the contrary, remained fixed immutably within a set orbit; it was entombed, as it were, between the covers of a book that she had largely written herself, the lines of which she knew by heart from the top to the bottom of every page. A closed book, perhaps, and of very limited interest, but it was her own, her very own composition, and within its dry rusty latitudes her step was sure and unfaltering. For all his agility in one small corner of his life, in almost every other sense he was about as nimble as an elephant, in the blind semi-comical way he blundered into people, into lives and situations, the secret tortures he went through trying to extricate himself from them while trying at the same time to preserve his bland equanimity, sipping fine wine and dabbling in delicate food and conversation with the desperate dexterity of a skater skimming over very thin ice, knowing a single unwise mistimed step would send him plunging into the cold void beneath. He was a grotesque contradiction, even in the glare of his own self-generated light, his solidity a mere matter of flesh, of poundage, masking an inner hollowness in which he could hear, if he dared to listen, the thin lonely echo of his thoughts like solitary steps in a bare room. More and more of late his thinking was mere capitulation to morbid whims and fancies, making him dread idleness such as now, for in the silences that should have been pleasurable he could not avoid hearing the dull thud of truth no matter how he might muffle his ears against it.

Marcie, too, had changed, was still changing, not only towards but away from him, growing further away from him almost daily, putting subtle ever-increasing distance between them; he could not pinpoint it or say with any certainty that it was one thing or another, but then he had no need to classify it, for it was there, it had begun, and he could feel it, now sharp, now vague, like an ache that was not easy to identify or locate, except that it persisted and was present all the time, below the surface of almost everything they said or did together, in the way she looked at him or, more and more, the way she did not look at him. About this at least he was convinced he was not being merely morbid, was not letting any subliminal hysteria get the better of him; it was something that was immediate because of its very subtlety, something that lingered in the air after her, like the faint but distinctive perfume she used. They could still talk, argue and laugh together without being too forced or determined about it; at any rate they could talk, argue and laugh as much as they ever had done before, and that had never been very much, but now her eyes seemed always to be elsewhere when they were together, over dinner and drinks in town or in the privacy of the apartment, in company or alone. She acted as though she merely shared the table and the small talk with him in hotel or restaurant while waiting for someone else to turn up, without doing anything as obvious or discourteous as looking about her as he chatted away with increasingly desperate affability.

He was fairly certain that there was no third party, that there was nobody else involved, at least not so deeply that she would want to exclude him completely from her life; had it been anything as ordinary and mundane as that, he would have approached it with a shrug and proceeded to cope with it accordingly, since at least it would have been something tangible instead of a buried suspicion hardening into indeterminate certainty. From almost the beginning of their affair there had existed between them a tacit understanding that, should someone else sufficient to arouse her interest arrive upon the scene, they would treat it entirely dispassionately, in a separate context, and not allow it to change the basic fabric of their relationship to any dramatic degree. It was like an unwritten contract between them, sealed if never signed, which through some strange yet honourable perversity both were resolved to observe and fulfil for as long as was practicable. The change now taking place, felt rather than perceived, lay instead in the very texture of her attitude, something sensed rather than confronted, maddeningly beyond words. If the contempt that in his more lucid moments he could feel flowing from her like a physical emanation were indeed true and not another morbid trick of his imagination, then it was a contempt upon which she thrived and grew strong, as most other people did on the plainer substance of love, and it had the effect not merely of dismaying him, but of making him covet her all the more vehemently. He knew this to be a sickness within him, but he was powerless to combat or deny it; he sought her as he would an antidote to some strange virulence that had seeped into his system and possessed him, and he tossed and writhed in the dilemma of knowing that she was both antidote and poison, the chronic cause of the complaint and the ineffective, indispensable cure. He loathed his dependence upon her; the free-and-easy ambivalence that had so pleased and fitted his purpose at the start had now changed into chains of subtle tyranny that threatened to throttle all sense and reason out of him, yet wishing it gone was as futile as wishing himself in another life, another body.

The place that most other men would call home was little more than a morgue to him, inhabited if not by corpses then at the very most by animated ghosts and his business life offered no succour; he hated it, despised its sordid inanities, its grossness, its shrill littleness, a vacuum filled by poseurs and imposters, insufferable braggarts and voyeurs of the most repellent kind, battening on the vanity and feeble talent of others, cannibalistic to its core; a hollow shrine where gaudy candles flared briefly overnight and were extinguished forever. More than ever his thoughts were drawn to the theatre; it beckoned with irresistible appeal, a perfect catalyst, an ideal crucible for the energies and ingenuities he felt he still possessed and which were still waiting to be properly mined and brought to the surface. It was, he felt convinced, his true metier, the one area in life where reality and fantasy were not continually at war, at loggerheads, were not so horribly irreconcilable, but could mingle and be transmuted into art, and he longed to immerse himself in that world, to become caught up in all its frenzy and suspense, where chance and certainty so often wore the same mask and held out the same enticements. He saw it as a separate universe, a world unlike any other, truly a place apart, and without any difficulty at all he visualised himself in it, come into his own at last, the land and climate he was born for; he saw himself in that near and future time, taking risks, spectacular gambles, meeting potent challenges, backing his latest instincts and intuitions with the hard currency of cash and idealism, bracing himself against the clash of motley temperaments, the wild and subtle swordplay of colourful rivalries and ambitions; learning the ropes by perhaps painful degrees, but avidly learning the dangers, the traps, the intricacies of planning and mounting productions of proven masterpieces and new works full of brilliant bombast and lucent nihilism, making obeisance to old masters and lending a platform to the new and undiscovered, those struggling in gifted infancy and those in mellow fame whose voices had long out-soared the eagle.

He smiled, knowing he was indulging himself in a perennial mythology, in the most blatant romanticism, but not caring a sweet damn; anything was better than the reality that enveloped him like a brittle caul. The sheer prospect was enough to dazzle and exhilarate him, like coming within sight at last of an exotic and mysterious place after a long and troubled journey. Soon, he promised himself, soon he would be free of the whole wretched recording business, with people who were true artists in the best and immemorial sense, true professionals for whom life and art were of the one and most singular substance, forged in the same lyrical fire; he would forever be free of strutting imbeciles twanging electrified instruments and yelling their empty heads off in a simpering sea of idolaters, without a morsel of music or sensitivity in their pampered bones; venal buffoons interested only in accumulating their little pile of manna before scuttling back into padded oblivion, into the obscurity that had spawned them, once more indistinguishable from the general flotsam of their kind. How he had endured that semi-world for so long, for so many Babel years without disintegrating himself into the same pervasive mechanical idiocy, he could not begin to comprehend even now; his reserves of strength, resilience, self-belief must be after all not inconsiderable, enabling him to survive a marriage and a business that both led precisely nowhere, and the thought warmed and consoled him and took the chill out of the moonlight.

'Yes, by God!' he exclaimed aloud, striking the cold stone of the window ledge, unable to suppress his excitement, inspired by his own lonely philosophising, by what struck him as a subtle insight into the central dilemma of his existence, the fruits of long and wearisome experience falling suddenly into his lap. 'That's what I'll do!'

And then intuitively he became aware that he was not alone; the realisation came to him slowly, with a sly almost stealthy ease, and with it the thought of what a terrifying thing it was not just to hear but actually to listen to the beating of one's own heart. It was like nothing he had ever known before; it was an exquisite fear, to sit there in the lifeless moonlight listening to the quiet pandemonium inside his ribs, sensing this other presence in the room; there was not a sound, not a creak, not the faintest rustle, but the knowledge, the certainty of someone else being there – not concealed, nothing as simple as that, but unrevealed, alert, watching his slightest movement, observing the very posture of his head etched against the moonlit window, tracing the tracks his mind was pursuing, waiting for the smallest hesitancy, the smallest hint in his intent self-concentration, not to pounce, but rather to sneak in, to subtly invade his consciousness simply by being there, by sharing the room, the hour and the night with him, making a patent mockery of his prized and pathetic privacy, his absurd isolation that was ultimately ridden with echoes of the world he could never escape from or convincingly deny. He felt quick outrage at this other unseen presence, this silent, blatant intrusion, yet perversely he welcomed it, he wanted it for reasons he could not remotely begin to define, let alone rationalise. He was being observed, closely, minutely, he knew, by eyes that were alien, hostile, even perhaps bale-ful, but which to his horror *knew* him, comprehended grotesquely the devious twists and turns of his nature and followed as the lines on a map its hidden courses. He felt deeply exposed; the room, the house, the night were no longer his own, were no longer uniquely his own province; he was being coerced into sharing this moment, this silent contemplation, this fragment of his life with someone else, supremely against his will, yet in strange warped accord with his unvoiced wishes that he despised but without which he would be laughably incomplete. It was all nonsense, he told himself hopefully, but terribly believable nonsense since he was at that very instant living it; he longed fiercely then to recapture his remedial necessary cynicism, but it was immensely beyond him, beyond his need.

The voice when it came struck him as coldly as the lightning that had moments before died from the sky. 'You could not sleep, Mr Sandford?' The heavily accented voice ignited the profound stillness of the room with noon-day resonance, hearty and nonchalant as a visitor newly arrived from the sea. He felt the coarse shadow draw closer, ponderous with stealth and confidence. 'Can I do anything for you, Mr Sandford? A cup of coffee, perhaps?' The blunt mannish fingers touched the empty glass on the window ledge, tracing the rim. 'Some more cognac, maybe? Whatever you want, Mr Sandford, you will let Gerda know, yes? That is after all what I am here for, is it not?'

He summoned authority from nowhere, hollow to his own ears, hoping it resounded in his voice. 'Why are you not in your room? What are you doing, may I ask, wandering about the house at this hour?' He did not turn around but sat almost hunched forward, staring out into the garden, feeling his will loosening like a tightly twisted rope inside him, feeling her shadow standing over him.

'But no, Mr Sandford, I have not been wandering. I have sat here all the time, in this room. I see you come in, but I make no sound. I do not wish to frighten you.'

He half turned his head, angry. 'Frighten me? How could *you* frighten me? Do you think I am a child?' He felt and heard the petulance in his voice, and returned his trapped gaze to the window. 'You should be in your room. The children or Mrs Sandford might need you, late as it is.'

'Ah,' came the unperturbed reply, as if grasping some latent understanding, her shadow nearer now, casting a solid replica on the floor, 'you have been to see Mrs Sandford?'

Again he felt the ire leap in him, and again he felt defeated. 'What the hell – .' He stopped and groped with stiff fingers for the empty glass, not finding it. 'Yes, I have been to see my wife. I was on my way down to look for a book and – ' Again he stopped, feeling he was standing in a witness box, making a guilty admission but unable to desist. 'I found her still reading. My wife is a great reader, a great lover of books, as you may have noticed. Myself, I hardly ever read, except when I'm extraordinarily happy or depressed.' He folded his hands tightly in his lap, her shadow now draping over him like a thick cloak. 'What is your name again? I seem to have forgotten – '

'It does not matter, Mr Sandford.'

'No,' he heard himself saying, with the quiet intentness of a man speaking to himself, keeping his eyes closed. 'It does not matter. Names never do, I have found. How long have you been with us now?' He was speaking mechanically, as if into a void.

'That does not matter either, Mr Sandford.' She was standing behind him, her large hands almost touching his shoulders, poised in the air in a strangely protective manner, as if about to cradle an infant, yet not wanting to wake it from its slumber. 'Mr Sandford, I have to tell you something. It is very sad.'

'Well,' he forced himself to ask when she did not go on. 'What is it you want to say? Can't it wait another time? It is really quite late and I'm tired – '

'Your wife is very sick, Mr Sandford.'

'Elinor – sick? Look here, I hardly need you to tell me that. I know you probably mean no harm, but she does happen to be my wife, and if I don't know her state of health by now – '

'But perhaps you don't know, Mr Sandford.' The voice for all its guttural thickness had fallen to a hushed sneering whisper, as if they were hatching a plot together. 'You are such a busy man, and sometimes a very tired man. Maybe you do not have time to see what I see, what I know.'

He swallowed, hearing the assured contempt in her voice, the detached insolence that was at the same time almost maternal, and fought vainly not to be intimidated, not to be excited by it. 'I'm aware my wife hasn't been very well lately, and tomorrow I am having the doctor over – '

'Your wife is dying, Mr Sandford.' The words were uttered with a kind of neutral glee, like someone revealing something they had discovered before anyone else and took much pride in.

He half started up from the ledge, raising his arm, fist clenched, as if to strike out not only at her, but at something else, some intangible force or presence that was infinitely loathsome to him, yet infinitely, horribly alluring, enticing, insinuating itself into the warped and secret recesses of his nature with mole-like persistence and purpose, sinuously evading and defeating his frantic attempts to crush it with consummate cunning and contempt, spelling out at every turn things

221

he somehow knew and recoiled from, an image in a mirror he longed to smash but could not, lacking even that small saving rage, that small impulsive strength. He could only stare at her as she stood before him, substantial as a wall, her broad bare shoulders confronting him like a marble shield, sturdy warrior legs planted firmly apart, as if daring him to move or advance.

'You – you lie!' he uttered finally, weakly panting, dropping his arm and sitting back down abruptly, almost quailing as she stood over him. 'You lie,' he repeated, passing a trembling hand across his eyes, his voice more hollow than before.

'I tell the truth, Mr Sandford,' she said, impassive, yet triumphant. 'I tell only the truth.'

He shut his eyes, willing himself futilely into insensibility, and when he reopened them she had gone and returned with the decanter of brandy and was filling his glass, like a nurse pouring out medicine for a patient, not so much offering it to him as putting it firmly into his hand.

'A little cognac, Mr Sandford. It will help.'

Obedient as a child latterly chastised, he put the glass to his lips and drank without in the least tasting the liquor, only minimally aware of the gesture itself. She emitted a slight satisfied grunt, and then with companionable ease poured out some brandy for herself into a glass she had brought back with her, taking up her position as before, immovable, implacable. Incongruously he found himself reflecting that for all her bulk the woman moved with surprising grace, stealthy as a cat and as grossly complacent.

'You feel better now, Mr Sandford – a little better, yes?'

He looked dully up at her, like someone struggling feebly out of an anaesthetic. 'Listen,' he mumbled, 'I grant you Elinor – my wife hasn't been at all well in recent months – she might perhaps be even rather more ill, more sick than I've had time or opportunity to fully realise. I grant you that much. But with proper medical attention, with expert care and treatment – '

He sensed rather than saw her smile of intimate and superior knowledge, the slow bucolic shaking of her head.

'Still you do not understand, Mr Sandford,' she stolidly intoned, a glint of moonlight beckoning as she lifted the glass to her mouth, precisely like someone holding a casual tête-à-tête at a cocktail party with a not over-bright guest. 'It is already, I tell you, too late.

Even now as we speak the poor lady is dying. For months you do not know, but it is true.'

'You're not a damned nurse, are you?' he whimpered, rather than demanded, pleading rather than flinging forth an angry retort. 'You speak as if you were a damned oracle.'

'But I know, Mr Sandford,' came her unmoved reply.

Something like fire flashed behind his eyes and he grasped at it hungrily. 'You *know*?' he cried, doubling the fist of one hand into a tight ball and almost beating it upon his knee. 'You *know*, do you? And what mythical medical knowledge, what hidden powers of – of divination do you possess to make such an assertion – eh?' He tried mightily to bring a sneer into his voice. 'You're only a bloody au pair person, for God's sake, not Marie Curie!'

'Please, I do not know of this lady, this Marie Curie – '

'Damn right you don't! You know damn all!' He was working up a weak puerile rage, deliberately, desperately evoking it, using it as a crutch to lean upon so that he should not totally collapse and crumble before the weird impregnable strength she exuded, facing him in the suddenly enclosed and claustrophobic room, unscalable as a sheer solid cliff-front. 'I must be quite mad, quite out of my senses to even sit here and listen to you, a mere damn servant, hired to do a specific household duty and nothing more – ' He stopped, shoulders heaving, and emptied his glass in a single gulp, glaring first at her, then down at her stolid encroaching shadow spreading across the tiled floor as if it would engulf him if she moved a fraction nearer. 'Since, however,' he went on, forcing himself to be calm, 'since you have the arrogance, the incredible audacity to speak so – so dogmatically on such a delicate, such an intensely personal subject, then it is my duty to demand an explanation, to have you tell me what you know, or more correctly perhaps what you *think* you know – '

'Yes, Mr Sandford. I understand.' Her voice was flat, detached, and utterly derisive, as if she was soothing a querulous animal, pampering it by her very patience.

'You cannot, you simply cannot – ' Again he tried feebly to rise from the window ledge, putting the empty glass down. 'You cannot go about saying such things, making such – such *bald* statements without some basis, even the slightest basis of fact. It's monstrous, as if you were quoting holy writ. It's a monstrous impertinence, a colossal liberty – ' He sank back down on the ledge once more, limp and out of breath.

'You are angry, Mr Sandford, because you are afraid.'

'Don't you dare presume to advise me!' he rasped, rallying his dwindling resources of anger, his waning store of pathetic dignity, gripping the edge of the window seat with both hands.

'Your wife, poor lady,' she continued, as if he had not uttered a sound, taking meditative sips of her drink, 'is dying of cancer. Of the liver, I think. Yes,' she said, nodding her close-cropped martial head decisively, 'of the liver definitely.'

'Once more I warn you – '

'With months only left of her poor sad life. Weeks now, maybe. It is, as you say, far ahead now, far advanced.' She seemed to come out of a momentary pensive trance and spoke briskly, as if to forestall any further interference from him. 'I do not lie, Mr Sandford. Out of her own mouth she tell me this.' Again came the subdued note of ghoulish pride, of smug triumph. 'We are – how do you say? – as sisters.' She almost sniggered, a deep guttural sound in her throat. 'Maybe more than sisters – who knows?'

'You bitch!' he muttered hoarsely, a terrible delectable panic fluttering inside him, tremulous with dread and revulsion, yet pulling him irresistibly beyond outrage into its dark orbit, lighting small hated fires he longed despairingly to quench. 'How dare you malign my wife with your filthy tongue – '

She laughed, placating him now. 'I joke, Mr Sandford, I joke. Do not take offence. But your wife, poor lady, has no one all the day to talk to, so she turn to me, to her friend Gerda, and I listen with much care, much pity, much heart.'

She spoke in a low vibrant monotone that was at the same time almost devoid of inflection, as if from a stage or podium to an entirely captive audience, now and then pausing as though to consult her carefully prepared script, her delivery suave, precise, supremely assured of being listened to and attended.

'So I take much pity on the poor lady, your wife, and she tells me everything. Sometimes she cries and then I wipe her tears away. It is very sad, is it not?'

He twisted savagely about on the ledge, writhing like an eel caught securely in an ever tightening net, having to wrench the words out of his burning throat.

'You're a damned filthy liar! My wife dislikes and distrusts you as much as I do – as much as we all do in this house – '

224

She contemplated her glass for a moment, slowly swirling its contents around. 'That is not at all true, Mr Sandford,' she said at length, softly. 'She loves Gerda. I am her friend. All the time you are away in the city I am her friend. I take care of her. As a poor sick invalid I take care of her. Even the times when she has maybe a little too much to drink.'

He stared at her, stupefied, his mouth hanging comically open, hands limp on his knees. 'Are you telling me – ' he stopped, diving for breath. 'Are you standing there and telling me that my wife drinks in secret?'

She gave a coarse chuckle, as if relishing some rich private amusement, taking slow loving sips of her drink, her lips making crude smacking sounds.

'In secret?' she echoed. 'But of course, Mr Sandford. She does not wish to distress you, to make you angry, so only when you are away in the city does she drink. Is it not brave and admirable of her, that she has such thought for you? She drinks only for the pain, you see, for the great pain the cancer brings. She does not drink for the pleasure – oh no.' She gave a profound sigh, rocking back and forth slightly on her splayed feet. 'But I do not mind. I do not get angry with the poor sick lady. I care for her as a child, a baby. I take her sometimes into my arms when she has too much pain or too much drink, and rock her to sleep – here – ' She let her hand stroll lazily over the flagrant promontory of her bosom barely concealed in the thin nightdress, her voice dreamy. 'As sometimes I do the youngest of the children, Mr Sandford,' she added, thick contempt once more clogging her tones. 'The little lady of the house.'

Sandford remained silent for some time, as if stricken dumb, then he groaned and held his head in his hands. 'I don't believe any of this! If what you say is true – but it isn't, it can't be! Dr Rubens would have told me – of course he would! He is the family doctor, our own personal physician – it would be his professional obligation to tell me – what am I thinking of, sitting here listening to such foul lies from a scheming amazon like you?'

'Ah, but you *are* listening, Mr Sandford, are you not?' she almost purred, draining her glass and putting it down on the table behind her, turning sideways as she did so, her shoulder gleaming white and muscular in the still remorseless moonlight; she turned back, looming like a granite sentinel in front of him. 'Why do you not go, Mr

225

Sandford? You have only to stand up and leave. Why do you not do so?'

He recoiled from her, into the shadowed recess of the window seat, his mind darting desperately about for an outlet, a mirage of escape.

'Lies, all lies!' he croaked. 'Rubens would know – he wouldn't dare keep anything like that from me – '

'Yes, the good doctor knew,' she said, nodding, sitting down on the ledge, silhouetted between him and the moonlight. 'All this time he knew, but Elinor – ' she paused, enunciating the name with laconic, apathetic familiarity, with affectionate odium and distaste, 'Elinor made him swear on oath never once to tell you. She does not wish to trouble you. She has this great thought for you. We all have, Mr Sandford,' she murmured, her voice descending to a grotesque lisp, fondling him with its sound.

He felt the blood on his tongue as he bit into his lower lip. 'By God, I'll sue Rubens – I'll have him struck off the register – he had no right – '

'Ah, do not be angry,' she said softly, with sensual insolence, the shape of her head squat and animalian etched against the glowing window behind her, the side of her face exposed to the moon chiselled in crude stone and lit by a sly venal elation, the corner of her wide mouth drawn down in a leer. 'It does not do you good to be angry.'

He cringed further away from her, against the wall, into the caressing folds of the curtain.

'Don't touch me – please don't touch me – '

She did not speak, nor did she have to, for at that moment he knew she discerned utterly the whole tapestry and complexity of his nature, and knew him with a sureness, with a dominance so complete that never again would he have strength enough to ignore or deny the merest intimation of her presence, either in his house or in his life.

In the midst of this fatal and spellbound awareness of her, the telephone shrilled, and like some caged animal being suddenly let loose he flung himself out of her shadow, out of the room and down the long echoing hall, grabbing at the instrument as if it had been a spar thrown to him out of the dark as he was about to go beneath the waves for the last time, almost sobbing into the receiver. It was Marcie, ringing from somewhere in Southampton, saying she had already posted a letter off to him, and that in it she had explained some of the reasons why she was sailing for South Africa the next morning.

PART V
Epilogue

15

WALKING along the thronged city streets in the fine misty rain of the autumn evening, taking little account of her surroundings or in which direction she went, she knew beyond the smallest relief of doubt that she was returning to a paradox, going back to the embers of something that had burnt itself out without ever really having caught fire, save briefly, in brilliant flares and conflagrations that had illuminated the whole world for her for sustained scintillating moments, before spluttering out and dying dismally, leaving both of them drained, dejected, as stranded and unknown to each other as before, fumbling again to find a foothold in the bleak ordinary light of shared existence, back once more in the comfortable and hateful world of predictable utterance and stereotype gesture, going into each day out of mere necessity, because there was nothing else to do.

There had, after all, scarcely been any true convincing flame in all the coloured smoke that had gathered about their lives; smoke that had swirled and cleared from time to infrequent time, letting them catch glimpses of immediate things whilst shrouding all broader vistas, any wider perspective of distant prospects that might lie in the future and be discerned, towards which they could have aspired with greater honesty and keener endeavour. She was filled with a vague amazement still that everything should have changed so utterly and leave her so little changed; she knew with a sense of bitterness that basically she was the same person now as she was at the beginning, when they had met for the first time, as if nothing even remotely momentous had happened to either of them, as if it had all been a precarious, passionate and quite perishable dream out of which she was now slowly, painfully emerging and learning to live without, like a cripple learning to walk without crutches.

She felt cheated of some obscure inalienable right, robbed of a virility of outlook, a certain indefinable but invaluable dimension that should have been hers, a natural process of growth that would have deepened her awareness and put her on a more equitable standing with life, with herself and other people. She could not understand why this had not happened, could not accept it, and it enraged her a little, so that she wanted to claw the charged air, to accost total strangers as they passed her shadowily on the pavements and demand an explanation, a clue to the conundrum, to scream out in protest and proclaim that life, surely, could not have played such a sly barbaric trick on her, to leave her unchanged and unprepared in the midst of the chaotic joy, bewilderment and pain that had come upon her in the span of so short a time. But she walked on, with bland impervious face, rooted in limbo, the loud sordid edifices and extravagant dens of the city leering, beckoning, setting up their insufferable and bewitching clamour.

She detested the deadness, the studied indifference inside her, and tried to force her mind to dwell on other less perilous things, the safe contingencies of real or imagined hurt, resentment, the easy outrage of disillusion and betrayal; she needed the sharp bite of pain or grief to break her frozen mood, needed the vital infusion of anger from whatever source to dissolve the icy waters of her zealous apathy and render all the conflicts and issues at war in her life at last real and raw and terribly menacing, as in her heart she knew them to be. Such facile reactions, however, such swift and simple sensations played truant on her now and did not rush to her aid; she walked zombie-like into the roar of the approaching night, feeling the soft rain, almost caressing, on her face, the fearful burden of wasted unused emotion clanking within her like ancient chains, dragging her down, her step deliberate, her heartbeat dull and regular.

She wondered if she had already ceased to exist for him back there in the apartment in Earl's Court, mulling over the latest score, plucking out its embryonic melody tentatively on the guitar, wandering dark and intense through the usual maze of musical hieroglyphics, absently drinking, no longer occupied with thoughts of her but simply getting on with the job, the task in hand, at that very moment handling his life quite competently without her and finding it not in the least difficult or daunting. She remembered he had not even looked up when, throwing aside the magazine she had been pretending to read, she announced she was going out for a walk, for a breath of even the gaseous city air; he had merely mumbled something and gone on scribbling notes into the large exercise jotter he used for work, guitar laid across his lap, a slow blues record playing remotely in the background. If she had told him then that she was catching the next plane to Hong Kong or Heraklion or Rio de Janeiro she was sure it would have made as much impact on him as if she had said she was taking a trip to Littlehampton for the weekend. He worked with a sort of bitter absorption that was unassailable, a sort of joyless intensity, like a convict on a chain gang mindlessly going about his allotted task, his prescribed toil, finding neither solace or excitement in the exercise, embroiled in diligence and discipline and nothing beyond that. He seldom now consulted her or sought her advice, and when he did it was with a sullen reluctance, as if he were merely doing her a favour by acknowledging her presence in the room with him, even though ostensibly it was still a working partnership and she was supposed to be involved at least in setting down the lyrics, which she had anyway to mouth and articulate in the final analysis. He seemed at times to begrudge her even that dubious distinction, as though it were an intrusion, an infringement upon the real nature of his work, little more than a necessary nuisance which eventually he hoped to be able to do without and discard.

She remembered, too, as she trudged the throbbing streets, his obsessive distrust of the future, how, in spite of the small success they had gained within the last couple of years, he treated tomorrow, any tomorrow, as an absurd abstraction, almost as an enemy, a potential traitor, something to be shunned, avoided and kept in wary abeyance for as long as possible. Tomorrow was a confrontation full of obscure omens; he never planned ahead, never predicted, theorised or prophesied about things that might happen next week, next month, next year; he considered that a childish diversion from the reality of the moment, whatever that reality might be, and this distrust, this lurking suspicion had lately begun to be applied to people as well, to friends they had made since their marriage and to those associates and near strangers they had of necessity to work with, so that it seemed he expected a razor blade to be hidden in every handshake, a faint snigger of derision to lie behind every kindly encouraging word, as if people were constantly and in secret sneering at him, at his origins, his music, his playing, and making unfair and cruel comparisons, labelling him an inept amateur, an overpaid failure patronised and pampered by a pathetic middle-aged pompous dilettante with nothing better to do with his money or his time and who – so they seemed to insinuate to him – rather fancied his red-haired long-legged lissom little songbird of a wife and would surely make her one of his more decorative acquisitions as soon as he tired of his current black mistress.

All these things she read daily in his eyes, in his morose silences as much as in his frequent outbursts of pique and occasional desperation, travelling the country, building up a small reputation. almost a small fan following in certain smaller cities and towns, seaside resorts and a few favourite nightclubs where they had become well known. His moods varied from the excessively buoyant to the implacably depressed, and there was nothing very remarkable about that, since most people, she observed, were more or less the same, except that with Art the two extremes appeared not to be extreme after all, but more and more often to blur and take on the same hue, the same tone and texture, to present the same face, so that she could not tell from one moment to the next behind which mood, which mask he was hiding.

Yet if on the surface he seemed hellbent on affecting the cliché-ridden life of the creative artist, sulky, irrational, morose and loquacious, aloof and flamboyant, reclusive and gregarious, with his work firmly at the centre of his universe, his only true and abiding passion when all was said and done – if he sought to ape and emulate that parody of existence – she all too wearily knew the reverse side of the coin, the long seemingly unending intervals when he lounged and loitered about in whatever place they happened to be, miserable as any callow schoolboy dreading the start of a new term, dithering at anything he did, reading silly detective or adventure stories full of improbable juvenile heroics, staring blindly, at television for hours without, she suspected, a single intelligent or original thought in his head; getting easily and wilfully bored for no rhyme or reason, loping about the room grumbling about the weather, the hotel food, the acoustics, the asinine audiences they were getting lately; kicking things out of his way, petulant as a child wanting new toys, rehashing things he had done before in the name of work, terrified of attempting anything new, reduced to an almost moronic state of indecision and ineptitude.

'What in God's name are we doing here?' he would often mutter, not expecting an answer, taking another surly swipe at his drink, sprawled in a chair or on the bed, glowering at the ceiling. 'What the bleeding hell *are* we doing, leading this shit kind of life?' Then he would lapse again into sullen lethargy, letting the weak waves of his discontent sweep sluggishly over him.

The cold clutch of possession was loosening for both of them, passively letting go, opening like a limp infant fist after a querulous broken slumber. Their life seemed already cruelly abbreviated, bleeding in some vital artery that had been severed almost without their knowing it; the shadow of something in the future had already fallen between them, as if the wounding words that now lay unsaid would one day be spoken, would one day be flung like arrows between them, heavy with bitter conviction, when all compassionate evasions and tender duplicities would no longer be of any help or solace to them and, bereft of even the thinnest and shallowest camouflage, they would be driven to murderous candour. Even when he asked her opinion, when he asked her to sit and listen to something he had written, something that excited him more than usual, she felt uneasy, unsure of herself, like being invited to a party at the last moment, as an afterthought, a kindness, because she just happened to be there and she might as well come along as stay behind. She recalled one such occasion, one sombre evening in some forgotten place near the sea, waiting for night to come when they were to play in some club in the nearby town.

'See what you think of this,' he had said as they sat out on the small balcony facing the grey veil of mist that was the sea. 'It just came to me this afternoon, while you were out shopping or whatever you were doing,' he added with a grin.

'I was shopping.'

'Sure.' He got up, went back into the shadowy room and returned with his guitar. 'I haven't tried to write anything down yet – it's just running around in my head.'

She watched the curious little charade she had seen so often before and knew so well; how he bent low over the instrument as if he were communicating with it in whispers, angling his head sideways to catch its reply; the fingers of one hand roved tentative and persuasive over the taut strings, gently seeking a response, while the other hand was engaged in an apparently aimless manipulation of the assortment of nuts and bolts along the base, fussing with them until he had got the right timbre; it was a ritual that had never ceased both to amuse and irritate her, and despite his efforts to explain the technicalities involved she had never got used to it. Then at last his fingers settled into a gradual stroke and he began to play. It was like nursing music out of an inanimate log of wood; there was about it something of the snake charmer's art; she was still not cynical enough to dismiss it as no more than uncouth skill. The main melodic line was delicate, unobtrusive, peripheral to the slumbering turbulence that lay coiled and quivering underneath, like the tremulous impending violence of an incoming tidal wave, gathering volume and identity as it surged inexorably forward, breaking off here and there from the central spine of the theme like high-flung spray, then falling back into the main current with a subdued crescendo, plunging and broiling with trapped strength, a baited primitive sound, a raw gangling thing caged and beaten into shape, sinking, ebbing tamely away, only to leap and surge upward again with renewed and fiercer intensity, lilting and snarling. He sat crouched forward on the chair, like someone hiding a wound, his fingers foraging for newer and more vibrant response, darting up and down the strings, plucking, teasing, caressing, lingering over a receding note, striking forth another, his eyes drowsily half open, mouth compressed, abstracted, absorbed in a private dialogue, no longer aware of anything else beyond the thing he was trying to forge and create.

Looking and listening, she felt once more excluded, isolated, an intruder not so much resented as ignored, her very presence an impertinence in a world he could at last claim and inhabit on his own terms, utterly without need of her or the sucking comfort of her love and concern. The music, and his absorption in it, bred in her a forlorn sense of departure, and she felt at that moment that they were both inescapably alone without the bleak benediction of farewell, alone in a way that would be made more intolerable if they remained together, feeding off the receding illusion that they could not face the future without each other. She knew then that, like herself, he was using music as a substitute for reality, or at any rate for a reality they could no longer share or retain; music was a force that was pushing them further and more surely apart instead of drawing them closer together, creating a gulf rather than a bridge between them, another subtle form of betrayal neither of them could have anticipated let alone desired. She closed her eyes and waited for him to speak, to become real again when the music had finished.

He had sat for a long time, there on the tiny balcony of that anonymous hotel, in the moist dusk, head bowed as if in prayer or contemplation, shoulders slumped, yet with a certain nervous rigidity about him, as though he had reached a conclusion he had not really wanted to face. He spoke at last, without moving.

'I'm waiting.'

She found it difficult to speak from her own deepening sense of desolation, almost of resentment, to come up with the words he wanted her to say; she felt cornered and knew it was absurd, and tried to keep her voice neutral, clinical.

'It's like nothing you've done before.'

He gave a grunt and shifted in the chair. 'Even *I* know that. Why be so bloody cagey? Either you like it or you don't.'

She went into the room, poured herself out a measure of whisky and water, and came back out on to the balcony, standing by the low parapet.

'Must things always be that simple for you – a straight yes-or-no to everything?'

'Must they always be so complicated for you, analysis just for the bloody sake of analysis? I could do with something of the same, by the way.'

She set down her glass on the parapet, fixed him a drink and brought it to him. He looked at it for a moment, then finished it almost in one gulp; she felt his mood tighten, darken, and felt a slow echoing response within herself.

'It isn't a question of whether I like it or not. It's a matter of understanding it. I want to understand it first. I'm sorry, but that's how I'm made.' She sipped her drink, catching the distant tang of the sea.

He put the guitar down upright in the corner next his chair. 'From where I stand you like or dislike something first, *then* you start trying to understand it. Response before analysis.'

'If that way works for you, fine. It doesn't work for me. I have to come to terms with things first before I can make up my mind about them, before I can know for sure whether I like them or not.' She sat down sideways on the parapet.

'You're a cold-hearted bitch, aren't you?' His voice was quiet, almost pensive, leaning forward, arms spread on the parapet, the chair tilting on its front legs. 'I wonder why you didn't bother to analyse me before you married me – but then you didn't have time, did you?'

'No.' She lit a cigarette; she knew it annoyed him when she smoked, telling her it would ruin her voice, but she did not care what he thought then. 'I'm sorry if you think I'm cold-hearted, let alone a bitch. I don't think I'm either, very much, and anyway it doesn't matter. I thought it was your music we were discussing, not my personality defects.'

'My music!' He threw himself back, the back legs of the chair crashing on the tiled surface of the balcony, twisting the glass round in his fist. 'Don't use words you don't understand. You don't give a shit for what you call my "music", with such a fine degree of contempt in your voice. You don't like what you heard just now, only you haven't the honesty to admit it, and you don't like it because you can't sing it –'

'Oh, don't be childish, Art, for God's sake.' She exhaled smoke angrily. 'Give me credit for being just a little bit more intelligent than that. And as far as I recall, I never said I didn't like it. Be accurate, if you can't be rational.'

He finished off his drink, went into the room, and came back with a full glass. 'You didn't like it because there aren't any lyrics for you to slaughter and mutilate.'

'That sort of remark doesn't hurt me any more, which must mean something.'

'Well, with that fine analytical mind of yours you've probably already worked out what it means.' He drank. 'I'm too dumb for that kind of high mental activity.'

The thin yellow eye of a lighthouse beacon winked on and off through the mist as if it were trying to attract their attention; she thought she heard the lonely foghorn of a ship passing in the distance, above the furious racing of her own heart, but could not be sure; in the courtyard below their window a few cars were beginning to draw up, doors slamming, people being happy and raucous, calling out to one another; she suddenly felt immeasurably sad.

'Let's not get sloshed tonight,' she said, stubbing out her smouldering cigarette. 'We're being paid for what we do, whether you like my voice or not, and I think we ought to give a fair return.'

'Oh, I'm all right,' he said, giving a short harsh laugh. 'I don't have to sing. Amazing how you can fool people when you're playing an instrument. You can cover up your mistakes in a flash – they think it's part of the bloody score. But when you're out there belting out a song

– now that's something else again. No room for bum notes there.' He spoke with bitter abandon, with a kind of despairing animosity, the words falling about him like shattered glass, each one meant to pierce and wound.

'It doesn't matter, Art,' she said wearily, putting down her glass, no longer interested in the fray. 'It doesn't matter.'

She had turned and gone back into the rather sparsely furnished room and lain down on the bed, not feeling anything, and after a while he had come in from the balcony and stood nearby, looking down at her, a slight unkempt silhouette in the dusk, hands bunched in the pockets of his jeans; he came and sat down on the side of the bed, brushing the hair back from his face.

'Christ, Janice, what's wrong with us?'

'Let's not start talking in clichés again.' She turned about on her side, away from him. 'It's so boring.'

'I'm not – I'm only trying to find out why things are so lousy between us – we don't talk any more – just hiss and snarl – '

'Let me get some sleep, can't you?' We go on at eight.'

'Janice – ' He leaned over her, his hands fumbling, going beneath the waist-line of her sweater, meeting at once her bare flesh, moving upwards, encountering the crisp cupolas of her brassiere, the satin rustling faintly under his fingers, impeding his quest; aroused, everything else swept aside, forgotten, supremely irrelevant, she turned over, searching for him with a fervour that matched his own, arching her body to allow him to unsheath her breasts, the nipples plump and erect nudging pertly against his cupped palms. The jeans peeled away from her and he sank down with a low relieved cry into the apex of her spread thighs, his hands caressing her hips, her soft sloping stomach, finding again her breasts, kneading, pressing with quick hurtful insistence, her throat smoothly uplifted, breathing evenly but hard; his body was now one tremulous beseeching demand, to which she was wholly, exuberantly responsive, his warm assertive potency drawing fire from her mute eloquent impatience, her heart pounding with a sharp exquisite captive pain, aching for him; and then with a soft little whimper of anguish it was over, a dull ordinary throb where magic had been, the outlines of the room returning, dimly discerned in the dusk, and once more the far away ghost wail of a ship coming to her out of the night like the moaning of someone lost and in need, wandering the earth . . .

*   *   *

235

Traffic screamed past her, the lights of the city flashing insanely, knifing downward at her like weapons wielded by madmen, the rain thickening, turning savage, blowing into her face with spiteful glee. Oblivious, not knowing, not caring where her steps took her, she sometimes blundered into people, caught the snide sniggering and crude suggestions of men as she passed, some reaching out, grabbing at her sleeve, jingling coins, flaunting pound notes, cursing after her as she walked on impervious and immune, fragmented images flaring in her mind like the lurid neon fantasies dancing everywhere about her; odd inconsequential disconnected pieces of her life swirling around her like fireflies, keeping watch, keeping step, accompanying her wherever she went in the furious labyrinths of the night, never leaving her, never letting her be, baleful and tender, caressing, bruising, making her weep silently, tearlessly for what had so brightly promised and so grotesquely ceased to be; things she could not even name, because they were of her heart only and therefore unnameable, shadows of dreams, intimations, nightmares trailing after her, consoling her, mocking her, damning her, the echoes of many lifetimes, of all the lives she had never led, following her like a blessing or a vengeance.

Grandmother dying in her square little bed, the long bright litany of a life drawing to a close, exquisite and tranquil; Grandmother that frail guardian telling her to be strong in hope with a strength and hope that had eluded her and would perhaps forever elude her because she did not know where to seek it or how she might recognise it whether in others or in herself; she had learned nothing after all either from the life or the death of the one person who might have taught her a little how to cope with her own life. Grandmother twinkling with sherry and exuberance, telling her fables out of the girlish fable of herself twisting life round her little finger, exploring and conquering worlds and not moving an inch from her humdrum glowing little plot of earth, and then no more, quite gone, fading already cruelly even from memory and not all the yearning and loneliness in the world would put her back where she had so gaily and so eloquently been, for that chapter was over and could never be reopened, shut tight as a coffin lid and as out of sight. It was neither better that way nor worse, neither merciful nor barbaric; it was simply so, and the years were already taking care of the sorrow.

'Naturally I hope you will be happy.' Her father tall and stooping and inadequate, wishing her not unkindly to be gone, back into the life she had chosen, so foreign to him, wanting only to be left alone with his figures and cabalistic calculations, placing precise premiums on other lives, trundling stolid and oxen-like up and down the small front lawn every other weekend of summer slicing with oblivious brutality the shorn and shrivelled grass, arid and sapless as his own existence gone beyond recall, falling into ponderous tight-lipped abstraction, not knowing how to cope with the three children he had to his perennial surprise helped to sire and bring into the world.

Her mother, a fading sepia figure, a stern still-life rigid and unalterable in the narrow honesty and pride of her ways, her hair lying in a ball on the thin nape of her neck, worn fingers moving like mice against the dark tweed skirt the only evidence, the only betrayal of emotion, facing that first and only declaration of selfhood from the child and daughter now almost woman she had up to then stoically reared and tolerated and never for once known.

Richard. He had not vanished completely from her world; now and then she would come upon a report or interview he had written for the local paper where he had gone to work and which would carry his name: 'Richard Treston'. It made her smile to see his name in print so bold and decisive when her usual remembrance of him was so different, and a small illogical ache would stir momentarily in her heart for she knew not what. Not often but sometimes in the middle of a song perhaps and even above the glare of the stage lights she would imagine that a certain face in the crowd alone at a table must surely be his, even though she could not very vividly remember it; the feeling would come to her that somehow he was not very far away, quietly observing her, engrossed in what she was doing, absorbed in whatever moment that held her, unaware of anything else. The fancy would pass quickly enough and once again she would be back with her own life, but always it left a certain warmth, a certain reassurance, a feeling that had nothing to do with time or if they would ever see each other again. She supposed other people would smile and think she was being silly and girlish and poetic, building things up in her mind, being sad and nostalgic about something in the past that had never really been there; but she knew she was being nothing of the sort, she knew she was not prone to idle myth-making. Nor was she being in the least disloyal to her husband; in a way Richard had never existed at all, that entire little episode, that small poignant idyll had been essentially unreal, keener and more charged in retrospect than it had ever actually been in what was often so flippantly termed real life.

If he had existed at all it was only as an ambiguous half-formed wish after something ephemeral and insubstantial as a cloud; a wish that, had it been granted, she would almost certainly not have known what in the world to do with, an absurdity too great even to think about. He belonged solely to a part of her that had risen and flown once before coming back firmly to earth; and yet she was surprised now and then by how much she wanted to see him again, even in passing.

Simon. He had come into their apartment one evening after they had not seen or heard from him for over a month; dragging his steps like one suddenly afflicted with a mysterious disabling disease, his face dreadfully sunken in some inscrutable despair or horrible exultation – it was difficult to tell which; his speech slurred, shrill at times to the point of effeminate hysteria, hands unsteady, splashing drink down his shirtfront, giggling inanely at one of his own feeble and increasingly coarse jokes or for no reason at all, looking convulsively over his shoulder in the middle of conversation or a meal, as though half expecting an assassin to be lurking in the shadows behind him, or falling silent, staring at the wall in front of him as if at a death-mask etched there, eyes slightly protuberant, glazed or lit with a bright unnatural alertness, plump moist lips tremulous, tongue-licked again and again, his suave corpulent bulk seeming to be shrivelled inside his expensive suit hanging loose and limp on him, the flesh of his neck riven and sagging in thick folds. He walked about like an insomniac, pudgy face a fearful pasty hue, drawn and haggard, jingling his car-keys or coins in his pocket, taking the brandy they offered him like a child accepting sweets, putting it absently to his lips, then setting it down on a table, forgotten.

They, for once united in discretion, had not queried or in any way referred to his abrupt non-appearance at his office or social haunts, and he had not mentioned it or proffered any explanation; for about an hour they had indulged in small talk of no consequence whatever, with many long silences in between, mostly on Sandford's part as he stood, staring into space, running the pink glistening tip of his tongue over his lips repeatedly in a way that she found somehow revolting and almost obscene, small gimlet eyes deeply ringed and sunken in his head. Then abruptly he had gathered up his white scarf and gloves and said he must be going. He paused at the door, as though remembering something, turned round and said in a matter-of-fact manner: 'Oh, by the way, Marcie's gone.' As they looked blankly at him, he had gone on with a faint abstracted smile: 'She's gone into theatre management. With – someone else. In South Africa.' He opened the door and stood on the threshold, slowly slapping the glove he had not put on against the palm of his other hand, pursing his lips, staring down at the carpet, as if trying to remember something else which he thought perhaps he should tell them. 'Incidentally, Elinor's not at all well. In fact,' he added apologetically, still faintly smiling, 'she's dying. So,' he sighed, shrugging his shoulders, 'I won't be very actively involved in the business side of things for some time to come.' He looked up at them, the sickly smile deepening. 'You could say I won't be involved at all from now on. Never mind,' he said with a frightful false heartiness, 'you're established now, aren't you, so it won't matter really, will it? Good night.' The door closed after him and he had gone padding down the corridor to the lift; above their stupefied silence both of them could have sworn they heard him humming.

She shuddered slightly now, seeing again that bloodless moon-face and the expression of cunning idiocy that seemed to spread over it and mask it as he spoke in such a dead voice of the violent mystifying change his life had undergone within the space of a few weeks. Fastidious as ever, he had left no loose ends dangling untidily; every aspect of the business in which, as he had himself so often put it, he had 'dabbled so extensively' was placed in the hands of lawyers and legally, scrupulously dismantled, disassembled and sorted out to the satisfaction of all concerned, from top executives to lowly clerks; he simply sold or otherwise disposed of his shares and dropped more or less completely out of both commercial and social circulation, leaving the usual and inevitable shoal of rumours in his wake, some scurrilous, some humorous and nearly all of them spiteful: he had absconded with most of the company's capital; he had been arrested and had bought himself out; he had contracted an incurable and altogether unmentionable disease and had only months to live; he had finally fled to Brazil with that damned supercilious black bitch of a mistress of his; his wife had sued for divorce, his wife had left him, his wife had died by her own hand; he had murdered her or had paid to have her murdered; he had simply gone insane and was locked up in an asylum – one for the very rich, of course. Fast and furious the tales of envious imagination flew and grew more fantastic until, inexorably, people tired of the game and in his absence the lugubrious dust settled at last and finally he was spoken of, if at all, only as an oddity, a fat-bellied Jew who had notwithstanding a perennial lean and hungry look and who was not even certain of his own sexuality, let alone his antecedents, a sly devious bastard who richly deserved to sink without trace under the weight of his own craftiness and duplicity. That hideous heap of his out in Mill Hill with its atrocious and unspeakably bad taste and decor was now little more than a mausoleum, and wherever he was now, said the former sycophants now turned pundits, they and London as a whole were well rid of him. So to all intents and purposes Simon was duly disposed of and buried more thoroughly than if he had been laid in the earth – which would at any rate have been a more magnanimous act than the vicious symbolic character assassination of him that ensued upon his voluntary withdrawal from that small segment of society in which he had so munificently and uncomfortably figured and moved, an outsider who dispensed largesse with remote and incurious prodigality and thereby incurred the wrath of those who most benefited from that irritating trait.

Except that for a certain few he was a very unquiet ghost that roamed the memory and was even glimpsed at times through the rain-spattered rear window of a taxi-cab or in a carefully isolated corner of a restaurant well off the fashionable beat, huddled over a drink wreathed in cigar smoke, not so much hidden as impassively indifferent to everyone and everything about him, his eyes vacant, his face once grossly rubicund rubbed smooth of almost all expression; and nearly always seated slightly behind or to one side of him a large formidable heavy-featured ample-bosomed woman with close-cropped hair that gave to her whole appearance a distinctive and disconcerting martial stamp, who sat inscrutably looking on, never taking her dark piercing eyes from him as he ate or drank or smoked or read the newspaper, who watched him with predatory pride, with hawk-like alertness, taking no interest whatever in her surroundings or in anyone else present, seemingly coming alive only when, on a rare occasion, someone made tentatively to approach their table, and then she would glare and positively bristle in such a threatening manner that, catching the unwelcome vibrations, the would-be intruder would hesitate and then scuttle hastily away with a startled backward glance or two at the incongruous spectacle at the table, the shrunken absorbed grey-faced man drinking or eating in such an animal way, and the vigilant absurdly comic yet frightening female so contemptuously devouring him with her black unyielding eyes; it was like something out of a baleful nightmare, a fragment of a malevolent painting kept out of sight in a cellar and seen only at fleeting and disturbing intervals, like the face of an owl in the dead hours when it is neither night nor morning.

Janice remembered. That dull undiscerning day, a cold dreary drizzle falling from leaden skies, and him waiting for them under the dripping melancholy trees in the park, blubbering forth almost immediately fragments of the truth alternately with swagger and tired casualness, the squalid little truth as miserable as the day itself, falling as spittle from his lips. Bereft then of any lasting shred, any lingering pretensions of manliness or self-respect, huddled beneath the trees, fatuous and sullen by turn, babbling, at times incoherent, as if drunk though with something infinitely more potent, more lethal than mere alcohol, clogging his veins and his sensibilities; the fairish thinning hair plastered to his skull with rain, dabbing at his wet cheeks with one of his pale exquisite handkerchiefs.

'So good of you to come.' Stammering his gratitude for meeting him there at that peculiar spot, at that peculiar time of day in response to the garbled phone call he had made earlier that morning; fumbling aimlessly in the pockets of his immaculate jacket, never quite meeting their eye. 'Still together, eh, you two? Well, well, whoever would have thought it, eh? There's hope for the human soul yet, my dears. Hope for the human soul.'

His voice petulant, then shrill, defensive, rising at times to falsetto jocularity more grotesque to hear than the hushed sombre whine it frequently sank to, chewing on an unlit cigar like a dog with a bone, dabbing constantly at his cheeks with the delicate lace handkerchief, stepping out on to the gravel path, walking a little ahead of them.

'Nothing remains the same – did you know that, hmm? Nothing. I find it irresistibly amusing to think that at my age my entire family appear to have disowned me. One of life's saving little ironies.' He slouched on, shoulders stooped, eyes darting about all the time as if on the look-out for something or somebody, gnawing at the useless cigar clamped in a corner of his mouth. 'Do you miss me back at the treadmill? A little? Glad to be out of that bloody rat race, my dears, out of that bloody hellhole. I am my own man now. My own man.'

The tone became wistful, gentle almost; white flurry of lace dabbing incessantly at streaming cheeks, head nodding, eyes darting.

'I sometimes miss the competition, of course. The rough-and-tumble. The thrill of spotting an exceptional talent now and then. Like you two, dear hearts. Also I miss avoiding the old knife in the back. There's a certain talent in that too, you know. A certain art. Like somehow twisting one's head out of the guillotine block as the blade was about to fall.'

Almost skipping ahead of them now, surprisingly small and dainty feet splashing carelessly in muddy little pools of rain, ruining the fine expensive leather of the shoes, besmirching the neat trouser-ends; voice lifting to a rasping chuckle.

'No room for imagination back there in the jungle. No room for flair, panache, the higher use of the intellect, to be pompous about it. I haven't quite made up my mind yet what to turn my hand to next, what to waste my money on. Perhaps you two bright young things might come up with an idea, a suggestion – eh?'

He turned on them abruptly a lost pale gaze, taking the slightly sodden cigar out of his mouth, a small sudden flicker of enlightenment passing over his face.

'I'm weak – I know that. Dreadfully weak. Always was, and getting weaker as I get older.' A meditative pause. 'I need strong people about me. Always did. No use denying it.' The plump eyelids drooped. 'I needed *her*. You've no idea, my dears, how I needed her. But what happens, hmm? She ups and goes off to South Africa – I ask you!' Hands outspread in appeal, beseechment. 'Bloody South Africa, of all the barbaric places on earth!' Again came that inane infantile chuckle, saliva trickling thinly down his creased unshaven chin, not bothering to wipe it away. 'Gone into theatre management, if you please – her! That cunning little black slut that I literally picked out of the Bayswater gutter, picking my brains all along and I the last to know, of course! No wonder they laughed at me behind my back. They had every right to. Ah well,' putting the cigar back between his teeth, walking on; 'at least I performed one useful function during my years before the mast – I amused them.'

Shaking his head in rueful bewilderment, drops of rain glistening on the expanse of rich worsted suit cloth drawn across his shoulders, silk neck scarf knotted and untidy, wound noose-like, limp with rain.

'"Be happy", she wrote to me. Be happy! My dears, happiness is a madman's dream, nothing more. One spends the best part of one's entire lifetime trying to be happy, deceiving oneself that one *is* happy. Such a deplorable waste. And my little dream, my obsession of a lifetime gone, vanished overnight. Sailing away first-class. With another man, another woman – who knows, who cares, and does it matter?'

At last he took the handkerchief and spread it out over the top of his head, giving him a pathetic clown-like appearance, hands again fumbling about in his pockets, foraging like rabbits in a burrow, feet kicking dead leaves out of his path.

'I may as well tell you. I'm done for now, dear hearts. Well and truly done for now. Oh, not money. Not anything as crude and simple as that. There's plenty in the kitty still. A viable cash-flow, as they say. No. I'm done for in another way, and my shrewd little brain won't get me out of this one in a hurry. Elinor dying fast in that clinic in Berkshire. Hating me, I suppose, with her last breath. If ever she had the strength or imagination to hate anybody, that is. The children gone too, boarded out like dogs in kennels. Too young perhaps to hate me yet, but they'll learn, they'll learn. So what is left? Nobody but me and that damned Teutonic amazon in all that big bloody museum of a house – '

He turned smartly about on his heels, a fixed lurid grin or grimace contorting his face, handkerchief clinging damply to his head, a sort of dying defiance starting out of his eyes.

'Don't tell me you don't know, that you haven't heard of her? My Wagnerian goddess, striding about from room to room without a stitch on her in broad daylight, ruling me with a rod of iron – oh surely you have heard the gothic tale? Surely it is the current gospel of Earl's Court and St John's Wood, poor Sandford smothered under all that Germanic poundage and suffering his fate heroically? No? I cannot believe it!'

He held his head high, eyes narrowed, peering through the dimness of the trees, nose seeming to sniff for a trace of that heavy familiar animal spoor in the raw air. Then he giggled, a slow sly sound rising in his throat, his eyes squeezed up tight with moronic mirth, whipping the cigar once more out of his mouth and waving it about like a baton.

'Oh my dears, what a pretty pass I've come to. You really should drop in sometime and see her. There she stands in the middle of the room, like bloody Goering addressing a Hitler Youth rally, a great damned beast of a woman, naked as the day she was born, sloshing down gin, brandy, whisky, vodka, pernod – any damned thing she can lay her colossal hands on, and coming at me winking and simpering, calling me all sorts of sweet names in her native tongue – it really is a sight to be seen!'

A bevy of laughing unchaperoned school children came running down the narrow windy path, bumping into him as he stood stationary in the rain; he cursed after them with ridiculous rage, shrinking away from the sudden physical contact as if they might infect him, face screwed up, shaking his fist as they scuttled off into the distance.

'Vile little buggers! No respect, no breeding, no manners. Drown them in the bloody Serpentine – that's what *I'd* do if I had my way with things. Children are the curse of the earth – never have a single one if you can at all avoid it. They pollute a man's bloodstream, take it from me.'

He became excessively polite and ordinary then, smiling a rather sheepish and disarming smile, taking the handkerchief from his head and stuffing it into his side pocket, a little abashed.

'You must forgive me for going on like this. I do most humbly beg your pardon. You two were the only real friends I ever made out of that whole imbecile bunch of swindlers, cut-throats and tricksters. It was so good of you to listen to an old fool talking absolute nonsense. But, you see, I get about so rarely nowadays that even talking absolute nonsense comes as an enormous and blessed relief. I heard that last single you made. Damned good. Is it selling well? Marvellous.' He pulled up the sleeve of his coat an inch or two, looking at his watch. 'Look, it's scarcely gone four. Do we have time for a drink, a meal perhaps? That cosy little place we used to go to sometimes – now where was it – Knightsbridge? Or was it somewhere by Marble Arch? We can hail a cab quite easily from here. What – you have to be in Ealham by six? Oh, what a pity.' He glanced at them shrewdly, eyes humorously appraising them. 'Sure you're not avoiding old Simon, too, along with the rest of my inseparable friends? Ah no, that was an

244

ignoble thought.' He had looked about him then with mild surprise, scanning the sky. 'Well, the rain seems to have eased off. Myself, I'll probably end up somewhere in the Black Forest, wherever the massive witch takes me.' He gave them a huge distorted wink. 'Nature will out, you know, just like murder. God bless you both, my dears, and please don't take it as a blasphemy.' He hid a hiccup behind a small pudgy hand. He had sauntered off down the path towards the magnificent carved gates of the park, waddling a little as he went, making a rather half-hearted effort to straighten his shoulders and strike a more erect and assured figure, stepping out round a curve of trees into the gathering early gloom of the November evening.

Conversation had been difficult and ragged between the two of them for days after that, both reluctant even to bring themselves to talk about it, as if hiding from each other a shameful private misdemeanour, a grievous secret wrongdoing, until at last one night after a show Art got rather drunk and loquacious, a pattern that was usual with him, and sprawled out in a chair, bottle at his elbow, had launched into a semi-coherent diatribe against the shambling imitation of a man that had been Sandford, a harangue addressed mainly to the amber-filled tumbler in his hand.

'Stupid old bastard,' he had burst out, a peculiar and unwonted venom in his voice, as though railing against someone who had done him a personal injury, or else raging against something he sensed in himself. 'It wants something like that to make you realise what a rotten con trick life really is behind all the kisses and flowers, the wine and candlelight, the soft bleeding words and congratulations.'

She poured herself a drink and sat down on the bed, shaking her hair loose from the band that held it caught up. 'Who are you talking about now?'

'Do you have to ask?' he leered, hitching one foot up on the seat, closing one eye and peering at the glass held aloft in his hand. 'That poor crawling slug Sandford. My God, it makes me want to turn in my membership card of the human race. It makes me want to puke.' He glared belligerently over at her. 'What do *you* make of it – what do *you* think?'

She studied a turn-of-the-century French poster print on the wall above the bed, trying to decide whether she liked it or not. 'I think it's all very sad.'

245

'Sad?' he had mimicked, putting on a great display of incredulity. 'You think it's all very sad, do you? It's nothing of the kind. It's bleeding ludicrous, that's what it is – ludicrous. A grown man letting himself down like that, letting himself be used by a fucking German giantess, a hireling ruling the roost and his wife dying of cancer, turning himself into the laughing-stock of London and not doing a thing about it. You call that *sad*? Sadistic would be nearer the mark, or more correctly maso-sadistic. The man's a raving lunatic – he has to be, to throw everything away like he has done. How can you find that sad or touching?' he had demanded, twisting about in the chair to face her.

'I don't defend him,' she replied, leaning back against the pillows and arching her neck, trying to ease the ache in it. 'He doesn't need mine or anyone else's defence. It's true what he said to us that last time in the park. In a funny way, in his own way, he *is* his own man.'

'Christ, you call that being a man, the sort of life he's leading? You must be out of your skull, or else your sense of values has undergone a drastic sea-change. The poor bastard would do himself a favour if he put a gun to his head and pulled the trigger.' He reached over for the bottle.

'I don't think we're in any position to advise anyone whether or not to live or die. What Simon does with his life is his own business.'

'You can't say that and him with a wife and three kids. Isn't what he does with his life their business too?'

'Yes, I admit that. It is their business. But it is certainly not ours.'

'Want to isolate yourself from the fate of others, do you? Whatever happened to your precious compassion?'

'I never for a moment suspected it was compassion you had in mind,' she said, closing her eyes rather wearily. 'You talk of him as if he was your bitterest enemy. Do be consistent.'

He had risen from the chair and begun to stroll about the room, an inordinate anger working in him, glaring at the furniture and other objects as he walked back and forth.

'At least Marcie had brains,' he muttered, gulping down his drink. 'She had style, class, a certain something about her that set her apart. As far as anyone knows, all this other bird has going for her is sheer bulk.'

'Maybe he happens to like sheer bulk.'

'It's sickening!' he insisted, pausing to look at himself balefully in the mirror as though at a rival. 'Just bloody sickening.'

'To each his own.'

'That bland middle-class liberalism of yours will be the death of you yet,' he flung back at her. 'Try feeling just for once, instead of stepping back and looking at things through a microscope. It might surprise you, knowing what it is to feel. Most of the human race do feel, you know, and I don't mean just in bed.'

She lifted the glass to her lips, slowly, as if it were a weight. 'I didn't think you did. And if by feeling you mean being fantastic and intolerant about other people's behaviour, then I'm rather glad I don't approach life with feeling.'

'You don't approach life with any thought beyond yourself, as far as my limited knowledge of you has been able to discern.'

'You know, that could very well be true, but like Simon I seem doomed to be myself, like it or not.'

That argument like many another they had, had fizzled out on a droning bickering note, leaving them both exhausted and perversely intensely dependent upon each other for reassurance that their love was intact and life still full of undiscovered promise for them if only they held back the cheap bitter word and kept faith however fragile with tomorrow.

They had been drinking at their 'local'. Then abruptly he had left her. She put her empty glass down, a little more fortified – though she didn't really know why – to face the future. She wondered if he was back at the flat, poring over his music sheets, if he was thinking of her at all, where she was, what she might be doing, or if he had gone out too somewhere in search of distraction and diversion and was at the moment as lost and despondent and at a loss what to do about life as she was herself. Before leaving the dim lounge she glanced across at the figure who had been her solitary companion for the last half hour or more; he had not moved a muscle, it seemed, and still she noted there were at least three more empty glasses on the table in front of him. She smiled, feeling herself in the presence of some sort of sorcerer or magician, swung the door to and stepped out into the street.

Discotheque music bawled and bellowed at her as she passed the blazing façades of entertainment lairs; an occasional drunk lurched against her mumbling to himself or half laughing, half crying, face cruelly exposed by lighted shop windows. She wondered if the light might be on in the front parlour of her parents' house, making a demure yellow square of the window, falling dimly upon the trim privet hedge and the shorn wet grass; she wondered whether the moon still struck at the same oblique angle upon the wall of her old bedroom, a shape sharp as any imagined by an artist that always seemed to be telling her things she could not decipher and fell often asleep with its stark light still throbbing behind her lids. The warning wail of an ambulance sounded close by, slicing the air; illuminated nude mechanical figures of women flashed on and off in sad garish allegories of lust; the aroma of hamburgers and fish and chips and Oriental food was everywhere prevalent insulting or titillating the nostrils; life lurid and loud pounded into the pavements, groaning, cursing, fuming with vivid retaliation, expectant beyond all reason, heedless and heartless and joyous in its desperate, solitary and garrulous singularity, its enforced bee-hive community and camaraderie making a mockery and a cruel reality of intimacy. All around her were voices and each voice was her own reiterating the lessons and prophecies she felt she must learn and understand and could not begin to comprehend were she to be granted the dubious boon of living several lifetimes.

Her steps slowed, recognising certain familiar localities, then quickened and assumed a certain rhythm, hands snug in the pockets of her anorak, the wind playfully teasing her hair, eyes steady and bright, returning to that inescapable paradox without which tomorrow would not exist and everything that had happened up to then a gloating smile of defeat on some unnameable face.

Down all the Days

The triumphant novel of the slums of Dublin

Pushed around the streets of Dublin by his boisterous brothers, the small crippled occupant of a boxcar is the silent witness of the city's joys and woes. Fully possessed of the thoughts and feelings of his sprawling family, he is the focal figure of the novel which relates his searing childhood and coming of age. At once tormented and relaxed, he is the detached observer of life in the slums of forties and fifties Dublin.

Written with the fearless discipline that Christy Brown had to establish over his own body, *Down all the Days* displays his lyrical gift with language to the full.

'Will surely stand beside Joyce and in front of all the others as Dublin writ large and writ for all times' *Irish Times*

'Deserves the highest critical acclaim, not because it was written with one foot but because it is the work of a real writer who just happens to be handicapped' *Daily Telegraph*

My Left Foot

The warm, humorous and true story of Christy Brown's supreme courage and triumph over the severest of handicaps.

Christy Brown was born a victim of cerebral palsy. But the helpless, lolling baby concealed the brilliantly imaginative and sensitive mind of a writer who would take his place among the giants of Irish literature.

This is Christy Brown's own story. He recounts his childhood struggle to learn to read, write, paint and finally type, with the toe of his left foot. *My Left Foot* is now a major Oscar-winning film starring Daniel Day Lewis as Christy Brown.

'A story of courage that is wise and in no way morbid'
Sunday Times

A Shadow on Summer

The ivory tower of success

The writer of a bestseller, Riley McCombe is anonymous no more. Crippled and publicity-shy, he is catapulted from the slums of Dublin to the wide blue sky of Connecticut and the full blaze of fame. Now he must write another.

While Riley stays with Laurie and Don Emerson, Laurie is only too happy to appoint herself hostess and mentor – and although he resents her criticisms, Riley responds to her warmth and femininity. Then, at one of his American publisher's lavish parties, elegant photographer Abbie Lang chooses to join in the curious tug of war for the young Irishman's love. But Riley, ever fearful of the responsibility of his craft, can only intensify the puzzled hurt of both women while he remains an intensely lonely prisoner of himself.

'Its sharpest insights concern the necessary privateness and privations of creativity'
Valentine Cunningham, *New Statesman*

'Christy Brown's *A Shadow on Summer* . . . maintains the remarkable energy of *Down All the Days*'
Martin Seymour-Smith, *Financial Times*

'It contains many flashes of insight into character and many descriptions of the New England countryside that take one's breath away with their rightness'
Francis King, *Sunday Telegraph*

Wild Grow the Lilies

The laughing drains of Dublin

Fond of the girls at Madame Lala's, eloquent reporter Luke Sheridan is fonder still of the sound of his own voice. Bursting with purple prose and ribald repartee, he even dreams of writing *the* Great Irish Novel.

But work comes first – especially when Dublin's evening newspaper is tipped off about the attempted murder of a German count. Going after the scoop of the year, Luke is helplessly and hilariously mixed up in the most wildly flamboyant goose chase that ever crossed the fair city's underbelly.

Wild Grow the Lilies, lively, fluent and derivative . . . is a grossly entertaining novel' *Times Literary Supplement*

'Christy Brown has an extraordinary gift for vivid language and imagery' *The Times*

'Christy's romp is thoroughly enjoyable . . . It is wildly funny, bawdy and vulgar and the writing, whether sonorous or broad Dublin, is a delight'
Catherine O'Faolain, *Irish Press*

Collected Poems

With an introduction by Frank Delaney

'Here was a man,' as Frank Delaney quite rightly declares, 'who had the true writer's gifts.' Christy Brown's first collection of poems, *Come Softly to My Wake*, was published to widespread acclaim. He went on to publish two more, *Background Music* and *Of Snails and Skylarks*, before his tragic death in 1981. In paperback for the first time, this *Collected Poems* incorporates all three volumes in a single edition.

'His verse, like his prose, is masculine, direct, unsophisticated and, above all, "a good read"'
Times Literary Supplement

'There is real talent here . . . a freshness of attack, a liveliness, energy and passion that remind one of Dylan Thomas'
Yorkshire Post

'Almost everything Christy Brown has written has the unique appeal of a writer whose primary concern is complete emotional honesty . . . All the time one senses behind the poems a creator whose delight in words is equalled only by his passionate candour of expression'
Sunday Independent

'Vigorous and sensual . . . of his sincerity and passionate commitment to language there is never any doubt'
The Times

A Selected List of Titles Available from Minerva

While every effort is made to keep prices low, it is sometimes necessary to increase prices at short notice. Mandarin Paperbacks reserves the right to show new retail prices on covers which may differ from those previously advertised in the text or elsewhere.

The prices shown below were correct at the time of going to press.

Fiction

☐	7493 9026 3	**I Pass Like Night**	Jonathan Ames	£3.99 BX
☐	7493 9006 9	**The Tidewater Tales**	John Bath	£4.99 BX
☐	7493 9004 2	**A Casual Brutality**	Neil Blessondath	£4.50 BX
☐	7493 9028 2	**Interior**	Justin Cartwright	£3.99 BC
☐	7493 9002 6	**No Telephone to Heaven**	Michelle Cliff	£3.99 BX
☐	7493 9028 X	**Not Not While the Giro**	James Kelman	£4.50 BX
☐	7493 9011 5	**Parable of the Blind**	Gert Hofmann	£3.99 BC
☐	7493 9010 7	**The Inventor**	Jakov Lind	£3.99 BC
☐	7493 9003 4	**Fall of the Imam**	Nawal El Saadewi	£3.99 BC

Non-Fiction

☐	7493 9012 3	**Days in the Life**	Jonathon Green	£4.99 BC
☐	7493 9019 0	**In Search of J D Salinger**	Ian Hamilton	£4.99 BX
☐	7493 9023 9	**Stealing from a Deep Place**	Brian Hall	£3.99 BX
☐	7493 9005 0	**The Orton Diaries**	John Lahr	£5.99 BC
☐	7493 9014 X	**Nora**	Brenda Maddox	£6.99 BC

All these books are available at your bookshop or newsagent, or can be ordered direct from the publisher. Just tick the titles you want and fill in the form below. Available in:
BX: British Commonwealth excluding Canada
BC: British Commonwealth including Canada

Mandarin Paperbacks, Cash Sales Department, PO Box 11, Falmouth, Cornwall TR10 9EN.

Please send cheque or postal order, no currency, for purchase price quoted and allow the following for postage and packing:

UK	80p for the first book, 20p for each additional book ordered to a maximum charge of £2.00.
BFPO	80p for the first book, 20p for each additional book.
Overseas including Eire	£1.50 for the first book, £1.00 for the second and 30p for each additional book thereafter.

NAME (Block letters) ....

ADDRESS ....

....

....